Managing the Data Center

Managing
the Data Center

ALLAN F. FROEHLICH

Lifetime Learning Publications
Belmont, California

A division of Wadsworth, Inc.
London   Singapore   Sydney   Toronto   Mexico City

Jacket Designer: Diana Ciardella
Designer: Nancy Benedict
Editor: Nancy Palmer Jones
Illustrator: Carl Brown
Composition: Computer Typesetting Services, Inc.

Printed in the United States of America
1 2 3 4 5 6 7 8 9 10—86 85 84 83 82

Library of Congress Cataloging in Publication Data
Froehlich, Allan F.
    Managing the data center.
    Bibliography: p.
    Includes index.
    1. Electronic data processing departments—
Management.   I. Title.
HF5548.2.F76 1982   658'.054   82-4622
ISBN 0-534-97942-4

Short Contents

Contents

Preface

As a data center manager (DCM), you must keep a complex set of resources (namely, hardware, software, and people) in balance and justify the cost and performance of these resources to your organization's top management. At the same time, as the organization's dependence on its information resources increases, the users themselves become more aware of and more interested in data processing. These factors combine to make the DCM's job more visible within the organization; in fact, they require that you truly *manage* the center. *This book describes how to manage (rather than simply "operate") a data center, and it defines the tasks that every DCM must accomplish in order to manage well.*

Experienced data center managers know that there is rarely a single, right answer to a data center dilemma. Rather, what's usually needed is an ability to make a sound decision from among a group of alternatives. *The theme of this book is that the data center should be viewed as a business enterprise and that you should make decisions much as a rational businessperson—a type of entrepreneur—would make decisions about a business.*

This book is written for the data center manager, for the manager of the data center manager, or for the person who is in line for appointment as a data center manager. In other words, the book looks at the DCM's job from the perspective of data processing *management* rather than from a *technical* data processing point of view. Thus, the focus is on such concerns as cost/benefit relationships and the effective use of the resources that have been allocated to the DCM. You will also find here several variations on data center "models," and the various parts of these models are discussed in order to understand why a data center works the way it does and to anticipate the parts of the model that are most likely to change over time.

Although this book contains a number of sample documents and forms, it is more than a simple "handbook." Rather, it provides a wide variety of recommendations and lists of specific things to do that will help you manage the data center better. The author's aim is to give you new insights into how the DCM's job can best be performed on a day-to-day basis and, in the larger sense, into what the DCM's responsibility is as a planner and leader of the data processing future of an organization.

Introduction

Defining the scope of the data center manager's job is an awesome task. Look, for example, at the following data processing trends that have emerged in recent years:

- Central processor capacity and power is increasing and increasing rapidly, even in what would have been considered a "small" installation just a few years ago.

- More on-line applications are being put into production.

- Distributed data processing is still a "young" concept, but the uncertainties surrounding it have not kept people from trying to implement it.

- Capacity allocation between central sites and distributed sites remains unsettled for the near term, but the trend toward distributed data processing will probably result in functional specialization among various processing locations.

- Data entry workloads are diminishing as a percentage of the total data center workload.

Each of these trends brings with it a set of changes with which a data center manager (DCM) must learn to deal.

In a recent conversation with a data center manager, the manager identified the following as areas that will change in the near future:

- Security and integrity of data will be improved.

• Production scheduling will be improved with the use of a job scheduler.

• Current CPUs will be replaced with larger, faster equipment since the growth of the company will create a larger volume of work than current CPU cycles can process effectively.

• Staffing characteristics will change (there will be less clerical effort, more emphasis on monitoring and control).

• The data center will be relocated because of insufficient space.

The startling thing about this list is not whether or not these changes will take place (they probably will), but the diversity of the events a data center manager is expected to manage.

If we reword the items in the above list to match terms traditionally used when a manufacturing process is revamped, the list would read something like this:

• Review personality profiles of all personnel; tighten access and availability to all facilities (local and remote).

• Study all work center loadings to determine optimum use of machine resources.

• Install totally new production line equipment.

• Retrain existing staff in needed new skills; hire specialists as needed.

• Move into a new production facility.

• Build additional plants, tying them into the main plant for operational purposes.

This is a formidable list of "things to do!" To deal with these tasks, the DCM must be a combination personnel director, industrial engineer, building services manager, production control manager, and computer guru. In other words, to be successful, a data center manager must tackle the job as though he or she were an entrepreneur striving to build a small company into an ever more efficient and cost-effective operation.

The major sections of this book are designed to help you develop this entrepreneurial attitude. Part I, "Managing," describes the difference between "managing" and "operating" a data center, defines the "total computer resource," and lays the groundwork for effective planning and measuring of the data center's growth.

Part II, "Organizing," describes the functions of every job in the data center and shows the relationship among these jobs. This section covers the importance of matching your employees' skills, backgrounds, and personalities to their positions and of providing realistic feedback on their performance.

Part III, "Getting Results—Managing the Information Factory," looks at the data center as a "factory" in order to show how to achieve the highest performance ratings from your "customers" (the users). The basic issues of production and inventory control, customer service, and optimal workflow are addressed in this section.

Part IV, "Handling the Business Details of Data Processing," gives specific practical advice on how to present the data center's budget, how to price data center services, and how to account for data center expenditures—all topics that must be handled well in order to obtain the support of upper management for the data center's activities.

Part V, "Living with Change," provides an overview of the issues that are becoming more and more important both as your own data center grows and as the industry as a whole becomes more complex. The concluding chapter (Chapter 22) provides a case study against which you can test your entrepreneurial skills, and the Summary provides a glimpse of the future from this author's point of view.

Throughout this book, the terms "data center" and "data center manager" are used as a matter of convenience to avoid ponderous lists of synonyms. These terms are meant to embrace all similar titles and designations, such as "operations center," "EDP center," "operations manager," "computer center manager," and the like. Likewise, terms such as "company" or "organization" are used in the generic sense and are intended to apply to a wide variety of business situations even though entities such as banks, hospitals, and nonprofit organizations may not usually refer to themselves as "companies."

The Selected Bibliography at the end of this book includes all the references cited in the text as well as books and articles related to data center management.

I

Managing

1

Managing Versus Operating
a Data Center

The purpose of this book is to show that the data center manager (the DCM) who manages the data center (by balancing all its resources—people, hardware, and software) will provide better computer service to his or her organization than the DCM who merely operates the data center. This chapter explains the difference between managing and operating, and it provides the model for a well-balanced data center that we will refer to throughout the book.

OPERATING THE "PRIMITIVE" CENTER

Operating a center, without managing its resources, means making "seat-of-the-pants" decisions and reacting to events rather than planning for their occurrence. Figure 1.1 illustrates this "primitive" organizational structure in a simple diagram. Here, the data center users are seen as the source of existing applications, and these applications make up the work profile of the data center. The DCM's job, then, consists of ensuring that the applications are processed and the results sent back to the users. From this point of view, the data center is part of a single processing loop, interfacing only with data center users.

"MANAGING" THE HARDWARE

Figure 1.2 shows the perspective of data center managers who view their jobs as managing strictly the computer hardware. These managers let the resource availability determine priorities for the workload, and they use the production results to review hardware utilization. In other words, all their focus is on the effective use of the hardware itself, which is why we label this the "unbalanced" data center.

MANAGING THE "WELL-BALANCED" DATA CENTER

Hardware is only one part of a rather complex set of resources that the DCM must manage. In fact, the DCM needs not only to use these resources effectively but also to maintain contacts or linkages with the rest of the organization. These linkages include the manager's routine dealings with users, with the systems analysts and programmers, and with the organization's top management. Figure 1.3 depicts these relationships and shows all the basic elements of a well-balanced data center. The service agreements, work profile, management

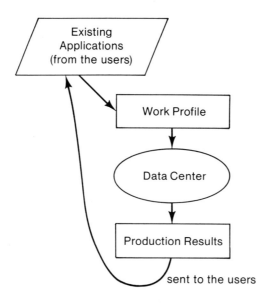

FIGURE 1.1.   *Primitive Organizational Structure for a Data Center*

policy, and data on resource availability form inputs to the data center; the performance review, production results, and resource utilization review form outputs from the center. Now the data center is part of two control loops—the *operating loop* on the left side of the diagram and the *planning loop* on the right side. The following sections describe these loops in greater detail.

The Operating Loop

Both users and data center personnel participate in the operating-loop activities. When an application becomes part of the data center workload (the work profile), a *service agreement* is negotiated between the user and the center. This agreement indicates the expected volume of work for the application (that is, the number of transactions to be processed each week or the hours of operation for an on-line system) and the expected performance levels (such as the delivery time for batch reports or the availability of the on-line system). User managers and the DCM must review regularly the operating results from the data center, comparing the results to the service agreement targets and noting any significant changes in the volume of

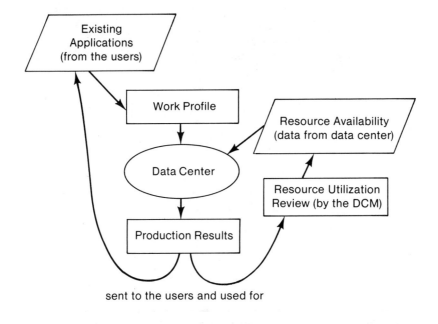

FIGURE 1.2.   Unbalanced Organizational Structure for a Data Center

existing applications or any performance areas that could be improved.

The Planning Loop

The planning loop involves users, organization management, systems analysts and programmers (that is, those involved with application development), and data center personnel. Given the existing service agreements from the operating loop and the expected workload levels from new applications, the DCM must review the use of the data center's total resources (people, hardware, and software) in order to anticipate future resource needs and must convey these needs to management.

When current resources appear inconsistent with the anticipated needs, management policy is needed to authorize significant changes in the resource mix or to consent to adjustments in the center's service levels. For example, staffing may be inadequate for the installation's planned workload, in which case upper management may authorize

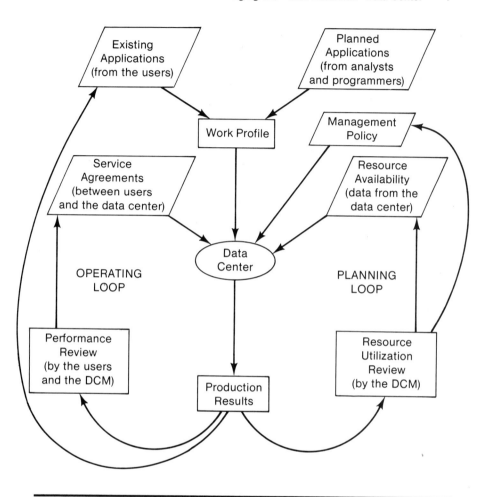

FIGURE 1.3.   *Balanced Organizational Structure for a Data Center*

the hiring of additional or specialized staff. Or, if the DCM anticipates a dramatic increase in the number of on-line terminals, the resource utilization review may indicate that the existing hardware or software resources are insufficient for this expected growth. In that case, corporate management may approve adding computer capacity or may direct users to live with extended response times at the terminals instead of installing additional hardware or software. These examples illustrate the linkages among data center staff and resources, new and existing applications, and the organization's management that the data center manager must maintain.

The Job of the Data Center Manager

Your job as data center manager is to manage the activities and maintain the relationships involved in both the operating loop and the planning loop. When the two loops mesh smoothly, then the users are active and enlightened participants in the center's activities, the data center is responsive to the users' needs, the total computer resource is put to good use, and management makes *policy* decisions (not technical decisions) about the level of resources available for serving the users.

There are certainly differences of scale among small, medium, and large data centers, but all of the essential functions of the center and its manager are the same. The functions that are carried out by data center staff specialists in the large center are handled on an informal basis in the small center. Perhaps without realizing it, the DCM in a small center has service agreements (usually in the form of verbal commitments to users), has performance reviews (frequently through face-to-face contact with user managers), has a work profile (often in the heads of a few people who know all the applications in the center), and is acutely aware of the use and availability of resources (since the DCM in a small center often gets directly involved in setting up, scheduling, and perhaps running jobs). The material in this book is focused on the medium- and large-scale data center, where more formal methods are needed and used, but the ideas that are presented apply also to smaller-scale installations. As the small installation matures and its workload increases, more formal, disciplined approaches are needed in managing the data center, approaches that are described in this book.

At whatever scale the data center exists, the job of the DCM requires expertise in a number of disciplines. The operating loop involves the skills of a *production control manager* (one who is able to respond quickly to changes in the operating environment), the talents of an *expert in customer service and public relations* (one who is ready to deal with possibly conflicting demands from several quarters), and the abilities of a cost-conscious *entrepreneur* (who can eliminate wastefulness whenever possible). The planning loop calls into play the skills of an *industrial engineer* (in trying to squeeze every possible drop of efficient production from the given resources), the foresight of a *long-range planner* (in attempting to anticipate future resource needs), and the perspective of a *general manager* (in per-

suading top management of the level of resources necessary in order
to meet present and contemplated service and cost objectives). *All of
these roles require a continual examination of the resource/service mix by
the DCM.*

    While computer technology is continually changing and influ-
encing the center from outside the organization, the needs and maturity of the center itself are also changing; the fact that these changes
occur at different rates adds another complicating factor to the DCM's
job. For those installations that have a highly integrated data resource
(such as the communications networks and data base applications typically found in medium- and large-scale centers), the basic functions
shown in Figure 1.3 apply, but additional functions must be evaluated
and divested or absorbed from time to time. For example, where
should the reporting responsibility be for such functions as word processing, communications control, and data base administration?
Wherever management eventually assigns the responsibility, you must
adjust to the situation. If such a function as word processing is assigned to the data center, you must take this resource into account in
terms of user or customer service (operating loop) and resource utilization (planning loop). If the functions are assigned outside the center,
you must provide linkages (such as data transfer and file interface) to
those functions in order to maintain the desired service levels for the
organization.

APPLYING THIS INFORMATION TO YOUR DATA CENTER

    At the end of each chapter in this book, we will provide a brief
list of questions that will help you to examine your own data center
and to apply the information in the chapter to your work as manager.
We will also provide hints or sample responses to these questions
wherever they are needed to trigger responses of your own.

    The following questions summarize the important points made in
this first chapter:

1. If you were to diagram the organizational structure of your data
   center, would it resemble the balanced picture shown in Figure
   1.3?

Hint: If yours is a balanced center, you should be able to identify representative activities for each part of the diagram. *Review the data center diagram regularly and list the areas where you feel the center is out of balance. (For instance, you may not receive information early enough on planned applications, or you may feel that user participation in performance reviews is unsatisfactory.) These items then become an agenda that points out what actions to take in order to achieve a balance and that helps you evaluate progress over the next few months.*

2. Do users regularly participate in the operating loop in your data center?
   Hint: To measure the level of user participation in your data center, ask yourself how often you meet with users to review service agreements and data center performance.

3. Does your top management understand its role in the planning loop?
   Hint: To ensure that your answer to this question is "yes," you can use the following recommendations:
   a. Keep management informed by periodically presenting information about resource utilization and availability.
   b. Give management an idea of where you expect the data center to be in the next two to three years and an idea of what type of management support you need to realize these goals.

These questions provide a partial checklist of goals to strive for in managing a data center. The remainder of this book is designed to help you accomplish these goals in your own data center.

SUMMARY

To achieve and operate a "well-balanced" data center, you should do the following:

- Understand what is going on in the data center among hardware, software, and people. Be able to explain underutilization of any of these resources, excessive overtime, or dramatic peaks and valleys in the workload.

- Establish and meet the service goals that should be reflected in written service agreements with users.

- Develop a data center forward plan and relay this plan to upper management. The plan should indicate the expected workloads and service levels, and the resources needed.

2

Managing the Total
Computer Resource

The total computer resource *includes people, hardware, and software. You can think of this total resource as a type of three-legged stool: when all of the legs are strong, they form a solid structural base, but if any of the legs are weak, the stool tips over. As a data center manager, you must ensure the proper balance among the three "legs" of the data center. This chapter introduces the main concepts that will help you manage each of the resource components effectively.*

MANAGING PEOPLE

The people resources of a data center consist of your staff, the data center users, and your boss.

Managing Your Staff

Anyone charged with managing a data processing area has a special responsibility when it comes to managing people. The general shortage of capable people dictates that the DCM be particularly sensitive to the handling, training, and development of the staff in the data center. Staff members need to see clear proof that they are important to the operation and that their contribution is recognized and appreciated. One way to do this is for you to delegate appropriate levels of responsibility and authority.

Delegating. The delegation of authority and responsibility is difficult for many managers, especially those who have come up through the ranks and have been used to doing many of the data center tasks themselves. It is hard to "let go of the reins," make an assignment, and then sit back and hope that the individual does the job as well as you would have done it yourself. *To provide development and satisfaction for your staff members, however, you must learn to delegate.*

One aspect of delegating is knowing who should take on extra responsibility and who should not. As a general rule, it does not make much sense to delegate responsibility to someone (like a data entry clerk) whose current tasks involve little decision making. On the other hand, someone like a shift supervisor or technical support specialist can profit from added authority, since this person can thus learn new management skills and improve his or her opportunities for promotion.

Most employees are eager to learn new skills, but they may have some worries about handling added responsibility. These worries can be solved if you provide a supportive structure for the assignments you make. First, you need to answer the following questions for the employee to whom you are delegating a task:

- What is the scope of the assignment?

- What form should the results take?
  - Report?
  - Plan?
  - Tangible results (such as a recommendation that reduces turn-around time by 13 percent or an off-site back-up procedure that simplifies the operator's activities while maintaining back-up integrity)?
  - Intangible results (such as taking responsibility for running a check-signing machine and returning it to the treasurer's office—this places responsibility where it should be and improves data center morale)?
  - Recommendations?

- What authority does the assignment carry?

- What limitations does the assignment carry?

- How will the results be measured?
  - By degree of improvement? In what areas?
  - By a reduction in costs?
  - By service level?
  - By productivity level?

- What resources are available for the assignment?

- When is the final measurement to be made?

- What interim checkpoints have been established?

You need to explain not only how *the results will be measured but also* what *specific results are expected.* For example, if you are assigning responsibility for the operation of a given shift in the data center, make it clear that you are expecting a productivity improvement of, say, 5 percent on that shift over the next year. (Of course, how productivity itself is measured must also be understood; Chapter Eleven covers measuring professional performance.)

Your employees need to have some "landmarks" along the way to help them measure their own progress. *Set some interim or incremental objectives against which the individual's progress can be measured.* On a six-month project, for example, have an in-depth review of the project with the individual at least every month to see how much progress is being made and whether help is needed. These reviews should be conducted with three goals in mind:

- To ascertain progress

- To enhance the individual's ability to manage an assignment

- To suggest follow-up for areas that may have been overlooked or that may need improvement

Judge the progress by asking specific questions and insist on specific answers. Questions such as "How are things going?" that are met with answers such as "Okay" shed no light on the situation. Open-ended questions such as "What additional resources do you need to complete the assignment?" may elicit responses such as "Two weeks more time" or "Four more people for six weeks." Each of these answers may lead to further questions, but the information exchanged is valuable and it may uncover problems in the project that would otherwise have been glossed over.

Once the assignment has been given, make sure that proper resources (such as people, money, and machine time) have been made available to get the job done. At the same time, make sure that unnecessary administrative chores have not been added to the task. In other words, if you want results from your employees, allow them to do the work that you are asking them to do: don't keep them from doing their work because they are too busy filling out reports, attending meetings, or generally doing administrative chores when they should be doing their assigned task.

Once you have delegated authority, there is a natural tendency for you to want to step back into the picture at the first sign of trouble. After all, the ultimate responsibility for whatever your employees do or fail to do rests with you. *In sum, to delegate successfully, you need some means of measuring and controlling the employee's progress (or lack of it), you need to give the employee every chance to work out problems for himself or herself, and you need a great stock of patience.*

Managing Your Users

In order to balance the demands created by the data center's users against your computer resources, you need to stay in touch with the user community within your organization. The "user community," of course, includes clerical people in various departments, supervisors and middle-level managers (such as the accounts payable supervisor or the cost accounting manager), and the managers of functional areas (for instance, the company controller or the production control manager).

If your users are new to computer applications, it is in your best interest to spend enough time with them (you may, at times, think that it is an inordinate amount of time) to explain how the application works, to listen to their problems, and to provide them with proper training. Many organizations view user training as strictly a systems and programming function, but remember that most systems analysts do not have a thorough understanding of the operations in the data center. Thus, it makes sense that the DCM take an active part in user training—you can then ensure that the "operations message" gets across to the users. This "message" includes your commitment to service, your use of service agreements (and the reasons for them), your organization, and to whom the user can talk when help is needed.

Among the issues that should be covered with users are:

- Why is meeting a batch transaction input deadline important? Briefly describe your batch schedule to the user and illustrate how a missed input deadline cascades through the data center system, resulting in other deadlines being missed.

- What happens in the data center when a user terminal goes down? Explain to the user the diagnostic and recovery steps that you and your staff take to ensure data integrity and prompt resumption of on-line service.

- What kinds of information can the user relay that will be helpful to data center personnel regarding the performance of the on-line system? The user may suggest changes in the sign-on procedure or may have a suggestion that would eliminate longer response times during certain periods of the day.

If this type of information is conveyed to the users, you will be able to use their "eyes and ears" to better your operations. For example, after hearing you describe your batch schedule, the user may realize—and tell you—that there has been an artificial deadline for the delivery of certain reports. If you adjust this deadline, the user's input deadline can also be adjusted. Similarly, a user's comments about on-line performance may help you "tune" the system so that more resources are allocated to on-line during certain times of the day.

Managing Your Boss

The management of your organization must be continually apprised as to whether the data center is keeping the total computer resource in balance. Your primary means of passing along this information is through your immediate manager. We have three strong recommendations for "managing your boss":

1. If you and your manager work in the same building or complex of buildings, *make a point of having a regular (weekly) meeting with the boss,* just to exchange information and keep the boss posted on specific data center accomplishments or potential problem situations.

2. In addition, *set a specific time for discussing computer resource usage and planning.* This special computer resource review meeting probably should take place on a monthly basis.

3. Between meetings, *keep a list of things to be discussed at the next meeting.*

Your boss has other sources of information concerning the operation of the data center: users, managers of user departments, and other managers (such as the marketing director, the manufacturing vice-president, the vice-president in charge of the Trust Department in a bank, and the vice-president of the Underwriting Department in an insurance company) are continually feeding your manager information about your operation. This means that your manager can work *for* you by helping to express the data center's needs both to the users and to the organization's top management. In other words, your boss communicates with a different set of people, usually at a higher level and on a more regular basis, than you do. If you arm your boss with a regular update on your problems, plans, and progress, then the boss, with the advantage of a higher management position, can help you by lobbying for hardware or software or personnel resources, by arguing in favor of funding for a project, or by placating a troublesome user (yes, this type of user occasionally exists!).

MANAGING HARDWARE AND SOFTWARE

Hardware and software are the other two elements of the total computer resource that the DCM must balance with each other and with the people element. The newest processor is of little use if the data center's hardware configuration is out of balance (if you have inadequate disk space, for example, or overloaded data channels). The most sophisticated software, whether it be computer control software (that is, the operating system) or application software, will not be cost effective if the hardware is inadequate to handle the complex program routines or if people are not properly trained to operate and use the software.

Typically, a change in any one part of the hardware/software configuration introduces whole sets of problems for the DCM. For example, a data center may experience the following four-step process as the center moves through various phases of information processing:

1. Primary applications (such as accounting or basic inventory control) are put on the computer with each application having independent, small-volume files.

2. Early attempts are made at integrating the data for various applications (such as tying basic inventory data to purchasing information).

3. Users become increasingly dependent on data processing as computerized information totally displaces manual systems (for example, clerical people grow to depend on computer terminals as a way to access information, and they finally throw out their index card systems).

4. A data base system is installed and used, with an increased number of on-line users and terminals; thus, the data resource moves front-and-center as a recognized organizational asset.

Step 1 brings with it many first-time users of the data center. This means that the DCM must train the data center staff to deal diplomatically with these users while still adhering to the center's standards and procedures and meeting the center's service commitments.

In Step 2, a control problem arises as multiple user areas begin to share common data. The DCM must renew emphasis on such data center procedures as establishing authorization to access certain files if the center is to avoid the destruction of data or uncoordinated updates of the same files.

The increase in the number of on-line terminals, found in Step 3, gives the data center high visibility within the organization. During this time, overall service levels, especially response times, are critical. The DCM should be ready to tune the system's resources or change the batch/on-line mix in order to maintain the desired service levels.

The advent of a full-scale data base in the organization (Step 4) will result in a new wave of first-time users (these new users are those who have a one-time request and want to tap the data base for some information). At this point, the DCM must emphasize data security and accessibility, without hurting response time for regular applications. Depending on the scope and frequency of the one-time requests, the DCM may need to provide additional disk work space or processing power.

You can see that each change affects the entire data center; thus, the real key to successful growth lies in forming a *plan* and operating within that plan instead of merely reacting to a current crisis in the data center. If the DCM, the staff, the users, and the management are all sufficiently aware of the overall plan for the data center, then the move from one level of complexity or sophistication to another can be accomplished with a minimum of surprises. Without a plan, you may solve an immediate problem, but your solution might work against the data center's larger goals.

For example, when the problems of the first-time users (Step 1) seem insurmountable, don't let the data center personnel do the users' work (such as correcting input data) in an effort to expedite that work. This approach is short-sighted—the workload in subsequent steps will force the data center to add staff to do the work that the users should have been doing all along.

In Step 2, don't take shortcuts around the data center controls simply because users are having trouble sharing a data file or planning the timing of an update. These shortcuts will come back to haunt the DCM (bad data live on!).

When the service levels in Step 3 begin to degenerate, don't rush out and order more hardware until you've exhausted other means of improving the service levels (such as allocating more hardware resources to on-line during the day and moving batch work to another shift). At the same time, prepare upper management for the likelihood of needing additional resources in anticipation of Step 4. *In short, the DCM must understand that current actions affect both the solution of current problems and the accomplishment of goals for the future.*

APPLYING THIS INFORMATION TO YOUR DATA CENTER

1. When was the last time you delegated a part of your responsibility? How much authority was delegated? Was it a successful experience for you and for the employee? What would you do differently next time?

2. In what ways have individuals on your staff grown through your delegating responsibility and authority to them?
   Example: The task of reviewing the first-shift processing schedule was delegated to a data control supervisor. This caused the supervisor to contact and interview a number of users and prepared her for the next assignment: scheduling supervisor.

3. Which of your users understand the most about how the data center operates? What is being done to educate the other users on this point?

4. What topics were brought up the last time you and your boss discussed computer resources? When is the next meeting scheduled?

SUMMARY

A balance must be maintained among the three parts of the data center's resources: people, hardware, and software. The following recommendations summarize things you can do to achieve this balance:

1. Develop your people by delegating responsibility and authority. Be sure to clearly state the assignment, identify the short-term and long-term goals, and provide adequate support so the person can successfully complete the project. With periodic reviews, reinforce the strong points of the person's performance and correct the weak points.

2. Make users aware of what goes on "behind the scenes" in the data center. Carefully consider user suggestions for improving data center service.

3. Keep your boss informed about the data center. Use the boss's position and contacts with upper management to aid in the resource planning for the center.

4. Have a mid- to long-range plan for the data center and let your boss know what it will take to bring the plan to life.

3

Managing the Data Center As a Business

A business looks at the level of services it provides, compares it to the customer demand for these services, and attempts to deliver the services at the lowest possible cost. Achieving this balance involves a variety of technical and nontechnical factors, such as the availability of resources, the ability to provide service within time constraints, and the quality of the service. In the same way, the data center manager must be aware of and must learn to balance the changing costs of resources and the changing demands for data center services, and decisions must be based on a broad range of business considerations, not just on the DCM's previous technical experience. In other words, as increasing costs and needs make the data center a significant part of corporate operations, the DCM must manage the center as an entrepreneur would. This idea of the manager as an entrepreneur may seem radically different from the traditional view. This chapter presents five major arguments for managing your data center as a business; Part Four in this book will discuss how to do this in greater detail.

CONTROLLING RISING COSTS

Although the cost of hardware on a per-unit basis is declining, total data processing costs continue to increase dramatically. From 1970 to 1978, aggregate United States data processing budgets rose almost two and one-half times from a total of $17 billion in 1970 to $42 billion in 1978. This trend is expected to continue in the 1980s. Aggregate spending for data processing is expected to top $78 billion in 1983—almost double the amount spent in 1978 (International Data Corporation, 1980). This means that, as more and more corporate applications are put on the computer, the DCM is managing a larger budget and the data center is becoming a very visible, integrated part of corporate operations.

To control costs, you should review them periodically "from the ground up." Don't simply extrapolate past costs and assume that they are still justified in a changing environment.

Rising costs and the increase in visibility are not problems that the DCM can solve on technical expertise alone; they are the problems typical of any growing business.

HANDLING THE RAPIDLY CHANGING TECHNOLOGY

Barry W. Boehm (1979) has noted that the degree of freedom in software engineering design has changed dramatically from the 1950s to the 1970s and that this trend will continue in the 1980s. For example, Boehm states that, in 1950, only about five choices of CPU equipment existed. In 1970, about 200 CPU choices existed; of these, one hundred were among the likely choices. There were no data management systems available in 1950, but by 1970 there were 100 possibilities with about thirty of these being the likely choices. Along with this proliferation of hardware designs, price-versus-performance characteristics continue to change. For example, the IBM /370 Model 138 had an attractive cost of $1,217,000 for a million-instruction-per-second (MIPS) performance compared to the older /370 Model 158, which cost $1,658,000 per MIPS (*Computer Economics Report*, 1982). Also, vendors regularly announce new capabilities or additional features for existing equipment components. The way in which the equipment components are attached or connected to each other is frequently modified, enhanced, or restricted.

All of these changing factors make the data center manager's task somewhat akin to trying to draw pictures in a surf-washed sand. Each time one looks around, the picture has changed or been washed away. No matter what combination of hardware and software one chooses, that choice can appear flawed when the next vendor announcement appears (usually, it seems, within days or weeks of one's most recent major configuration decision). *You should test such an announcement against your corporate data center plan and identify the total impact of the changing technology (that is, the changes needed in staffing, training, software, and procedures, and the cost/benefit relationships of these changes). In other words, you must use good business sense to determine if each change affects the corporation, if the change should be assimilated into the data center, and how the change should be assimilated so that it either improves service or reduces costs.*

COMPETING FOR QUALIFIED PEOPLE TO DO THE JOB

Qualified data processing personnel are in short supply; thus, the DCM is competing in a seller's market for qualified employees. However, people enjoy being a part of a well-run organization; they enjoy being a part of a winning team. *To help make your people feel that they're winners, hold brief but regular meetings with your staff members and point out how their work has helped the company make more money. Mention cost-saving ideas that have been suggested by users and by the data center staff.*

The DCM who can manage the total computer resource to produce a winning combination will find it easier to attract good people to the operation. Specifically, a data center with good operating procedures, one that has a high on-time performance record and a reputation for reliability with its users, and one that makes good, cost-effective use of its people and equipment will tend to draw better people to the company than a data center that is poorly run. These same characteristics will help the well-managed data center keep the good people that it already has.

MEETING THE INCREASING DEMAND FOR SERVICES

In spite of occasional flurries of resistance to a computerized application or to computers in general, users most often come to accept the use of a computer in their daily business lives. In fact, not only do they accept it, but, after an application has been in production for a time, users will actually resist the removal of the automated application and will usually ask for the automation of additional applications. As the number of applications increases, the computer becomes a very visible part of the user's operation. Consequently, user department managers become more aware of what a computer can do for their departments and of the generally falling prices of hardware. This combination of a desire for more applications, an increased awareness of the potential of the computer, and more attractive pricing for computer equipment leads to a greater demand for computer services.

You should stay in close touch with your users so that you can anticipate increased demand and respond creatively while holding costs down. For instance, explore ways of documenting job set-up procedures so this task can be done by the user. This puts more control in the user's hands, reduces the data center workload, and frees up data center resources.

COMPETING WITH DATA PROCESSING ALTERNATIVES

Finally, the data center should be run on a cost-effective basis because of the presence of competitive alternatives. If you do not do an effective job of managing the data center, someone else will. The DCM's goal is to "stay in business," and this applies both to the data center and to himself or herself. To put it another way, the DCM, by providing the best service possible (service whose costs the users can justify readily because of the benefits obtained), will have a facility that is more economically attractive than the facilities and services available from others.

Viable methods for processing data now include time sharing, facilities management, contract programming, packaged programs, and the like. Vendors selling these alternatives routinely make their pitch to top management and to the users. For this reason, the DCM must be continually aware of what a given service costs the organization and of what that service would cost from others. *With the wide array of equipment and software available, the DCM should be prepared to help users evaluate alternatives and to counsel users as to the most cost-effective way of doing the job. In addition, you should seek out friendly users who will "pilot" new technology on a limited scale before it is introduced to broader areas of the company.*

THE PERSONALITY OF THE ENTREPRENEURIAL MANAGER

These aspects of the DCM's job may lead you to ask, "Who in his or her right mind would want to manage a data center?" It is clearly not a job for those who like a steady, unchanging routine day after day. It is also not the position for those who do not want to change themselves, since the DCM must grow with the job, must expand his or her knowledge and interest areas as the operating environment continually changes. The successful DCM takes a broad view of problems as they arise, assesses their impact in corporate terms, seeks new solutions, and is not content with a "We have always done it this way" attitude.

The DCM's job involves continually examining the resources at hand (that is, the hardware and software installed and the people who operate them) and comparing them to the resources potentially available (that is, to vendor offerings in hardware and software and to the personnel in the marketplace). The results of this comparison must be matched against the expectations of the DCM's users, management, and staff. Discrepancies between the realities and the expectations must be explained, rationalized, or corrected. To be effective, then, the data center manager must be a skillful negotiator, be tenacious, work well with others, communicate clearly with top management, have an awareness of the business climate, be inquisitive, and have a realistic outlook as to what can and what cannot be accomplished. A good DCM should be able to respond positively to the following questions:

- Do you willingly seek a compromise solution to a problem?

- Do you attempt to compromise while persevering on basic principles?

- Can you talk easily with users? With data processing technicians?

- Can you relate well to a user manager's problems?

- Can you make a succinct case for gaining approval of a data center budget?

- Do you know what the company's operating results were for the last four quarters?

- Do you know how your company compares with competitors in terms of product line, sales volumes, and profitability?

Every decision you make must be evaluated in terms of its overall effect. Thus, you must operate like a successful business entrepreneur, continuing to provide the best service at the lowest cost and willing to challenge all comers.

FINDING OUT HOW TO RUN A BUSINESS

If you are a data center manager whose background is technical, you should make every attempt to expand your business skills. There are a number of ways to do this, such as:

- Enroll in an evening business course (or courses) at a local college or university (especially accounting, marketing, finance).

- Obtain an MBA degree (several universities have intensive programs in which you attend one day per week while working or in which you take leave from work for ten to thirteen weeks).

- Enlarge your reading list (regular reading should include *The Wall Street Journal, Fortune, Forbes, Harvard Business Review*). Pay special attention to articles on organization, cost accounting, leasing, and profiles on competitive companies.

- Go to a seminar on a non-DP subject (accounting for nonaccountants, motivation, and contracting are perennially popular topics).

- Find a mentor, someone you respect who is in a management position. Observe how the mentor makes decisions and handles personnel (hiring, firing, promotion, reorganization). Ask questions of the mentor, such as why a certain action was taken or not taken.

- Mentally try on your boss's problems and job—would you make the same decision your boss made?

- Establish and maintain a network of management contacts. Make a point of including several non-DP people in this network. Keep in touch with these contacts, observe how they manage, how they run their business, what special problems they face, and how they deal with their environment and business conditions.

APPLYING THIS INFORMATION TO YOUR DATA CENTER

1. Think through several recent decisions you have made that affected the data center. Select an example that dealt with hardware (such as installing additional disk storage units from your mainframe vendor), one that concentrated on software (such as selecting a data base management package), and one that involved personnel (such as deciding which of two people to promote to customer service supervisor for the data center).
   - Were these decisions made solely on their technical merit?
   - Were broader management implications, such as customer service or rapid implementation, taken into account?
   - Were you satisfied with the outcome?
   - Faced with the same decision, what additional factors would you consider next time?

2. What information sources (newspapers, periodicals, seminars, meetings) do you have available that can give you a broad perspective on business, management, and the activities of your company?
   - Can these sources be used more effectively?
     Example: *When an article appears about your company's line of business, make a point of discussing it with someone in management at your company. Find out how your company compares with the competition and with companies cited in the article.*

- Is your management aware of your need for this information?
- Are there other sources of information that you could use?
  Hint: Consider textbooks, autobiographies of business leaders, and discussions with management personnel.
- Does your boss know of the specific management topics in which you're interested?
  Hint: If your boss knows of your interest areas, he or she can pass on information about these areas and may direct you toward meetings, seminars, and conferences that will further your education.

3. Is your management aware of the demands for services that are being put on your data center? In other words, does your management know who your top three users are, which user's data center workload is changing most dramatically (growing or shrinking), how much excess capacity is available in the data center, and what your personal top-priority project is?

4. What is your management's general feeling about the amount of money being spent on the data center?
   - Too much?
   - Too little?
   - Not getting their money's worth?
   - Cost effective?
   - Don't know? (Better find out!)

5. What are your users' general feelings about the amount of money being spent on the data center?
   - Too much?
   - Too little?
   - Not getting their money's worth?
   - Cost effective?
   - Don't know? (Better find out!)

SUMMARY

The successful DCM must control rising costs, manage rapidly changing technology, acknowledge the scarcity of well-qualified people, deal with an increased demand for service, and be cognizant of competitive alternatives in the data processing industry. Thus, the DCM must function like a successful business entrepreneur, continually looking at the costs, benefits, and effectiveness of the center and evaluating possible changes in personnel and processes. The goal of the DCM is to provide the best service at the lowest cost to data center "customers."

4

Measuring the Data Center's Current Status

If you are to use this book to make cost-effective changes in your management of the data center, first you must know where your data center stands now and what its needs are. This chapter shows you how to assess the current status of your data center; it provides guidelines for measuring the center's cost/benefits to the organization and the level of its expenditures, for looking at the data center through the eyes of others, and for gauging the center's participation in corporate planning.

QUANTIFYING THE CENTER'S COST/BENEFITS

The importance of the data center to the corporation can be measured by considering the benefits that the corporation experiences from computerizing various applications. These benefits can be quantified in terms of revenue, cost avoidance, and cost reduction.

Measuring Benefits

If the data center directly generates revenue for the organization—it might act as a service bureau for outside clients—these monies can be measured as a benefit to the company (of course, you will want eventually to net the revenue benefits against the data processing costs). Most data centers, however, exist solely for internal purposes—that is, they are *cost centers* rather than revenue-generating entities or *profit centers*. Thus, the corporation is more likely to benefit from cost avoidance and cost reduction than from revenue from the data center.

Measuring Cost Avoidance

To measure cost avoidance, evaluate each application and assign a dollar value to costs that are *not* incurred because the application is on the computer. For instance, as volumes increase for the application, are you able to maintain constant levels of clerical staffing (in both the user area and the DP area)? In other words, because the application is computerized, are you able to avoid the costs of additional staff? Similarly, are you able to defer the costs of additional record-keeping facilities or equipment, even in the face of increased volumes for the application?

Measuring Cost Reductions

Cost reductions can also be quantified by looking at the expenditures that have been reduced because an application has been put on the computer. You may find areas where the clerical staff has been reduced or reassigned to more productive duties. Costly processing steps may have been eliminated since the work was computerized. In assigning dollar values to these savings, do not be overly concerned if the dollar amounts are not very "firm." Make estimates when necessary, identify these figures as estimates rather than definite dollar amounts, and then test these estimates for reasonableness. (For example, are the cost estimates of the wages saved consistent with wages being paid to the rest of the staff?)

Of course, you also need to net cost reductions against any increased expenditures in other areas of the application. For instance, if more people are added or if more equipment is being used in the data center because an application has been put on the computer, these added costs must be netted against the savings realized in the user area. A meaningful cost reduction results in a net operating savings that is large enough to pay for the reduction effort (that is, the one-time costs) within one year.

MEASURING THE LEVEL OF DP EXPENDITURES

A further measure of the status of the data center within the corporation can be obtained by analyzing the amount of money spent on data processing. The level of DP expenditures will rise and fall as the organization moves through various stages of growth. Thus, the data processing budget can be compared to some corporate financial base to determine whether the corporation is in an expansionary, stabilized, or retrenchment posture regarding data processing. By industry, here are some guidelines (International Data Corporation, 1980):

Industry	DP Budget
Manufacturing	0.7% of sales
Financial	0.2% of assets
Retail	0.3% of sales
Transportation	1.0% of sales
Utilities	0.6% of sales

Factors that can contribute to reducing the DP budget as a percentage of corporate revenue include:

- Intensive cost controls

- Recent cost-cutting measures

- Old equipment, fully depreciated

- Retrenchment, no new development

- Lack of investment in updating existing applications

Factors that can contribute to increasing the DP budget as a percentage of corporate revenue include:

- Few or no cost controls

- No cost-cutting program

- New equipment, high depreciation

- Massive new development projects

- DP industry salaries escalating

- Many units of old equipment, not replaced by more efficient equipment

In measuring the importance of DP within the organization, you should take into account the above variables regarding the level of data processing expenditures. Check periodically to see where your installation stands with regard to these guidelines. Be prepared to explain differences, either plus or minus, between your level of expenditures and the guidelines. Few, if any, installations will match the guideline levels exactly or will remain at the guideline amounts for any period of time. At some points, your spending levels will be less than the guidelines, at some points more than the guidelines, and at some points exactly equal to the guidelines. It is more important to measure your spending levels and to understand the reasons behind them than it is to match the spending guidelines. Specifically, ask yourself why your company is spending substantially more or less dollars on data processing than others in the industry. (You can also expect your management to ask you these same questions.)

MEASURING HOW OTHERS SEE YOU

The data center does not exist as an island within a company; rather, it survives by being a service center to the organization. As such, it is very dependent upon whether the users and management feel that it produces a fair return for the money that is spent on data processing. In other words, if you think of the users as "customers," then you can see how important it is to measure what these customers think of your business, of your service, of the way your employees deal with them, and of your prices. Just as in an independent business enterprise, if your customers are not satisfied, they will eventually take their business elsewhere.

Quite often, the "feelings" users have toward the data center are at least as important as the actual service being provided. Some users, for instance, look at data processing as a service function within the company; they consider data processing employees to be nothing more than a subservient group providing marginal or questionable benefits. These users often impose unilateral demands on the DP staff and expect immediate, flawless results. Other users feel that the computer is a necessary evil, something that must be tolerated. These users tend to have as little contact with the computer staff as possible. The third group of users actually recognizes and appreciates the genuine value provided by the data center.

On the other hand, DP staff members quite often hold a similar range of attitudes toward the user, and these attitudes may widen rather than bridge the gulf between themselves and the users they serve. To help you pinpoint the feelings of your users and of your own staff, we have provided the following lists, which name the various ways that both hostile and positive attitudes can be expressed:

1. Users . . .
   - Are ambivalent toward DP
   - Feel DP costs too much
   - Are intolerant of poor response time
   - Fear the computer
   - Resist the discipline and inflexibility of DP
   - Feel DP is indispensable
   - Do not understand DP
   - View the computer as "magic"
   - Feel the computer invades privacy
   - Use a different vocabulary from DP specialists
   - Feel DP staff members speak jargon, not English
   - Think DP development time is too long
   - See DP as not involved in planning
   - Think on-line systems are "down" too often

- Consider DP people as strictly technicians
- Feel DP people don't want to be part of the company
- Would like DP to understand the company's priorities
- Think the computer is a necessary evil
- Recognize that some DP has been beneficial
- Want faster turnaround
- Must depend on computer systems
- Feel some systems are unreliable
- Think the DP solutions are not correct for the problem
- Feel performance falls short of design expectations

2. Data processing people . . .
- Think users are overly dependent on DP
- Resent the "yours" versus "mine" attitude of some users
- Realize that service levels are critical and very visible
- Recognize that users want more information more often
- Know that ineffective output distribution gives DP a "black eye"
- Want more user involvement in the early design phases
- Feel DP frequently suffers from "growing pains"
- Think user departments resist change
- Sense that users see DP as a threat to job security
- Regret that users are impatient and that DP cannot respond quickly
- Feel users do not understand the priorities of DP
- Know that the DP image is only as good as the last service level
- Realize that early resistance to an application often changes to user dependence on the computer
- Feel users do not understand what happens in DP
- Sense users' increased expectations for computers
- Think users have little empathy or sympathy for DP problems
- Resent "negative recognition" (for down time or late deliveries, for example)
- Think users fear loss of control over user operations

The best DP/user environments exist where the negative items on the above lists have been minimized or eliminated, and the best tool for accomplishing this is a continuing dialogue between the data processing people and the users. If you are doing a good job, the users should know and understand it. If you and the users are not satisfied with the service levels you are providing, let the users know what is being done to improve service. Chapter Six will discuss ways in which this type of dialogue can be established and maintained.

MEASURING YOUR PARTICIPATION IN THE CORPORATE PLAN

The degree of participation (or lack of it) that DP enjoys in the area of corporate planning gives another perspective on the importance of data processing to the corporation. Relatively immature data processing installations will be viewed by the users and management as staff departments rather than line operations, and DP will not play a significant role in corporate planning. (For our purposes, *staff* departments are those areas that are not directly involved in producing or delivering a product or service; *line* departments are those that are directly involved. For example, the data center is usually considered a staff function, along with the accounting and personnel departments, while the teller operation in a bank or the production control department in a manufacturing company are considered line functions.)

As the DP role within the company changes and grows to the point where it is perceived as a more integral part of the company's day-to-day operation, its role in corporate planning will also be expanded. When the installation reaches a relatively mature level, as characterized by a good applications mix, a reasonably well-informed user community, and a proven record for efficient, effective performance, the DP area will be looked upon as more of a line function.

The recognition of DP as a line function is also a realization by users and management that the data processing staff and the computer are indispensable to the company's operation and that the computer managers should rightly be included in the planning for the company. At this point, the plans of the company will have a very direct bearing on the level of computer service needed, and these company plans, in turn, provide guidance as to what amount and level of people, hardware, and software the DCM needs for the long term. Chapter Six discusses in greater detail the evolution of the data center from a staff position to a line function.

For now, a few quick indicators can help you assess where your data center currently fits in the corporate picture. If you, as DCM, are informed only *after the fact* of changes in procedures for processing work (such as new order entry deadlines), then the data center is clearly not viewed as an integral part of the operation. If, on the other hand, you are brought into discussions early and made part of the decision to change procedures, then the data center is considered a key part of the operation.

APPLYING THIS INFORMATION TO YOUR DATA CENTER

1. What benefits (cost reduction, cost avoidance) can be identified and quantified for applications being run in your data center?

2. How does the level of data processing spending at your installation compare with average spending levels for your industry?

3. How does the present spending level compare with the spending level three years ago? Five years ago?

4. What additional benefits have come to the data center because of additional spending? Could the money have been spent more wisely? What benefits have disappeared because of reduced spending?
   Example: An expense cutback may have meant elimination of a quality control position in the data center, resulting in a gradual decay in the quality of work and eventually leading to more reruns.

5. Who are your most supportive and least supportive users? Why?

6. How would you assess the relationship between data processing and top management in your organization?

SUMMARY

This chapter has emphasized the need to understand your data center's status in the organization. The information included here is summarized in the following recommendations:

- You should assess the current level of workload, staffing, and equipment in the data center.

- Periodically measure the costs and benefits of having the data center and be prepared to explain spending levels (and changes in spending levels over time). A data center "snapshot" taken from time to time should show a decrease in the cost of processing a given unit of work, a higher level of service or quality to the user, or a combination of these two factors.

- Work continually to satisfy users' (customers') needs from the data center. Fold the demands caused by these needs into a forward plan for the data center and be ready to make this plan a part of your participation in the corporate planning process.

5

Defining the Data Center's Future

This chapter presents ideas on how to compare the data center's actual position (in terms of services and applications) with where you want your data center to be in order to serve your users and management better.

ANALYZING FUNCTIONAL STRATEGIES

A *functional strategy* defines the way in which the data center performs the work required by a user. *As the data center manager, it is your job to ensure that your functional strategy matches the way in which the corresponding user approaches the work.* (You must also ensure that your functional strategies meet the corporate objectives for the use of information resources.)

Perhaps one user manager sets a high priority on service to customers, even at the risk of paying some premiums in the form of wages or extra capacity; as the DCM, you should slant the data center's services to coincide with this user's objectives and methods. In other words, you might provide equipment and other resources to support the peak periods for this user's workloads, although you realize that there will be surplus capacity during other periods. Conversely, if a user manager emphasizes minimizing costs in his or her area, you should concentrate on minimizing that user's operating costs in the data center, perhaps by installing lower-speed, less costly communications devices.

Note that, in the first example, the user's strategy does not give you carte blanche for wild, unnecessary spending. Instead, it means that this user is willing to spend extra amounts for premium service to customers. The task of the DCM is to suggest ways to achieve this high level of service at the most reasonable price. You may, for example, suggest installing extra terminals in the user area or make a commitment to rapid turnaround for this user's jobs.

Similarly, in the case of the cost-conscious user, you face the challenge of providing the best possible service at the lowest cost. You might suggest overnight processing or exception reporting, which would reduce the amount of printing required.

Steps to Take for Adjusting Functional Strategies

To analyze and adjust your functional strategies, you need to take the following steps:

1. Examine the types of work done in the data center for various user areas. Identify the critical applications for each user *and rate the level* *of service that each user receives from the data center.* A level of service consists of the data center making available a computer resource (such as a terminal) or delivering a result (such as a batch report) within a particular time limit and for a particular cost.

2. Meet with the user manager *to be sure that your service levels agree with his or her objectives.* Discuss these services in terms of on-time delivery, the quality of the product produced, and the cost of providing this product.

3. Explain to the user manager the reasons for input deadlines *in the data center.* Explain, for example, that if the user does not meet these deadlines, the data center may be late in delivering the work, or the extra effort required by data center staff to make up the lost time may result in higher costs to process the work.

4. If the quality of the work is not as good as it should be, find out why *this is so.* Perhaps your staff does not have adequate resources to do the job properly. You may need additional employees, equipment, or work space. These additional resources will cause, of course, additional costs, but the per-unit cost of doing the work may not necessarily increase if the productivity and quality improve. Poor quality work that has to be reworked costs as much money, or more, as doing the job correctly in the first place.

5. Consider the interrelationships that exist between users. *Notice how the work of one department or division agrees with or differs from the concerns or strategies of other departments.* The delivery or availability of output to one user, for instance, may be part of a critical timing or information flow between two user areas. By understanding these connecting dependencies, you can do a better job of scheduling and assigning priorities in the data center while attempting to satisfy all of your users.

LOOKING AT THE DATA CENTER'S HISTORY AND ITS PROSPECTS

Looking at your data center's history can help you plan for the work to come. Determine the applications that were considered to be critical two years ago and five years ago. Analyze just why these applications were key applications at that time. Note the volume of the workload for these applications in terms of absolute levels of work (for instance, five years ago, the center processed 1,500 transactions per week for the accounts payable application) and in terms of the relative workload within the data center (five years ago the accounts payable application represented 12 percent of the center's workload). Compare the total number of people in the center today with the numbers for two and five years ago, and identify the major applications on which these people spent their time. Compare today's budget with the budgets of these past years, and note how the spending levels were distributed among various applications.

Once you have compiled this information, use it to answer the following questions:

- What do all these figures tell you about the changes that have been made over the past five years?
  Example: "Five years ago, the data center workload showed an emphasis on accounting applications; now, the majority of the data center resources are devoted to manufacturing applications."

- Has the data center become a more efficient operation?
  Example: "We are running the computer 38 percent more hours per month and the cost per hour has decreased 3 percent compared with five years ago."

- Do these figures indicate trends that can help you plan for the future?
  Example: "If present trends continue, manufacturing applications will take over 65 percent of the center's resources within the next three years."

- What do these figures tell you about your staffing needs for certain workloads?
  Example: "We will need more trained people for on-line applications and less staff for batch processing during the next three years."

The overall corporate business plan provides another source of information about the data center's prospects. More mature centers will have a workload distribution that closely parallels the mainstream business activities of the corporation, as Richard Nolan (1979) has concluded in the studies he has made of data processing installations. The DCM can create functional strategies for the data center based on knowledge of the corporate plan for the next three to five years. *Be aware of plans to add new products or services, to reduce or drop existing products or services, or to maintain the status quo in some areas of the corporation.* This information can easily be obtained by having regular (at least monthly) contact with the user managers through informal chats or scheduled meetings.

GAUGING THE ECONOMIC HEALTH OF THE COMPANY

Successful data center managers learn to stay abreast of the economic health of their company in order to gauge what equipment may be needed and what processing alternatives to explore. *By staying in regular contact with user managers and with your boss, you should be aware of which divisions or product lines are enjoying good years, which are encountering bad times, and which are in a flat or stabilized period.* For the division with a "hot" product and with expanding sales, you can expect increased processing volumes, requests for additional capabilities (such as more terminals or increased storage capacities), and demands for faster turnaround or response times. These needs seldom take the form of neatly packaged, formal requests to the data processing area since, in the dynamics of the user's business, there is usually little time to spare when a product is doing well. This means that, unless you make a point of following the economic status of user departments, you may be given far less time to provide additional services than you or your staff would like.

By contrast, the division or product that is having a rough year will probably scale down requests for data services. Numbers of computer runs, numbers of copies of reports, or numbers of terminals in the user areas may all be cut back as volumes shrink and cost-cutting moves are made. Like the profitable divisions, the division that finds itself in trouble will want you to act quickly to reduce expenditures.

To face these demands, you must be prepared to advise the user managers as to the effects of various courses of action. In the case of the user who wants to reduce costs, you may not be able to extricate the company from equipment commitments without incurring pay-ment penalties, or the apparent cost savings may not be realized if the downturn in this user's sales is expected to be of short duration and the equipment would have to be reinstalled as sales volumes pick up.

Similarly, cutting costs by reducing the number of skilled person-nel in the data center may backfire if capable people are hard to find when the need arises a few months down the road. Often the user who wants to cut costs will say to the data center manager, "You figure out what you are going to do with those people. They work for you!" In this case, you must decide whether to assign the people to other duties, keep the people in the hope that business will improve, or release them. Again, to make this decision, you need to be a party to the orga-nization's long-range needs and its plans for information resources. If these plans call for increased service from the data center, the staff should probably be retained. If the outlook for the future indicates reduced service demands, the staff should be reduced.

The data center is also affected when a division or product line has stabilized within the company or within its marketplace. Stabiliza-tion is characterized by a relatively mature product or service, one for which demand, competition, and sales volumes can be predicted with a fair amount of accuracy. In this situation, you should be prepared to advise the user as to the most economical means for doing the job.

When a product or service is "taking off" following its initial in-troduction, there is often a sacrifice in cost effectiveness in favor of simply getting the job done. *More rigorous cost-accounting studies usu-ally take place after the product or service has settled down, in an effort to enhance its profitability. At that point, you can suggest the evaluation of alternate or additional vendors for equipment (for mainframes, peripherals, modems, or terminals), for software (such as the line control programs or utilities), or for supplemental services (such as maintenance, expendable supplies, or microfiche).* You must also advise the user of the pros and cons of these cost-cutting moves in terms of quality, availability, and vendor reliability. There is not necessarily a direct correlation be-tween quality and price (either high or low).

Whether it is a case of serving an expanding product or service, one that is retrenching, or one that has stabilized, it is very important for the DCM to know what's happening in the user divisions. If you have any luck at all, the seemingly conflicting requests and demands will allow you to reassign resources (in the form of both people and equipment) to serve all of the user needs best. In order to do this, you must have a good deal of information as to the current "health" of each user area and what the plans and future needs of the user area might be.

The changes that occur in the data center will be dictated by the current status of the center (as discussed in the previous chapter), by the economic vigor and information needs of the organization (as noted in this chapter), and by the changing aspects of the data processing industry. The following chapter examines the effect that these changes can have on a data center.

APPLYING THIS INFORMATION TO YOUR DATA CENTER

1. As the DCM, do you have a clear idea of the objectives of the corporation?

2. What are the operating objectives of the key users of the data center facilities?
   • How have these objectives changed over the past three years?
   • Are there noticeable differences in objectives among the key users?

3. How is the data center structured to respond to these user objectives?
   Example: Are procedures regularly reviewed to eliminate unnecessary steps that may result in extended turnaround time? Have you analyzed the cost effectiveness of the data center equipment?

4. What assistance can be offered (people, hardware, software) to help management get information that it needs?
   Example: Do you have software with a new graphic display capability that might be useful to the marketing department?

SUMMARY

This chapter can be summarized by the following recommendations:
   • You should look for consistency among the functions provided by

the data center, the service desired by the users, and the service and cost objectives of the organization.

- Make a point of talking regularly with users to review delivery or availability of data center resources, the quality of the center's work, and the cost of producing this work.

- Take note of the changing workload, staffing and application emphasis over a three- to five-year period.

- Be attuned to the business "health" of the company and its various operations.

6

Managing the Changes in Data Processing

As the data center manager, you can expect changes in three significant areas as your data center matures and becomes an information utility in the corporation. These areas are: (1) the technology of data processing, (2) the terminology of data processing, and (3) the role of data processing in the corporation as DP moves from a staff position into that of a line function. In this chapter, we discuss these changes, placing particular emphasis on your responsibilities as the changes occur.

MANAGING THE CHANGES IN TECHNOLOGY

The following statistics illustrate the rapidity and the magnitude of the technological changes that have occurred in data processing in recent years (Wagner, 1979):

---

1. Processor speeds (multiplications per second):
1952	2,200
1964	12,000
1980	240,000

2. Processor memory capacity (in bytes):
1960	32,000; 64,000; 128,000
1980	millions

3. Processor memory costs (monthly per million bytes):
1952	$222,000
1964	$28,000
1980	$430

This type of change is likely to continue. To keep both the data processing staff and the data center user informed of technological changes that may affect operations, the data center manager must stay abreast of activities in the data processing marketplace. Your prime sources of information are the trade magazines, such as *Computer Decisions*, *Datamation*, and *Infosystems*, and vendor announcements.

Technological changes influence how data services can be provided and how expensive they will be. These changes also influence the availability of personnel or the attractiveness of your company to skilled DP personnel. In other words, if your company is running equipment or software that is considered outmoded, it may be very difficult to get people to come to work for you.

Technological changes may take the form of expanded product lines offered by a vendor or the form of more vendors offering the existing technology. For instance, an existing vendor may announce new magnetic tape capabilities that allow more devices on a given configuration, or the vendor may now be offering more than one model to choose from so that you have a choice of speeds and capacities. On the other hand, if additional vendors enter a given segment of the equipment market (modems, for example), they stimulate competition and give the buyer more options. *Your job is not only to stay informed of these new technological developments but also to analyze how you can use them to the advantage of your data center and the organization.* The following subsections provide a starting point for this analysis.

Assessing Corporate Policy on Technology

Some companies have a management commitment to stay on the leading edge of computing technology. In these companies, any new hardware or software announcement is welcomed eagerly, and substantial resources are made available to integrate the new equipment or software into the existing configuration. If yours is such a company, you will probably serve as your management's main source of information about technological developments.

In addition, vendor announcements have a dramatic impact on applications that involve the leading-edge technology (such as massive data bases, widespread networks, or communications using satellite transmission). The leading-edge company may have to designate one or several people in the data center whose sole purpose is to deal with vendor announcements, coordinate prereleases of software, and perhaps control the installation's activity as a vendor test site. If this leading-edge orientation applies to only one application or for only a short time, the DCM must decide what is to become of these specialists within the data center after the application has been installed and is productive.

Finally, not all the new, relatively untried hardware or software will perform as you thought it would, or it may be replaced by a better version fairly quickly, and this may require reinstallation. These possibilities must also influence your plans for the data center's future. *It is your job to keep upper management informed of both the benefits and the costs of the commitment to stay at the leading edge of computing technology.*

At the opposite extreme are companies who feel that it is less expensive to buy tried-and-true equipment and software and to hire already trained and experienced personnel than it is to serve as a proving ground or training center for new technology. This philosophy obviously affects your plans for the data center; for example, it may make service levels more predictable while it also places some restraints on what people you can hire. For this type of installation, vendor announcements may not have a dramatic impact, but the changing technology does have a direct impact on economies of scale. For instance, a technological development might put processing power and memory within affordable reach for a company that had previously restrained its data processing growth because of the cost of a particular class of computer. Similarly, at some point, a cost/benefit analysis might make placing terminals or minicomputers in user areas overwhelmingly attractive. You (as DCM) then have to determine how this "extended machine" will be absorbed and managed within the organization.

Neither corporate philosophy toward the changing technology is inherently good or bad; what is crucial is that you understand clearly what the philosophy is so that your management of the data center helps to meet corporate objectives.

Communicating the Risks of Using New Technology

Part of your job as data center manager is to inform both the user and upper management of the results expected and risks taken when they invest in some aspect of the new data processing technology. To do this, you need to understand that technology, in any field, proceeds at various speeds through different stages of development and maturity.

Figure 6.1, for example, depicts the relative technological maturity of various processing modes. Batch processing and remote job entry (RJE) are shown as mature modes; there is relatively less risk or less that is unknown when embarking on projects that involve batch or RJE than there is with other modes. With a mature technology, there is less of a research-and-development (R&D) aspect to the project; more solid information, experience, and methodology are available. If the company does not have the right people on its staff, or doesn't have the proper equipment, these resources can be obtained in the marketplace. Admittedly, the usual cautions must be observed

State-of-the-Art

Technology	Infancy	Adolescence	Maturity
Batch			XXX
RJE			XXX
Time sharing		XXX———XXX	
On-line inquiry		XXX————————————XXX	
Data base	XXX—————————XXX		
Distributed computing	XXX		
Learning curve	HI---		---LO

FIGURE 6.1. *The Maturity of Various Data Processing Modes*

as when buying anything, but the point is, the resources are available with some degree of certainty.

In contrast to the mature technology, the mode of processing that is still in its infancy involves more risk. For instance, if a user invests in a project that calls for distributed computing, make sure that the user expects the usual developments that surround high technology in its infancy: namely, there tend to be a series of very encouraging announcements, some failures, some delays in development or in delivery of products, a steep learning curve for the people initially involved, incompatibilities among various products or vendors' offerings, and a dearth of available documentation. Very often, the hardware and software for a new technology are made available before the ability to assimilate them into day-to-day operations has been worked out. This results in high start-up costs for the organization.

The user needs to know that, in a project that involves the latest technology, estimates as to cost and development time may vary greatly as the project progresses. Two important reasons for this variance are:

1. There may be restarts, in which work already put into the project may have to be scrapped and the task begun anew.

2. The availability of software, equipment, or supporting services may

not meet their original schedules, or what is offered may be changed due to discontinuation of the product or slippage in the schedule by the vendor. This can cause the project schedule to slip in varying degrees or can cause the project to come to a virtual (or real) halt while alternatives are explored.

If the user thinks that the project has little uncertainty associated with it, the increases in cost and time will come as a shock, give the impression that the project is totally out of control, and erode the confidence that the user has in the data processing group. By advising the user in advance of the uncertainties, you may not make these variances more palatable, but at least the surprise factor will have been minimized.

In contrast, your responsibility in projects that involve mature technology lies largely in ensuring that time and cost variances do not occur. If substantial variances do occur on this type of project, management can rightly question the DP staff's abilities in estimating and managing a project. After all, this type of project, by definition, is helped by the ready availability of compatible equipment, software, and personnel. The success or failure of the project, then, rests on the ability to define precisely the project requirements and to control the expenditure of resources during the course of implementing the project. Thus, the type of technology required for each project helps determine your major responsibilities as DCM.

Communicating with Upper Management

One of the key responsibilities of the DCM is that of interpreting or translating computer marketplace announcements into terms that make sense to upper management. What, for instance, is the importance of a vendor announcing a new processor that has a rated internal speed four times that of the processor already installed at the company (which was among the fastest processors available eighteen months ago, when the decision was made to install the machine)? It may well be that nothing need be done in the face of the new announcement, but even this information should be passed on to the management. You must assume that management will be hearing and reading about the vendor's announcement and will be curious about it. Rather than saying nothing or assuming that management will come to the same conclusion as you do about the new equipment, you can allay management's possible apprehensions and reconfirm that you and your top management are thinking along the same lines regarding equipment by communicating actively. The following section discusses communication in greater detail.

MANAGING THE CHANGES IN TERMINOLOGY

The rapid changes in data processing technology dictate that data processing terminology change just as rapidly. In fact, the changing terminology can prove the major obstacle in your attempts to communicate with both users and upper management. Some users are not interested in learning data processing jargon at all, while those who do try are frustrated by how quickly a new set of buzzwords appears. No sooner had a user understood the concept of "Management Information Systems" (MIS), for example, than it was replaced by "Information Resource Management" (IRM).

Still, it is crucial for the data processing staff as well as for the user and upper management that users and management understand the changing technology and its impact on corporate operations. How can you bridge this communications gap? Here are some suggestions:

- In talking with users, mention new DP developments, and use the terminology that the users understand.

- Point out DP advances in the user's specialty area. For example, a new point-of-sale terminal may be of interest to the marketing department. Lower communications costs may help the traffic department shape plans for a distribution network.

- Publish an information bulletin or newsletter that keeps users and management informed about DP developments.

- Offer to give a short talk about DP developments at the next management meeting. Do the same for the next general employee meeting or the next employee club meeting.

MANAGING THE CHANGES IN THE ROLE OF DATA PROCESSING

While the technology of the computer industry as a whole changes and matures, changes also occur within your particular organization. Richard L. Nolan (1979) has produced several studies that have become standard reference points for analyzing the maturity of a data processing installation. Nolan's work indicates that data processing evolves within an organization through the following stages:

1. Initiation

2. Contagion and proliferation

3. Consolidation and control

4. Integration

5. Data administration

6. Maturity

In the first stage, data processing is rather "self-centered" within the organization. The second and third stages reflect periods of expansion followed by conflict as the users and management are, by turns, euphoric about the possibilities of computer applications and disenchanted with the uncontrolled costs and unmet promises of the data processing areas. This is followed, in the later stages, by periods of cooperation and maturity, in which users recognize both the value of computer applications and the need to become involved in the management of the data as an organizational resource. (Chapter Nine covers this maturing process in greater detail.)

Concurrent with and as a part of these changes, the "mix" of activity within the data center changes. Changes in users, applications, equipment, data center staff, and organization are to be expected. There are no guidelines that can be used to forecast just when an installation will progress from one level of maturity to another. Since it appears certain, however, that all installations will continue to change and mature through the stages noted above, the data center manager must be prepared to adapt service levels (by extending on-line hours, for example), training plans (such as regularly scheduled user training sessions), and management style (by delegating more authority and responsibility, for instance) in order to respond to these changes.

APPLYING THIS INFORMATION TO YOUR DATA CENTER

1. What steps have you taken to inform the users of changes in DP technology?

2. Has new DP technology been presented in a context to which users can relate?

3. Does the organization look largely at conservative estimates of tangible benefits for justifying new technology in the data center? Is the organization a "leading edge" DP installation?

4. Are users made aware of the relative maturity of the necessary technology when new applications are discussed? Do they understand the risks involved in using the new technology?

5. What changes have occurred at the installation that indicate the maturing process of data processing and the data center at the installation?
   Example: A disenchanted user may recently have become a DP believer.

6. Is management aware of these changes?

7. Are users aware of these changes?

SUMMARY

You have a responsibility to your organization and management to keep them abreast of changes in DP technology and terminology and of the changing DP role within the organization. *Specifically, advise your organization as to whether a new technology is suited for the organization in terms of state of the art, risk, opportunity, and the organization's ability to absorb the technology. You should also inform your users and management as to which of the Nolan "stages" your installation is in, and you should warn them of expected changes as the installation moves toward the next stage.*

7

Building an Effective
Management Style

This chapter discusses the tools that you have for improving the data center's relationships with upper management and users. These are the tools that make up your management style. First we look at the most effective way to present the data center's changing "product" to management and users. Then we discuss how you can change your management's view of data processing, create an ongoing dialogue with the users, and develop a steering committee that helps guide the data center to a successful future.

PRESENTING THE CHANGING DATA CENTER "PRODUCT"

The basic "product" of the data center (and the reason for the data center's existence) is *service*. This product includes the following elements:

1. The accessibility of data

2. The security of data

3. The custody of data

4. The availability of data center resources

5. The production of agreed-upon outputs

6. All of the above delivered to customers (that is, users) in a useful form, on a timely basis, and at a competitive cost

Any change in the data center (in its workloads, its resources, and so on) creates a change in one or more elements of the data center product. As the data center manager, your job is to ensure operational success in all these areas of service so that your users and management will not take their business elsewhere. To do this, you must learn how to make top management aware of the factors involved in and the resources needed for providing good service as the data center changes.

The Switch to On-line Applications

For example, as the job mix in the data center changes from a heavy orientation toward batch processing to one of a batch/on-line combination, the DCM must inform management of what this increased dependency on the computer implies. With the new conditions in the data center come the following needs:

- For overload capacity for the on-line applications (through additional memory, more terminals, or higher speed communications lines)

- For better training programs for data center personnel and for users (such as operations management classes for shift supervisors and internal training sessions for users)

- For formal operations recovery plans (such as the committed availability of an alternate processing site)

- And for alternate equipment

Upper management must understand these needs if the data center is to continue to provide the desired product in the new on-line environment. For example, management should be informed of the potential business exposure if a key on-line application is inoperative for a period of time, such as an order entry system being down for two hours. (Incidentally, this is a good opportunity for you to get help from users in persuading top management of the application's importance and, therefore, of the need for backup and recovery provisions.)

The Need for Data Custody Procedures

A second example of changing data center needs lies in what happens to concerns about *data custody,* a specific type of service that is provided by the data center, as the applications portfolio grows at the installation. When applications are processed as independent jobs, the organization can "get by" with loose or nonexistent procedures for cycling generations of data files and for providing secure, off-site storage for back-up files. When several data files are tied together and shared by several applications, however, any weak spots in the data custody procedures are magnified, and massive problems can occur. Your first priority, then, is to rewrite procedures (or, perhaps, to write them for the first time) and to possibly hire additional personnel for the data center.

Management must understand clearly why these additional efforts (that is, expenses) are being made. What appear to be additional costs for structuring and maintaining a data custody program are actually forms of insurance and the hallmarks of an informed data center (and corporate) management.

One of the most effective ways of explaining the importance of data custody is to present management with a well-reasoned cost/benefit analysis that indicates both the direct costs and the business-interruption costs of reconstructing lost data. If your management understands the impact of the move from a series of disconnected data files into an integrated data resource, then you are more likely to receive the proper support (such as the authority to hire data administration specialists, to train your staff, or to enter into a back-up site agreement) for creating, maintaining, and securing the integrity of the data resource within the organization.

CHANGING MANAGEMENT'S VIEW OF DATA PROCESSING

The previous section emphasizes the importance of keeping upper management informed of the data center's needs. Sometimes, however, in order to communicate effectively, you need to change the image that the data center and its staff hold within the organization. This section describes the tools of businesslike communication that will help you change this image. First, consider the following two positions that a data center manager can take:

1. The *outsider* is a top-notch operations technician who has come up through the data center ranks (an operator, for example, who moved into the technical support position, became a shift supervisor, then became DCM). This person regularly reads data processing professional journals and frequently attends technical seminars and meetings, but is hard-pressed to explain the company's product line in any detail. The outsider, further, is proud that the data center has the latest and largest piece of equipment that the vendor makes. This outsider's world consists of the data processing world, the world "outside of" the company.

2. The *insider*, by contrast, is well-grounded in data processing but is also attuned to developments within the company. Frequent conversations with user managers and regular contact with top management keep this person in touch with the operational climate of the company. As business conditions put pressure on the line managers, the insider relates to these pressures and attempts to respond quickly to special requests that come to the data center. The insider regularly meets with user managers to learn what their problems are, advise them of new or expanded capabilities in the data center, and warn them about operational restrictions within the center. The insider makes a point of attending professional meetings and seminars to stay current on data processing technology and to avoid becoming too nearsighted regarding company data problems. The user managers and upper management look at the data center manager as a management partner, one who provides realistic evaluations of processing and service alternatives and who provides this information in terms that users and management can understand.

Obviously, the "insider" DCM has the most effective communication with users and management because he or she has learned to present data processing activities and the data center's plans in busi- nesslike, dollars-and-cents terms. *Thus, your equipment, software, and staffing proposals should include:*

1. An analysis of current workloads

2. Projected resource demands

3. Cost/benefit projections based on varying sets of assumptions—In putting together the various assumptions, you are really testing a range of tolerance for your conclusions. For instance, will a proposed equipment configuration still do the job if the transaction volume is 25 percent greater than expected? Will the equipment still be cost effec- tive if the workload drops to 85 percent of the anticipated level? What are the "safety valves" if either of these assumptions come true? Can equipment be added? Reduced? All of these considerations should be discussed in your proposals.

You should become facile in synthesizing technical data and pre- senting it in terms to which top management can relate. *If the rapidly changing technology and shifting costs make it difficult to come up with firm data, use best case, worst case, and expected case scenarios in your analysis.* In this way, management will have more confidence in the data and in you and will be better able to make decisions that support the data center's needs.

After a few tries, you will find that this type of analysis and pre- sentation is not really as difficult as was imagined and that the issues that are brought to light during the analysis would not have been revealed through a broad-brush, seat-of-the-pants approach. Management, in turn, will recognize that you have general management talents useful outside the realm of data processing, and this can broaden your opportunities for growth and promotion within the company.

CREATING AN ONGOING DIALOGUE WITH USERS

Another essential element in effective data center management is good communication with your users. To create an ongoing dialogue with users, you should use all of the following tools: formal meetings, informal meetings, task forces, conversations and lunches, tours, and newsletters.

Formal Meetings

The *formal meeting* is a very structured occasion designed to present information efficiently within a given time period. Quite often, a written agenda guides the formal meeting from one topic to another, thus leaving little room for informal discussion among the attendees. Figure 7.1 shows a sample agenda for a meeting that covers a proposed order entry project.

A good deal of factual information can be disseminated in these meetings—information such as status reports, project planning or review reports, and equipment or project proposals. This type of meeting is frequently used when presentations are being made to upper management, such as budget reviews, progress reports on given projects, and final proposals for equipment and software acquisition.

Since the tone of the meeting is formal and the agenda tends to limit the topics being discussed, it is imperative that enough time be spent in preparing for the meeting to ensure its success. Discussion devices such as charts, graphs, presentation slides, and topic outlines all take time to prepare, but the time is well spent when the meeting serves its purpose and accomplishes the objective set for it. If the meeting deals with a particularly detailed topic, such as a remote terminal network, it is often advisable to issue topic outlines and meeting

Order Entry Project Proposal Agenda

I. Introduction of participants
II. Recommendation for new order entry system
    A. Capability highlights
    B. Cost/benefit highlights
III. Order entry existing procedures
    A. Workload
    B. Service levels
        1. To customers
        2. To field staff
    C. Standard reports
IV. Order entry shortcomings
    A. Outmoded system
    B. Rising workload
    C. Sales analysis is fair to poor
V. Proposed order entry system
    A. On-line terminals for order processing
    B. Field office remote inquiry
VI. Cost/benefit analysis
    A. Computer costs
    B. Systems and programming costs
    C. User costs
    D. Expected benefits
    E. Payback analysis

FIGURE 7.1. *Sample Agenda for a Formal Meeting*

notes in advance of the meeting to allow the participants sufficient time to familiarize themselves with the material and the issues to be decided. Figure 7.2 provides a checklist of the things you need to think about in preparing for a formal meeting. The formal meeting is further characterized by the keeping of some form of meeting minutes as a record of the occasion. These minutes are distributed to the participants and to others, such as top management, following the meeting.

The data processing staff can use the formal meeting to advantage for educating and presenting to users such information as new developments in computing and progress reports on large-scale projects. A very useful technique for making these presentations is to have the user department make part of the presentations wherever possible. For example, the user could discuss the existing workload and

- Have all participants and guests been notified of the meeting time and place?
- Has a room been reserved?
- Are all audio/visual equipment needs known, and has the proper equipment been reserved?
- Will the meeting involve a meal (such as breakfast or lunch)? If so, has the meal been arranged?
- Has an agenda been sent to all participants and guests?
- Should an information packet be sent to all participants and guests in advance of the meeting?
- Do all participants know their roles in the presentation?
- Has someone been designated to take minutes and to publish and distribute the minutes to participants, guests, and top management?
- Has the presentation been timed to start and finish within the time allocated for the meeting?

FIGURE 7.2.   *Preparation Checklist for a Formal Meeting*

procedure as part of a proposal to upgrade an application. This has the obvious advantage of shared participation, and it also serves as a kind of "checkpoint" as to just how much (or little) the users understand about the data processing aspects of the project. Conversely, these meetings also reveal how much or little the DP staff understands about the user's problem.

The formal meeting usually is limited in duration in deference to the other demands on the people involved. The time factor underlines the importance of adequate planning so that the most information can be transferred in a limited amount of time.

Informal Meetings

The *informal meeting,* as its name implies, is less structured than the formal meeting; it often takes the form of a workshop or working session when major pieces of a data processing project must be put together and the talents and know-how of several people are needed. In this atmosphere, the participants are more relaxed, since the tone of the meeting is one of accomplishing something together rather than of having to present a finished product to an audience. For example, assignments can be made beforehand, and participants can be expected to come to the meeting having done their "homework."

The work sessions frequently take place over a longer time period (hours at a time, with multiple meetings held until the job is completed) than do formal meetings, and the informality of the situation also encourages people to be more candid than they would be in a formal meeting. Thus, these working sessions provide an opportunity for data processing people to work closely with users and to get to know each other's problems, preferences, and persuasions. Remember, however, that the DP staff must not come across to the users as "know-it-all" technicians, or the users will get the impression that there is no hope for getting their needs expressed to the computer staff.

Examples of the workshop approach are the planning of a network of remote terminals (which would probably require the users, systems analysts, communications specialists, and vendors to get together to work out the details of the arrangement before presenting the plan to management for approval) or the planning connected with relocating the data center (requiring that data center people, building engineers, security specialists, and vendors get together for detailed planning).

Task Forces

A special variation of the informal meeting or the workshop approach is the *task force* assignment. While the workshop is usually a gathering of people who are prepared to accomplish something within the context of the meeting time, the task force is usually of a longer duration, and the participants are chosen for their particular background, experience, or specialty that relates to the topic.

In contrast to the workshop, where the bulk of the work is done during the meeting and in concert with others in the group, the task force generally involves independent research and the reaching of tentative conclusions by the participants, who then exchange information and ideas at the task force meeting and proceed to work out a solution or recommendation.

For instance, if computerizing a new application is being considered, users might be assigned to research workload and volume data for the past five years and to develop a projection for the next three years. Data center personnel might be asked to report on the hardware and software available to support the application.

Conversations and Lunches

Periodic informal *conversations* between you and your users provide a very effective means for keeping each other up to date and informed about recent activities and planned actions. The spontaneity of these conversations, whether they take place in the office, over lunch, or whatever, breaks down barriers between you and the user and usually leads to both of you gaining a better appreciation for the other's problems.

As one might expect, these meetings are generally unscheduled and occur with random frequency. The DP manager may have to take the initiative in setting up these meetings or in keeping up the contact on a regular basis, but, as time goes on, this type of exchange can prove invaluable. Once an atmosphere of mutual trust has been built up—and this may take quite a long time to develop in a recalcitrant user—one can glean bits of information from these meetings that would not be obtained through any other medium. For example, the user may discuss anticipated changes in his or her operation, such as significant changes in workload volumes or a reshuffling of the staff, with concurrent surpluses or shortages of personnel.

The data processing manager, in turn, can take this opportunity to tell the user manager about new or planned developments in the DP world. This is a good chance to point out changes in computer personnel with whom the user manager may come in contact, to give a brief sketch of how a new project is coming along, or to outline new computer industry announcements and what they might mean to the user manager's area or to the company in general. Given the informal atmosphere, the DP manager can use the time to advantage in order to enlist the support of the user manager for mutually interesting projects—support that both the user and the DP manager will need in the future when top management is asked to make a decision on a related expenditure.

Tours

Yet another way to establish communication with users is to have them *tour* the computing facility periodically. Years ago, a tour of the data center was a mandatory part of the company's orientation for new employees and was often the "showcase" stop on company tours for visitors. An increased awareness of the need for security in running the data processing area has resulted in a change in attitude: from a plate-glass-windowed, high-visibility workroom, the data center has become an innocuous-looking, solid-walled bastion containing the computer equipment. In the process, the data processing people have become even more isolated from their users, and this isolation has contributed to the mystique about computer professionals being "outsiders" who are aloof and not interested in the company.

Another reason for the elimination of tours of the data center is that, as data processing becomes a more integral part of the company, it is assumed that the users know what computer personnel do and, specifically, what is done in the processing of that particular user's job. This is not always a safe assumption as procedures and personnel assignments change over time.

For these reasons, it is helpful to have the users tour the data center: the tour allows them to update their perspective on DP personnel and on what happens to their jobs in the DP area. These tours should be conducted on a controlled basis. (We do not mean to advocate a return to the wide-open, "anybody's welcome" approach that was in vogue some years ago.) The user usually leaves these brief tours with a better appreciation for what goes on in the center and a greater understanding of the center's operating environment.

Newsletters

For the data processing organization that has a good deal of activity in terms of new projects and new equipment installation, or that has a fairly large network of terminals, or that often has changes in personnel assignments, a *data processing newsletter* forms another effective means of developing and maintaining user communications. There are two types of information that are passed on via the newsletter: official or procedural information and unofficial or "nice-to-know" information. The official newsletter is intended to be filed in a procedure book by the users; the unofficial newsletter is not meant to be part of the installation's permanent procedures.

The procedural information should include such items as new protocols for signing on to a terminal network, new operating hours or availability hours for the data center, and revised procedures for requesting project work from the systems and programming areas. The official newsletter contains the type of information that the user needs to know in order to function effectively with the data processing organization.

The unofficial information, on the other hand, is not absolutely necessary for the user to have in order to interact with the data processing areas, but having this type of information makes life a bit easier for the user. These "nice-to-know" items are things like the announcement of new personnel assignments (especially for data processing positions with high user visibility, such as a data control clerk or a network troubleshooter) or planned changes in equipment. (These changes are announced in very general terms as an "advance warning." When the new equipment is installed, that information would be in the official newsletter.) The newsletter can also be used to spotlight different user departments or to give a "pat on the back" to user areas that have made good progress with a data processing application.

The newsletter, while usually written by the data processing people, will be more interesting and informative if the users themselves contribute certain portions of it. For example, the user might describe how a new on-line application differs from the previous way of handling the job. In other words, take advantage of the user's special insight into an application. By highlighting a specific user activity, the rapport between the user and DP is enhanced.

CREATING AND GUIDING THE STEERING COMMITTEE

Almost every installation, at one time or another, decides that a data processing steering committee must be established. Many steering committees, however, are ineffective. An effective steering committee: (1) is comprised of the right people and (2) makes decisions on the right questions.

Let us look at the effective steering committee more closely. This committee has the following attributes:

- It has the authority to decide general data processing priorities.

- It consists of decision makers from user areas, data processing, and corporate planning.

- It provides data processing direction to support the expected corporate information needs (that is, it helps decide such things as application priorities and the general type of hardware to be used).

The emphasis in this committee is on setting general policies and priorities that reflect the corporate plans. For example, the type of decisions it makes includes assigning a high priority to an on-line application development because the application is in one of the company's rapidly growing product areas. General hardware plans to support this type of application are also approved by the committee because the committee understands the risk of inadequately equipping a key, high-visibility application. The committee meets quarterly, recognizing that, with the broad guidelines that the committee provides, monthly meetings are not necessary. (The steering committee does not take the place of detailed project review meetings, which are held as needed.) Programming priorities and detailed hardware decisions are left to the respective data processing managers, since they are better trained and equipped to make these types of decisions.

A typical decision from this type of steering committee in a bank, for example, would be expressed as follows:

Highest priority should be given to the development of an on-line system that will provide inquiry and update capabilities for demand and time deposit transactions at the main office and at each of the metropolitan branches.

Notice, in this statement, the key phrases that define the scope of the problem: *on-line, inquiry, update, demand deposits, time deposits, main office, branches.* Notice, also, that specific technical characteristics are *not* mentioned; there is no mention of the number of terminals, the size of the processor, amount of disk space, communications protocol, or response time. These items will, of course, become a part of the detailed specifications for the project and will be of concern to those directly involved, but the steering committee is not asked to make a judgment on these matters.

For contrast, let us look at an example of an ineffective steering committee. This committee has the following attributes:

- It is a rubber stamp for decisions; it has no real authority.

- It includes the wrong level of people (that is, they are not decision makers).

- It makes decisions on the wrong types of questions (such as program priority or detailed hardware decisions).

This committee starts out with good intentions. The first meeting is usually attended by an impressively high level of management (vice-presidents, division heads, and the like). The early meetings cover such issues as what programs are being worked on by the systems analysts and programmers and how much overtime is being put in by the data center crew. When the question of programming priorities is put to the committee members, they feel somewhat ill-equipped to decide which programs should be completed first, but they gamely take a stab at the question and do set some priorities for program development. After a few meetings, however, the vice-presidents no longer attend, since they have more important matters to attend to, and they send surrogates to represent them. These deputies are not in a position to make decisions on anything of import without first checking with their bosses. Priorities are still decided, but everyone on the committee has the feeling that what they are doing is not all that important. This feeling is justified from time to time when the committee's priorities are overridden by management.

To have a successful steering committee, (1) assess the corporate strengths and weaknesses regarding information, (2) assess the data processing strengths and weaknesses, and then (3) formulate a plan to bring these two areas into line with each other. Many installations designate a steering committee without first educating the users who become committee members about the different types of applications and about the importance of data as a corporate resource. Other installations start a steering committee prematurely, at a time when the data processing group is understaffed, undertrained, and ill-equipped to respond to significant new directions upon which the corporation may wish to embark.

You can use the following checklist to measure the strengths and weaknesses of the corporation and data processing. If you can answer "yes" to all of the questions, your steering committee will probably be effective.

1. *Corporate:*
   - Do users realize that data integrity is their responsibility and data custody is a data center responsibility?
   - Do users take an interest in data as an information resource?
   - Is management willing to invest in information resources?
   - Do several users share an information base?

2. *Data center personnel:*
   - Do they show an aptitude for staffing, equipment, and software planning?
   - Do they request additional money but give solid reasons and ample advance notice for the request?
   - Do they have a helpful attitude toward users?

A steering committee can be an important resource to the data center manager if the committee consists of the right people and is asked to make decisions at the right level. If either of these elements is missing, the steering committee will probably be a waste of everyone's time and a source of frustration to those involved.

APPLYING THIS INFORMATION TO YOUR DATA CENTER

1. Are you an "insider" or an "outsider" as far as users are concerned?

2. Are you comfortable with presenting data center plans and proposals in dollars-and-cents terms, rather than relying on technical jargon to persuade the listener?

3. What methods do you use to maintain regular contact with users and with management?

4. Is your steering committee effective? How can you make it more effective?

SUMMARY

You must strive to improve your data center "product" —that is, your service to users. You can expect changes in the data center job mix as the installation moves from a batch to an on-line orientation and as there is an increased emphasis on data as a corporate resource. *The successful DCM is one who has an "insider's" attitude toward serving users and the organization while staying current on DP industry developments.*

To be effective, you must present staffing, equipment, and software proposals in the dollars-and-cents terms that top management can understand. These proposals should include an evaluation of alternatives and take into account likely variations in workloads and costs.

Keep in touch with users through meetings, workshops, informal lunches, newsletters, and tours of the data center. If a steering committee is contemplated, take special efforts to make it an effective vehicle, one that will help both you and the users.

8

Preparing the Data Center Annual Report

To manage the data center well, the DCM must perform a periodic review of the money spent to run the center and of the level of service provided for this money in order to determine whether the corporation is getting a fair return on its investment in the data center. One method of organizing and structuring this review is to put together a data center annual report. *This chapter provides a standard format for the annual report, describes how to prepare it, and discusses what the annual report can tell you about data center operations.*

THE PURPOSES OF THE ANNUAL REPORT

The annual report puts costs into perspective in comparison to the services provided, and it tests data center activities for their relationship to the mainstream activities of the company. It also forces data center management to think in upper-management terms regarding costs and benefits, it causes an examination of costs on an overall and unit basis, and it analyzes the service mix (that is, the number of batch versus on-line applications) in the data center. By standardizing the way in which unit costs are categorized, it provides a means of comparing costs from year to year.

In short, it provides a measurement of the progress of the data center over the recent past and a means of communicating this measurement to upper management.

THE GENERAL FORMAT OF THE ANNUAL REPORT

An example of a data center annual report for a manufacturing company is shown in Figure 8.1. At first glance, the report appears to be oriented to the hardware portion of the data center, using measures such as average cost per job and average hours per job. These elements, in fact, measure the total data center resources since they are a function of the total center cost (people, hardware, software) and the gross output of the data center (expressed in average hours per job).

Notice the general format for the annual report. The significant accomplishments of the past year are briefly summarized, then the major objectives for the coming year are itemized (Part 1 of the figure). These two sections are followed by the performance analysis data (Part 2). This information can usually be presented in two or three pages. Again, the purpose of the annual report is to present a *capsule summary* of the data center's activity, not to present a detailed justification of how or where the money was spent in the center. It is presumed that you will have given more detailed treatment to accomplishments, objectives, and budgets in project plans, project review reports, and budget worksheets and narratives throughout the year. Parts 3 and 4 of Figure 8.1 contain the detailed worksheet calculations that support some of the data presented on the previous pages of the report.

As you examine Figure 8.1, remember that this annual report is based on a somewhat hypothetical data center. Therefore, the numbers and percentages used may not relate directly to your data center. In setting performance goals, select targets that are realistic for your center—for example, a 4 percent reduction in cost for a certain application may be overly ambitious, or it may be so trivial as to remove any incentive for trying to reach the goal.

This sample annual report covers a four-year period. *Obviously, any time frame could be represented, but four or five years is probably the best choice; at least three years are needed in order to give some indication of the trends in the data center, but a longer period of time, such as eight or ten years, is probably not pertinent to today's operations.*

DATA CENTER ANNUAL REPORT

Significant Accomplishments for 19n4:
- Improved availability of on-line system from 96.6 percent of planned hours in 19n3 to 97.4 percent of planned hours while planned hours increased from 2,600 hours per year to 2,860 hours per year
- Reduced batch job rerun rate from 2.9 percent (in 19n3) to 2.2 percent of jobs, while batch meter hours per year was increasing from 1,622.4 to 1684.8
- Converted data entry section from card keypunch equipment to key-to-disk equipment, resulting in annual net savings of $6,700
- Installed automated tape library system, resulting in better control and utilization of magnetic tapes—estimated savings in first year: $5,100
- Initiated user contact position in data center, resulting in improved user information, better use of on-line equipment

Major Objectives for 19n5:
- Increase on-line system availability to 97.5 percent or better.
- Reduce batch rerun rate to 2.0 percent or less.
- Reduce operations cost of accounts receivable system by 4 percent while maintaining service levels.
- Develop formal disaster recovery plan.

FIGURE 8.1—Part 1.   Data Center Annual Report

Performance Analysis

Expenditures Levels (in thousands)

	19n1		19n2		19n3		19n4	
Labor	45%	$441	48%	$ 594	49%	$ 667	51%	$ 857
Hardware	44	431	41	507	38	517	36	605
Supplies	6	59	7	87	9	123	8	134
Services	5	49	4	49	4	54	5	84
Total	100%	$980	100%	$1,237	100%	$1,361	100%	$1,680

Staffing Levels (average number of people)

	19n1	19n2	19n3	19n4
Data entry	16	15	12	10
Quality control	8	12	14	14
Operators	10	12	13	15
Management and administration	4	4	5	8
Total	38	43	44	47

Service Load (in percentages)

	19n1	19n2	19n3	19n4
Accounting and finance	10	9	8	5
Sales	30	30	31	33
Corporate staff	3	2	3	5
Manufacturing	28	33	36	40
Engineering	22	21	19	15
Other	7	5	3	2
Total	100	100	100	100

Productivity Highlights

	19n1	19n2	19n3	19n4
• Cost per available hour	$282.94	$267.58	$311.37	$431.98
• Average cost per job	$2.63	$2.87	$2.85	$3.47
• Average hours per job	0.009 hr	0.011 hr	0.009 hr	0.008 hr
• Cost per thousand data entry keystrokes	$0.727	$0.735	$0.689	$0.719
• Interactive availability	96.8%	97.1%	96.6%	97.4%
• Batch rerun percentage	4.3%	3.2%	2.9%	2.2%

FIGURE 8.1—Part 2.   Data Center Annual Report

* * * *Operations Cost Worksheet* * * *

	19n1	19n2	19n3	19n4
1. Shifts per day	2	3	3	3
2. Days per year	260	260	260	260
3. Shifts per year (line 1 $\times$ line 2)	520	780	780	780
4. Hours per shift	8	8	8	8
5. Raw hours per year (3 $\times$ 4)	4,160	6,240	6,240	6,240
6. System state	37%	40%	40%	44%
7. Available %	63%	60%	60%	56%
8. Available hours (5 $\times$ 7)	2,620.8	3,744	3,744	3,494.4
9. Total cost	$980,000	$1,237,000	$1,361,000	$1,680,000
10. Less data entry cost	$238,480	$235,170	$195,220	$170,490
11. Net cost	$741,520	$1,001,830	$1,165,780	$1,509,510
12. Cost per available hour (11 $\div$ 8)	$282.94	$267.58	$311.37	$431.98
13. Job steps per year	282,308	349,440	408,850	434,668
14. Average cost per job (11 $\div$ 13)	$2.63	$2.87	$2.85	$3.47
15. Average hours per job (8 $\div$ 13)	0.009 hr	0.011 hr	0.009 hr	0.008 hr
16. Planned on-line hours per year	2,080	2,080	2,600	2,860
17. On-line available hours	2,013	2,020	2,512	2,786
18. On-line available % (17 $\div$ 16)	96.8%	97.1%	96.6%	97.4%
19. Batch hours per year	998.4	1,456	1,622.4	1,684.8
20. Batch rerun hours per year	42.91	46.55	47.02	37.02
21. Batch rerun % (20 $\div$ 19)	4.3%	3.2%	2.9%	2.2%

FIGURE 8.1—Part 3.   Data Center Annual Report

* * * Data Entry Cost Worksheet * * *

	19n1	19n2	19n3	19n4
A. Data entry operators	14	13	11	9
B. Data entry average wages	$9,400	$10,100	$10,700	$11,300
C. Data entry wages (A × B)	$131,600	$131,300	$117,700	$101,700
D. Data entry supervisors	2	2	1	1
E. Supervisor average wages	$13,000	$13,800	$14,700	$15,600
F. Supervisor wages (D × E)	$26,000	$27,600	$14,700	$15,600
G. Total wages (C + F)	$157,600	$158,900	$132,400	$117,300
H. Plus 30 percent benefits	$47,280	$47,670	$39,720	$35,190
J. Total wages + benefits (G + H)	$204,880	$206,570	$172,120	$152,490
K. Equipment cost	$33,600	$28,600	$23,100	$18,000
L. Wages + equipment (J + K)	$238,480	$235,170	$195,220	$170,490
M. Percentage of total budget (L ÷ 9)	24.3%	19.0%	14.3%	10.1%
N. Hours per year per person	1,952	1,952	1,952	1,952
P. Strokes per hour	12,000	12,600	13,200	13,500
Q. Thousand strokes/year (N × P)	23,424	24,595.2	25,766.4	26,352
R. Annual group output (A × Q)	327,936	319,737.6	283,430.4	237,168
S. Cost per 1,000 strokes (L ÷ R)	$0.727	$0.736	$0.689	$0.719
T. Typical record cost				
40 strokes	$0.029	$0.029	$0.028	$0.029
60 strokes	0.044	0.044	0.041	0.043
80 strokes	0.058	0.059	0.055	0.058
120 strokes	0.087	0.088	0.083	0.086
160 strokes	0.116	0.118	0.110	0.115

FIGURE 8.1—Part 4.   Data Center Annual Report

USING THE ANNUAL REPORT AS A MEASUREMENT TOOL

The following sections discuss specific items on the report and the information that both you, as DCM, and your upper management can glean from it.

Expenditures

Examine the expenditures portion of the performance analysis for the total expense levels, for the rate of change in spending levels for each of the components, and for the percentages spent on each of the cost components for each year. First, note the overall expense levels and trends (the "total" line under expenditures):

Year	Amount	Percent Change
19n1	$ 980,000	
19n2	$1,237,000	+26.2%
19n3	$1,361,000	+10.0%
19n4	$1,680,000	+23.4%

If you were the DCM for this data center, you could relate this information to your experience and to the unit costs shown in the expenditures section in order to make the following analysis. Part of the increases in total expenditures can be attributed to inflation, but productivity increases should be expected to offset the inflationary impacts. (This will be reflected in the cost per job under productivity highlights.) The percentage increases in the costs between 19n1–19n2 and between 19n3–19n4 are substantial and are caused by the jump in the staffing levels for these periods. The staff increases were the result of adding a third shift between 19n1 and 19n2 and the addition of three managers in 19n4. The labor percentages, which are larger than the hardware percentages, seem to confirm the data processing industry trends.

Somewhat surprising is the decrease, albeit small, in the supplies expenses. Perhaps the explanation lies in a major application now running on-line that had previously taken up a hefty portion of the supplies costs. This would be one item on the annual report for which the DCM should have a ready explanation.

Another item that should be explained is the rise in the amount spent on services. From 19n3 to 19n4, this amount rose by 55.6 percent. While the dollar amount is relatively small, large percentage increases such as this must be explained by the DCM. (Perhaps there were unusual, one-time expenses, such as consulting fees, associated with the data center in 19n4.)

Staffing

The next section shows modest additions to the staff over the four-year period. Compare the distribution of the staff for the four years, and you can see that a transition is in process between data entry staff and quality control:

	19n1	19n2	19n3	19n4
Data entry	16	15	12	10
Quality control	8	12	14	14

These figures suggest that there has been a recent emphasis on quality control within the data center. Such an emphasis tends to increase the apparent costs of running the center, since the quality control salaries may, at first glance, be considered overhead or nonproductive expenses. But better quality control can pay off in better service and, if that strategy is working, a lower unit cost is to be expected for the work produced in the data center. That is, better quality control will result in fewer reruns, which means that a given resource in the data center can be used on productive work rather than on reruns, that relatively fewer resources are needed to do a given amount of work, and thus these factors will result in a lower unit cost. This is confirmed by looking at the batch rerun percentage (under productivity highlights); note that it has dropped each year:

	19n1	19n2	19n3	19n4
Batch rerun percentage	4.3%	3.2%	2.9%	2.2%

The other trend to be noted in the staffing levels is the doubling in the management staff from 19n1 (four people) to 19n4 (eight people).

There doesn't appear to be a ready explanation for this increase in the high-salaried staff positions since the net gain in data center personnel (three people) is completely accounted for in the management category. This category should be explained by the DCM and the additional costs justified.

Service Load

The service load breakdown shows a healthy trend toward the data center becoming aligned with the mainstream activities of the company (note the percentages for "manufacturing"):

	19n1	19n2	19n3	19n4
Accounting and finance	10%	9%	8%	5%
Sales	30	30	31	33
Corporate staff	3	2	3	5
Manufacturing	28	33	36	40
Engineering	22	21	19	15
Other	7	5	3	2
Total	100%	100%	100%	100%

Note that, in 19n1, sales took more of the data center resources (30 percent) than anyone else in the company. Manufacturing, the company's focus, was second with 28 percent. In 19n2, manufacturing became the dominant user area, and this trend has continued in 19n3 and 19n4. When the data center workload parallels the major activities of the company, we can assume that the installation is relatively mature.

The engineering department is also a substantial user of data center services, but the accounting and financial area represents only 5 percent of the workload in 19n4. This is somewhat surprising, especially since this area had been a larger user in the previous three years. The percentage drop in usage is no doubt due to an increase in the overall workload while the accounting volumes remained fairly constant. The data processing management should look into this area to determine if there are accounting needs that are not being serviced by the data center at present.

Productivity Highlights

The productivity highlights reflect a generally healthy operation. The following paragraphs discuss each line in this section of the annual report and describe how the figures were derived.

Cost Per Available Hour.   The cost per available hour represents the cost of running the data center (except for data entry costs) for one elapsed hour of available computer time. To calculate this figure, take the operations cost minus the data entry costs and divide it by the annual hours of computer time available in the data center.

The cost per available hour in this data center has been steadily increasing and has increased substantially from 19n3 to 19n4 (from $311.37 to $431.98 per available hour). From this, we can infer that equipment and staff were increased substantially from 19n3 to 19n4. This is, of course, borne out by looking at the staffing level section, where it is clear that the non-data entry staff increased by 15.6 percent (from thirty-two to thirty-seven people) in that time period. The increased labor and equipment costs are distributed over a fixed number of hours per year (namely, 6,240 hours per year between 19n2 and 19n4); thus the cost per hour is increasing.

Average Cost Per Job.   The average cost per job reflects the cost effectiveness of the data center. If, in a given amount of time, an average job costs less to process than it cost in another time period, the center is more cost effective than it had been. The calculation is:

$$C \div J = c$$

where C = net annual cost = (total cost) − (data entry cost)
     J = number of job steps per year
     c = average cost per job

An analysis of the average cost per job in Figure 8.1 indicates that the data center was operating more efficiently in 19n3 than in

19n2 in the face of the overall rising costs, but the average cost per job rose sharply between 19n3 and 19n4. This conclusion is only true, however, if the job characteristics are reasonably consistent from one year to another. Calculations such as average cost per job and average hours per job are based upon an underlying assumption that the workload mix is reasonably consistent from year to year. If there is a significant change in the mix from one year to another, this must be footnoted in the annual report. (A sudden change in the mix could occur, for example, in an installation that puts its first on-line application into production. This would consume resources throughout, say, an eight-hour period of the day, but it would only count as one job step.)

"Job step" is a somewhat arbitrary measure since a job step can consist of one or more executable program steps. The intent here is to provide some reasonably consistent measure of work for your data center. The number of job steps in your center will remain fairly steady from one year to the next unless there are substantial increases or reductions in the number of applications that you run in the data center. Thus, the job step provides a means of comparing your current workload with your previous workload.

The point here is that data must be understood in the context of the data center's actual history; the figures cannot just be taken to be "good" or "bad" numbers. The cost per available hour increased 38.7 percent from 19n3 to 19n4 while the average cost per job increased 21.8 percent during the same period. This indicates that gains in efficiencies are still being made, but at a slower rate than in previous years. As noted above, the DCM should be able to explain the reasoning behind the increase in management positions from five to eight people in just one year. This would obviously increase the total budget and increase the unit costs if the productivity levels and the volumes had remained constant.

Average Hours Per Job.   The figure for the average hours per job reflects the processing efficiency of the data center. If this figure is diminishing between two equal time periods (and if the workload mix is consistent), then more work is being accomplished in the same amount of time, which means that the center is more efficient. The following formula produces the figure for average hours per job:

$$H \div J = h$$

where H = available hours
      J = number of job steps per year
      h = average hours per job

Cost Effectiveness Versus Efficiency. The difference between the average cost per job and the average hours per job can be illustrated through the following cases:

Case	Number of CPUs	Cost	Jobs	Time	c	h
A	1	$1,000	1	1.0 hour	$1,000	1.0 hour
B	2	$1,000 + $1,120	2	1.8 hours	$1,060	0.9 hours
C	2	$1,000 + $ 980	2	2.4 hours	$ 990	1.2 hours

Case A shows a single processor that costs $1,000 to operate one hour and a single job that takes one hour to run. The average cost per job, c, is $1,000, and the average hours per job, h, is one hour.

In Case B, there are two processors, one costing $1,000 to operate one hour and the other costing $1,400 to operate one hour. The first processor runs the given job in one hour, and the second processor runs the same job in 0.8 hours. Therefore, running the same job on both processors would consume 1.8 available hours and cost $2,120; that makes the average cost per job $1,060 and the average time per job 0.9 hours. This is more efficient but less cost-effective processing than in Case A. (To show the cost effectiveness and efficiency relationships, we are assuming that the same job would be run on each processor. In practice, of course, you would run the job on only one processor.)

In Case C, two processors are again available, costing $1,000 and $700 respectively to run for one hour. As in Case A, the first processor runs the given job in one hour, but the second processor runs the same job in 1.4 hours. Running the same job on these two processors consumes 2.4 available hours and costs $1,980 for an average cost per job of $990 and an average hours per job of 1.2 hours. This is less efficient but more cost effective than either Case A or B. In short, adding resources to the data center should make the center more cost effective or more efficient (ideally, both will occur if you can install a processor that is both faster and less expensive than your previous one), and the average cost per job and average hours per job are measures of these qualities.

Look again at Figure 8.1. Note that, between 19n2 and 19n3, the average cost per job decreased slightly (0.7 percent) while the cost per available hour rose by 16.4 percent. This indicates effective use of the data center resources in spite of an increase in the total cost. The cost per available hour and the average cost per job increased 38.7 percent and 21.8 percent, respectively, between 19n3 and 19n4. This suggests a relative improvement in the cost effectiveness, since the cost per job is rising at a slower rate than the cost per available hour, but the increase in volume was not enough to offset the big increase in cost and the decrease in available hours during the year. The cost increase can be traced to the increased overhead represented by the system state, which went from 40 percent to 44 percent between 19n3 and 19n4. If the system state had remained at 40 percent, the cost per available hour would have been $403.18, illustrating the direct effect that system overhead has on operating costs.

Cost Per Data Entry Keystroke. The cost per data entry keystroke has generally been declining during the four-year period, although it rose by 4.4 percent from 19n3 to 19n4 (from $0.689 to $0.719). This increase could indicate that economies of scale have been exhausted in the data entry area. In 19n3, eleven data entry operators were supervised by one person, while, in 19n4, only nine data entry operators were used, but they still required one supervisor (and the supervisor's wages increased from $14,700 to $15,600). The cost of having the supervisor is being spread over the lower productive output of the nine operators, contributing to a higher per-stroke cost. As the staffing dwindles for data entry (perhaps because of increases in online applications or distribution of data entry functions into user areas) the cost of the supervisor will become a bigger part of the per-stroke cost, thus losing the economies of scale that were present with a larger data entry staff. At some point, the supervisory position will probably have to be eliminated (with data entry supervision absorbed by another supervisory position) in order to bring the data entry cost down.

Interactive Availability.   A key measure of data center operation, especially in the eyes of the users, is the availability of on-line system resources (sometimes referred to as "system up-time"). The on-line availability percentage is equal to the actual available on-line hours divided by the planned available on-line hours. The example in Figure 8.1 shows a respectable interactive availability percentage, but these figures must be evaluated against the center's availability goals. If the goal was to provide availability 98 percent of the time, the performance obviously fell just short, but if the goal was 95 percent, the performance is commendable.

Batch Rerun Percentage.   The batch rerun percentage is equal to the number of hours spent rerunning batch work due to data center errors (such as setting up a job incorrectly or using the wrong tape or disk file), divided by the total number of hours of batch processing. This is a key measure for the data center since, obviously, reruns consume data center resources. It is important to note that, in this example, only those jobs that are rerun due to data center errors are considered in the rerun rate. Of course, reruns can also be caused by others, such as users, but these are not directly controllable by the DCM. Therefore, only the reruns caused by data center errors are counted in this measurement.

A high rerun percentage (that is, a percentage defined as unacceptably high for your installation) calls for intensified quality control measures. The center reflected in Figure 8.1 has, in fact, responded to the rerun rate by adding quality control personnel, and the move apparently has paid off in a lower rerun rate.

Summing Up the Performance Analysis

The following conclusions can be reached on the basis of the data presented in Part 2 of Figure 8.1:

1. The general cost trends conform to the expectations for costs in the data processing industry.

2. An increasing percentage of the data center dollars are being spent on labor, which also conforms to industry trends.

3. These two pieces of information indicate that the data center manager is recognizing the changing picture in data processing ex-

penses and concedes that increased amounts must be spent on staff salaries and benefits.

4. The amounts spent on supplies and services should be observed carefully for the next several years to determine whether the trends in these areas establish a firm pattern. These expenses should remain a relatively small part of the total budget, but the costs should be kept under control.

5. Changes in the staffing levels suggest that the data center is in a period of transition; the data entry area is being deemphasized while a new emphasis on quality control in the data center has emerged.

6. Additional management positions have been established; this could be the result of increased workloads, but reasons for the increase in these positions should be thoroughly explored.

Not only is this measurement information useful to you as data center manager but it also can be used to report the progress and activities of the data center in a nontechnical fashion for top management. One warning, however: the service level data (on-line availability and batch rerun percentage) are useful, but a problem develops in attempting to arrive at consistent units of measure from year to year and from one application to another. These service level measurements are directly tied to the service agreements you have established with users. As the application mix changes, you must adjust the on-line availability and batch rerun percentage goals.

COMPILING THE OPERATIONS WORKSHEET CALCULATIONS

The data shown on the worksheet calculations are used mainly in support of the information presented in the performance analysis. The worksheets probably contain too much detail for presentation to upper management and should be retained for back-up, but the DCM must have the worksheet data in order to put together the annual report and must be familiar with the data in order to respond to questions that arise during the discussion of the performance analysis.

Cost per available hour and average cost per job were calculated using the data at lines 1–11 of Part 3 of Figure 8.1. Some lines are self-explanatory, but several lines in the worksheet require additional comment. The days per year (line 2) account for a five-day-per-week operation.

The total available machine (central processor) resource is represented by lines 6 and 7, since the total resource is made up of processor overhead (the *system state* or the resource consumed by the operating system), the problem program state, the idle state, and the wait state. These latter three factors are combined, shown as line 7, and labeled as "available percentage" of processor time. Put in the form of a simple equation:

$$S + A = 100\% \quad \text{or}$$
$$S + (P + I + W) = 100\%$$

where S = system state
A = available processor time
P = problem-state time
I = idle-state time
W = wait-state time

Clearly, as S increases, A decreases, leaving less resource for productive work. This has happened between 19n1 and 19n2 and again between 19n3 and 19n4, according to the worksheet. (The increase in available hours, shown in line 8, from 19n1 to 19n2 is due to the addition of the third shift in 19n2.) When the system state increases, if the costs are constant or rising, the productivity must be picked up somewhere else in order to hold the unit costs steady. In other words, more jobs must be run through per hour because there are fewer production hours available on the machine.

The cost per available hour (line 12) is *not* the same cost as that used in a chargeback system. A *chargeback system*, where data center costs are charged back to users on some prorated basis, should be constructed using a number of factors; charges should be based on a direct relationship between the costs of these factors and the specific user's consumption of the individual resources. These factors include hardware, software, labor, supplies, overhead, and the interactions among these factors. In other words, the charge to the user should reflect the usage of *l* units of labor, *m* units of machine resource, *n* units of supplies, and so forth, with each resource appropriately priced. (Chapter Seventeen discusses chargeback systems in more detail.)

The cost per available hour makes no such distinction among the resources. Instead, it is a way of normalizing costs within a changing environment. It views the processor utilization as a finite, measurable resource unit that can be used to express, for comparative purposes, the relative cost of operating the data center. To that end, the net operations cost (that is, the total cost minus the data entry costs) is divided by the available hours to arrive at the cost per available hour. Again, the cost per job (line 14) would not be appropriate for use in a chargeback system unless there was uniformity in the resource utilization mix across all jobs run in the data center. That is, all jobs would have to use the same percentage of hardware, of labor, of software, and so on for the cost per job to be valid as a chargeback rate.

A closer look at lines 5, 6, and 7 confirms what was observed earlier regarding the operation of the center. Between 19n3 and 19n4, the available hours decreased due to more of the processor resource being spent in the system state. With no increase in the raw hours per year, the cost per available hour jumped dramatically (by 38.7 percent). A 6.3 percent increase in the job step volume was not enough to compensate for an increase in the cost and a decrease in available hours: therefore, there was a 21.8 percent rise in the average cost per job. The data center manager will have to pay particular attention to the center's productivity (by being alert for excess personnel, and rising overhead costs) in the next few years in order to keep the unit costs at an acceptable level.

The planned on-line hours value (line 16) is calculated by multiplying the planned elapsed on-line hours per day (given as 8, 8, 10, and 11 for 19n1 through 19n4, respectively) by 260 (the number of days the center operates each year). This, in effect, is a target service level established each year in conjunction with the user managers.

The on-line available hours (line 17) is the actual number of hours that the on-line resources were available during the year (for example, if the system was down for one hour, the resources were not available to the on-line users for that hour). Dividing the on-line available hours by the planned on-line hours yields the on-line available percentage (line 18). This percentage should be compared with a target available percentage that had been established as a data center service objective at the start of the year.

The batch hours per year (line 19) is simply the total amount of batch work for the year, as given by system measurement data. The batch rerun hours per year (line 20) are the hours consumed in rerunning work due to data center errors. There is some judgment involved in identifying data center errors versus user-induced errors, but, given that ground rules can be established for such a determination, the rerun hours represent nonproductive time in the center. That is, reruns use up resources that could otherwise be used for other work.

The batch rerun percentage (line 21) is calculated by dividing the batch rerun hours by the batch hours. As with the on-line availability percentage, the batch rerun percentage should be compared with the center's annual objective for the rerun percentage.

COMPILING THE DATA ENTRY WORKSHEET CALCULATIONS

The data entry worksheet calculations are based on the costs and productivity data for only the data entry portion of the data center. They are expressed separately because they are readily isolated from the other functions of the data center in terms of levels of expenditures, productivity, and usage. The details are labeled lines A through T in Part 4 of Figure 8.1. Line N, the hours per year per person, is computed as follows:

365	days per year
−104	weekend days
− 10	vacation days
− 7	holidays
244	net days
× 8	hours per day
1,952	hours per year per person

Examining the data at lines L and R, it is apparent that the increased cost per stroke between 19n3 and 19n4 is due to the group output rate (line R) falling faster (at 16.3 percent) than the decrease in the cost of equipment and wages (line L, dropping at a rate of 12.7 percent). This reinforces the notion that the economies of scale are no longer being realized in the data entry section. As long as a data entry supervisor (that is, a nonproductive position) remains in the section, the productivity slack must be made up by the remaining data entry operators increasing their productivity rates each year.

The costs of typical record lengths are presented for those who wish to convert the per-stroke costs to a per-record cost. The variability of record lengths and the desire of some installations to key and verify while others key and do not verify makes the per-stroke costs more universally applicable.

APPLYING THIS INFORMATION TO YOUR DATA CENTER

1. Have you attempted to present your data center results in the form of a data center annual report?

2. What are the strong and weak points of your data center as revealed by the annual report?

3. How can your annual report be made more meaningful to your users and management?

   Hint: Draft an annual report for your center and circulate it to a few users and some management people. Solicit their comments. The report should be useful to them after they have been given some basic definition of terms.

SUMMARY

Data presented in this prototype data center annual report is intended to give a businesslike picture of activity in the data center. It is a means of communicating with top management in terms of dollars and cents and productive output rather than in data processing's technical jargon. *As DCM, you should consider this form as a way to assess performance during a given time period and as a way to compare performance between various time periods. Appropriate modifications should be made to adapt the annual report to your particular installation. For example, if you are just starting to develop an annual report, complete historical data may not be available. Until these data are built up, you may have to omit some areas of the report (such as service loads). Over time, the complete report should be issued.*

II

Organizing

9

Mapping the Organization of the Data Center

This chapter uses various organization charts to show some of the many ways in which data centers can be organized. Remember that an organization chart, however, cannot represent the informal *structure of an organization, a structure often based on individual personalities and specific events in the development of the organization. This informal structure is often more effective than the formal one, and you must keep it in mind as you set up or simply examine the organization of your own data center. On the other hand, an organization chart does communicate the scope of authority for each position, the reporting structure, and the final authority within a given span of control, and, if it is reviewed and revised periodically, it can help you ensure that all functions of the data center are operating at peak efficiency.*

ORGANIZING THE DATA CENTER STAFF BY FUNCTION

Before you can draw a useful organization chart, you need to understand clearly the relationship of each data center staff position to its general function within the data center. The following areas represent the functional elements of the data center: preparation and review, execution, support, and control. All of the specific positions held by staff members within the data center fall under one of these functional groups. Figure 9.1 classifies data center positions by function and indicates the type of work and the level of creativity that each position involves.

As you can see from this figure, the data center serves as an organizational unit for people with a wide range of skills and levels of creativity. One of the real skills needed by the DCM is an ability to orchestrate this disparate group. With a full spectrum of jobs to manage—from the clerical, repetitive, highly structured assignments such as data entry to the creative, ad hoc, unstructured positions such as technical support—the successful DCM is one who can blend this pool of talent for optimum results. The following paragraphs discuss briefly the characteristics of each functional group.

The Preparation and Review Functions

The *preparation and review* group is characterized by a set of jobs that are clerical in nature—that is, they are fairly routine and predictable.

The data entry jobs are probably the most labor-intensive positions in the data center in that they have a steady flow of repetitive work. The emphasis in these jobs is on grinding out the work at a high productivity rate. Supervision of the data entry group involves good direction, well-documented procedures for each task, and ample advanced staging of future tasks. Controls are available in the form of production statistics and error rates for individuals and for the data entry group.

The other positions within the preparation and review group (those relating to job set-up, the tape library, check-out, and dispatch) may have peaks and valleys in the volume of work to be done throughout the shift, but the work must be done efficiently whenever it

Function	Type of Position	Level of Creativity
1. Preparation and Review:		
Data entry	Clerical	Low
Job set-up	Clerical	Low
Tape library	Clerical	Low
Check-out	Clerical	Low
Dispatch	Clerical	Low
2. Execution:		
Team leader (CPU)	Technical	Low/medium
Network monitor	Technical	Medium
Tape monitor	Clerical	Low
Forms handler	Clerical	Low
3. Support:		
Technical support	Technical	High
Quality control	Clerical	Medium
Data base administrator	Management	High
Administrative assistant	Administrative	Medium
Standards and procedures	Technical	Medium
Planning	Technical/management	High
User contact	Administrative/management	High
4. Control:		
Data center manager	Management	High
Shift manager	Management	Medium
Operations standards manager	Management	Medium

FIGURE 9.1.   *The Functions of Data Center Staff Positions*

is presented. Controls for these tasks include monitoring rerun rates for the job set-up people, making a periodic physical inventory of the tape library for the tape librarian, and monitoring user reaction or complaints for the check-out and dispatch positions.

The Execution Function

Positions within the *execution* group have a combination of clerical and technical attributes. The workload tends to be sporadic; there may be flurries of activity while tasks are being initiated or closed out, and then there may be slack periods during long-running execution of the jobs on the computer. Monitoring rerun rates and verifying that all assigned tasks have been run successfully during the given period of the day are means of controlling these positions.

The Support Function

The *support* tasks within the data center are truly a mixed bag as far as type of position and work characteristics are concerned. The people selected for these positions are generally more mature and experienced than those chosen for other positions; therefore, they need less direct supervision than others in the data center. Controls and measurements of the effectiveness of these people generally consist of evaluating the quality, thoroughness, and timeliness of their work and thus are more subjective than the controls employed for other jobs in the data center.

The Control Function

The control positions in the data center, of course, are those positions that directly involve the management of the center. Here, the volume of the work is unpredictable, and the type of work varies greatly. For example, these managers have to deal with upper management, contact vendors, handle personnel problems, and participate in the general management of the data center. The final judgment as to the effectiveness of these managers or supervisors is usually made by people outside of the data center—namely, the users and the organization's management.

PLACING THE DATA CENTER ON THE CORPORATE ORGANIZATION CHART

Where does this conglomerate of jobs, functions, and people fit into the corporate structure? The answer varies for each installation. Every company tends to go through a maturing process with regard to data processing. This process may occur relatively rapidly or it may occur slowly, depending on the attitude of top mangement toward DP, the skills of the data center people, and the degree of user involvement. Whatever the time frame involved, the data center occupies a different spot on the corporate organization chart at each stage of this maturation process.

When Data Processing Is Dedicated to a Single User

Early on, data processing tends to find an organizational home within the specific department or user area that has the first application on the computer or that shows particular interest in the way in which computers can be used within the department or within the company. Thus, early DP organization charts often take the form shown in Figure 9.2.

In this structure, the data processing positions are fairly well "blended in" with other people in the department and there is little, if any, differentiation within the DP group as to "operations" or "systems." The people involved in data processing may have come from within the department, or they may be "outsiders" whose job functions may not be understood completely by the rest of the department. For the rest of the company outside of this department, the data processing function is usually all but invisible, since the type of processing being done relates only to the immediate department.

These early data processing groups are often found within such departments as accounting or engineering. In fact, within the corporation there may be multiple, concurrent data processing activities (some of which might use an outside time-sharing system rather than an in-house computer) at this level of organizational maturity.

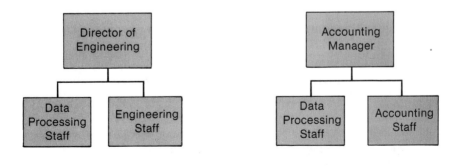

FIGURE 9.2. Dedicated DP Organization

In terms of management issues, the computer people usually find themselves reporting to a manager who knows nothing or very little about data processing and who is mainly concerned with running the department in general rather than paying a great deal of attention to the specific problems that arise in the data processing area. This situation may create difficulties in the recruitment and retention of qualified data processing personnel, since these people may be concerned about the type of professional development available to them in the small, self-contained department. On the other hand, this organizational structure does provide the departmental manager with direct control and accountability over the data processing activities.

When DP Expands to Serve Several Users

The tight, functional reporting structure remains in effect until several departments or functional areas are included in the company's computer activities and another level of management is justified within data processing. Now the data processing group starts to come into its own in terms of visibility and recognition within the company since the workload is enlarged, and computer applications can no longer be attributed solely to a single user department or area.

How does this change in organizational structure occur? Sometimes it is caused by several users quietly lobbying for more influence over the work done for them in the data processing area. More often, the change is made in response to the complaints of one or more irate user managers who feel that their work in the data processing area is being slighted in favor of the work of the "home" department (that is, the department to which data processing reports). When this type of change has been made, the organizational chart resembles that shown in Figure 9.3.

Although the data processing areas have now broken away from the tight alliance with a single user department that was prevalent in the organization shown in Figure 9.2, the first loyalty, naturally, still tends to be to the DP manager's immediate superior (often the corporation's controller). This means that the data processing group has not fully emerged as an organizational entity, but it is moving in that direction. In the process of this emergence, moderate visibility within the corporate organization is achieved. Top management and other departmental areas are more aware of the presence of data processing. Typically, additional workload is given to the computer staff as user interest in and demand for services increases.

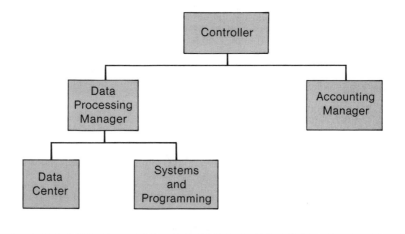

FIGURE 9.3   Expanded DP Organization

Since this organizational structure allows data processing to serve multiple user disciplines, the data processing functions become more intertwined in the day-to-day activities and problems of the corporation. A successful data processing manager, in this environment, comes to be a valued advisor and information source for the rest of management on such issues as computer usage and capacity and on the decision to extend computer service to new parts of the organization. At this point, the data processing area is considered to be a corporate or divisional *staff* function rather than a *line* operation, but the data processing manager becomes more involved in such matters as budgeting and, to some degree, advance planning for the DP areas.

With the structure shown in Figure 9.3, it becomes somewhat easier to attract qualified data processing people due to the higher visibility of the group and the more professional image that the data processing people carry, but it is difficult to keep these people if interesting and exciting projects and applications are not forthcoming in the data processing area.

When DP Becomes the Information Utility Within the Company

With the addition of more and more applications, the staff is generally enlarged in the data processing area, budgets get bigger, and the importance of data processing continues to increase to the point where the organization chart resembles that shown as Figure 9.4.

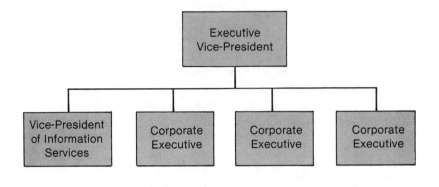

FIGURE 9.4   Data Processing as an Information Utility to the Corporation

Under this arrangement, data processing provides a data service function; in other words, because the DP group now provides a wide range of services (such as batch processing, on-line processing, data transmission, data base custody) and handles a diversity of applications, we can say that data processing has grown into an *information utility* within the corporation. An information utility, as we use the term here, is a facility that provides a broad spectrum of computer expertise and capability, including systems and programming talent, data base administration, and on-line, batch, and communications facilities.

At this stage, users see the person heading the data processing area (that is, the Vice-President of Information Services) as the "computer expert" within the company, and this person is frequently sought out for counsel and advice on data-related matters. As a group, the data processing staff has significant visibility within the corporate organizational structure. This is a result of the increased dependency on data processing by the user areas (although this dependency cannot be equated with widespread popularity, since some users may still harbor fear or resentment toward data processing).

During this stage in the maturation process, centralized control of computer expansion and procurement develops. *One of the pitfalls during this period is the tendency to expand in all technological directions at once, adding staff and equipment without a thorough cost/benefit analysis or without thinking through the long-term impact that such expansion has on the corporation.* This can easily lead to increased overhead expenses as specialists are added to the staff and as special equipment is made a part of the overall configuration.

Also during this stage, the exploration and development of many new data processing areas within the corporation make the company professionally attractive to data processing personnel.

As one might expect, all of this activity has a plus and a minus side to it. The positive aspects include the consistency of approach and economies of scale that result from a centralized organizational structure. The negative aspects include the user frustration that results (1) from more and more users wanting more and more services from data processing and (2) from the lengthened response times as the computer staff attempts to standardize terminals, configurations, and so on.

In some organizations, this evolution takes one additional step as an *information services group* is formed at the corporate staff level. This group takes on the responsibilities for long-range information research and planning, for data administration, and for advanced studies on technical developments and their applicability to the corporation. The data center may assign its own people to positions such as technical support (for the operating system, for instance) and data security and control, but the long-term planning on these issues is controlled by the information services group.

The DCM charged with the responsibility for an organization of the type shown in Figure 9.4 must possess varied skills including those that cover production control, quality control, and installation planning. In addition, with the growing diversity of the data processing activities, comprehensive processing procedures must be developed and followed.

ORGANIZING THE INFORMATION UTILITY

Figure 9.5 is a detailed organization chart of the fairly advanced, medium- to large-scale DP organization that we are calling the "information utility." In this organizational structure, the senior manager for data processing carries the title of "Vice-President of Information Services." (Of course, this title may vary from one company to another; in some companies, for example, the top data processing manager has the title of "director" instead of vice-president.)

An *administrative assistant* reports directly to this vice-president, and the position exists because of the steady flow of paperwork and

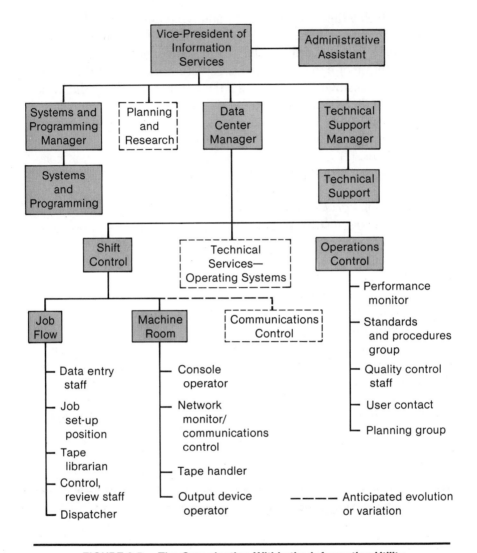

FIGURE 9.5. *The Organization Within the Information Utility*

reports that seems to be a part of any reasonably large organization. The duties of the administrative assistant include the monitoring and processing of personnel actions (such as pay increases), new-hire processing, and terminated-employee processing for all personnel assigned to the general data processing area. Additionally, the administrative assistant takes care of the processing of vendor invoices and maintains a suspense-file system to alert management when a review of a contract is due or subject to renewal. Any operational or productivity data is also maintained (and perhaps converted to graphic representation) by the administrative assistant.

The Technical Support Group

The *technical support* group has the responsibility for customizing technical software for the installation (such as operating systems, utilities, compilers, and the like), for fine-tuning the operational performance of the hardware and software combinations in use at the installation, for trouble-shooting operational problems, and for assisting programmers, systems analysts, and data center personnel in improving the efficiency of data processing functions. Instead of calling the group "technical support," some companies call this group "systems programming" (not to be confused with "systems *and* programming"), "systems support," or similar names.

The technical support function often begins as an additional duty for a talented or interested person within either the data center or systems and programming. When the workload and complexity of this function become more than can be handled as an "additional duty," technical support is recognized as a separate position within either the data center or within S&P. As the workload continues to build, the support function is then split off as an entity of its own. This organizational structure reflects the fact that technical support serves the activities of both S&P and the data center.

Care must be taken to ensure that the technical support staff members properly document their actions and that they stay in close touch with the DCM regarding changes to operational characteristics of equipment and software. Technical support people usually like to work independently, want little supervision, want maximum flexibility as to working hours and availability of resources, and have a loyalty to the technical discipline in which they are trained rather than to a particular company. Thus, documentation and communication from the technical support staff are imperative in order for the installation to have any consistency in operation should the technical specialists leave the company.

The Systems and Programming Area

The traditional role of the *systems and programming* area is well understood to be the definition, design, and development of applications and will not be reviewed here in detail.

The Data Center

Figure 9.5 shows two major sections within the *data center* itself: shift control and operations control. It must be noted that this is but one of a variety of organizational structures that are workable for a data center. Essentially, the shift control group is responsible for repetitive, day-to-day operations and functions. The operations control group is responsible for the overall review and planning of data center operations and is concerned with how the data center's performance meets the present and planned information processing needs of the corporation.

Shift Control. Two major sections are found within the shift control group. The *job flow* section deals with setting up work for processing on the computer, and the *machine room* section handles the actual processing of work on the computer.

Functions such as data entry, job set-up, tape library maintenance, post-run control and checking, and work dispatching are located within the job flow section—in other words, these are the positions that take care of the preparation and review functions (Figure 9.1). These positions are marked by jobs that are generally clerical and repetitive, with the workload varying from steady (data entry) to sporadic (job set-up, job check-out, work dispatch) to on-demand (tape library). Emphasis in these positions is on consistent procedures—that is, the establishment of work routines that optimize the efficiency of the group and allow quick spotting of any variations from these procedures. For example, the late arrival to or dispatch of work from the center, or the existence of error rates that are higher than usual should be easily detectable based on the data center's standards.

The position of *job flow supervisor* can be a very good one for someone who formerly headed the data entry department, for example. As the data entry workload is reduced with the advent of more on-line applications, the data entry supervisor often represents more overhead than is tolerable; in this case, moving the data entry supervisor into the position of job flow supervisor is advantageous for the individual's career and is good for the data center, since this individual probably has significant experience within the company.

The machine room group is responsible for the efficient and effective utilization of computer machine resources—these are the positions that accomplish the execution functions. Specifically, this group must operate the central processor and associated peripherals to achieve optimum throughput on batch operations and to provide the expected availability of computer resources (such as the processor, peripherals, and terminal equipment) for on-line operations. Tasks within the machine room group involve a combination of technical and clerical skills and are marked by a sporadic workload.

The team leader of this group, who may well be the senior console operator, and the network monitor or communications control supervisor have jobs that require good technical training and skills. They must watch the activity levels and patterns on the various pieces of equipment and must make decisions as to which resources to allocate or reallocate at certain times.

The other jobs on the machine room team are that of tape handler (one who mounts and unmounts tapes as needed for specific jobs) and output device operator (one who monitors printers and ensures that continuous forms are in adequate supply). These jobs are clerical in nature with a sporadic workload.

Within this organization, meeting predetermined schedules is the responsibility of the *shift control manager*. The determination of these schedules is a joint effort involving people such as the DCM, systems analysts, and users. Since meeting these schedules can involve resources and tasks that are found in both the job flow group and in the machine room group, the shift control manager is directly responsible for the use of these resources.

Operations Control. Advance planning, performance monitoring, monitoring of standards and procedures, quality control, and user contact are the responsibilities of the operations control section. These positions handle the support functions listed in Figure 9.1. The difference between these activities and the activities of the shift control section is that operations control is responsible for establishing a climate for efficient operations, and shift control is responsible for efficient operation within this climate. In this sense, the operations control section is more externally oriented and the shift control section is more internally oriented relative to the data center. Shift control, undoubtedly, has regular contact with users and those outside of the data center, but operations control staff members must have more of an external view as they carry out their assigned responsibilities. In other words, their perspective should take into account user needs, changing technology, workload, future capacity requirements, and good data processing practices.

Performance monitoring, as part of the operations control group, reviews data such as machine utilization, available on-line hours versus planned on-line hours, total batch hours, total batch rerun hours, data entry keying rates, and data entry error rates. These data are used in putting together information for the DCM's performance review with user department managers and are used for long-term resource requirement planning.

The *standards and procedures* group is responsible for setting standards and reviewing adherence to these standards on such things as operating documentation and operating procedures. This group is interested in the documentation of new applications before they are put into production as well as in ways to improve the operating documentation of existing applications. The operating procedures are reviewed from time to time by this group to try to find ways to eliminate inefficient procedures.

Quality control (QC), in some respects, overlaps the functions described for the standards and procedures staff. The primary difference between the two areas is that the QC people look at specific applications and their performance, while the standards and procedures people take the specific situations and attempt to generalize them for wider application within the data center. By periodically intercepting production output (or copies of the output) from the shift control group, the QC staff checks the quality of the work being produced in the production environment. Thus, QC serves as a bridge between the user and the data center.

The *user contact* group also contributes to the bridge between user and data center. This group maintains direct contact with the users, and the users know that these people can provide ready assistance on operating problems and procedures within the data center. At the same time, the user contact group relieves the rest of the data center staff from interruptions by users. This is especially important when equipment or system outages occur. By providing a source of information to the users during problem periods, the user contact group allows the other key people in the center to concentrate on getting back into production as rapidly as possible.

The *planning* group is responsible for the advance planning of the data center. Specifically, this group evaluates current capabilities and capacities against existing workloads, then projects these conditions into the future to determine the resource mix and the skill levels that will be needed to satisfy expected workloads. These projections, of course, include a look at the amount and type of equipment, at the training and background of the data center personnel, and at the level of data processing education and understanding that exists in the user community within the corporation.

The issues that were discussed in Part I of this book are especially applicable to the planning group. For example, it is essential that the planning group know the direction that data processing is expected to take for the next few years so that the right amount and type of resources can be available when they are needed. If, for instance, the company is shifting from batch processing to more on-line processing, the planning group must assess correctly the changing needs of the data center and of the users. These needs can include the installation of more random access storage devices, of transmission lines, line concentrators, terminals, and other equipment. At the same time, the planning group must ensure that the supporting software is compatible with the new hardware capabilities. Finally, the group must schedule the necessary courses for the users and the data center staff in plenty of time before the new configurations are installed.

In a sense, the operations control section acts as a staff to the data center manager, and the shift control section acts as a line operation within the center. Clearly, the two sections must work closely together, but separating the two sections (with separate supervisors) allows for efficient functioning of all areas—the shift control people are free to go about their duties with major emphasis on getting the work out and maintaining resource availability; the operations control group has the luxury of taking a more studied look at the operation of the center without the pressure of the immediate workload.

Expected Variations

It was pointed out earlier that the organizational structure shown in Figure 9.5 is but one way to align the data center staff. Consider some basic variations that may take place in this organization.

The importance attached to a particular function by the corporation (or at least by the DCM) is indicated on an organization chart by the level at which responsibility for these functions occurs. As the installation continues to grow, certain functions will become more important and will thus rate a higher level manager. For example, as the network expands, more terminals will be added and more on-line time will be required in the data center during a given period. When this happens, the network monitoring function may be taken away from the machine room group and given to a *communications control* group that is placed on a par with the machine room group and headed by the network monitor. The expanding network could also result in a realignment of other functions within the data center, such as those of the user contact area (for instance, the network monitor may become the users' primary contact in a widespread on-line network), and it may result in a reduced level of activity and importance in the job set-up and dispatch areas, since more of the work will be done on-line than in a batch mode.

Figure 9.5 shows several other anticipated variations. The *planning and research* box, for example, indicates the group that will eventually become an information service group. The *technical services* box represents a group that may evolve in very large installations where new versions of operating systems software are constantly being tested.

Yet another area where change can be expected is that of data base administration and control. Like the evolution of the technical support staff discussed earlier, the data base administrator (DBA) can emerge from either the S&P area or from the data center staff. It is typical that, in the early days of a company's DBA activity, the requirements for this position focus on a strong technical background. As time goes by and more applications are tied to the data base, the skills needed by the DBA change to a combination of technical, organizational, and operational skills.

Another area that is likely to change is the data entry function. Most likely, the workload will diminish for data entry within the data center as more on-line applications are installed and as users obtain remote-job or distributed-computing capability. At the same time, the quality control function may experience a rise in stature within the data center organization. Depending upon the importance that is attached to data processing quality control and audit activities in the corporation, quality control may achieve the same level in the organizational structure as operations control.

Figure 9.6 illustrates a mature data processing installation that combines centralized and distributed computing capabilities. Here, the centralized staff reports to the vice-president of information services as in the typical medium- or large-scale computer center; the distributed capability is shown, for illustrative purposes, in the marketing area of one of the company's divisions. (Distributed computing,

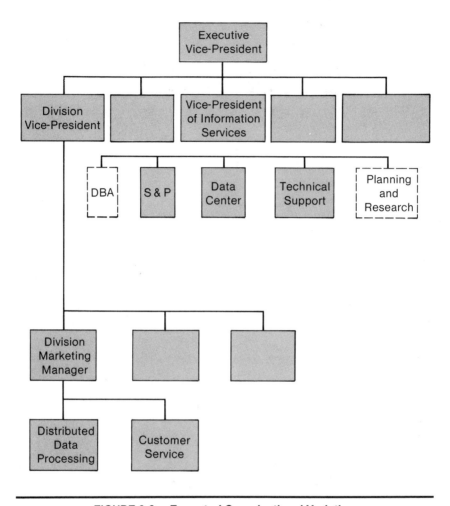

FIGURE 9.6. *Expected Organizational Variations*

of course, involves the installation of microcomputers or minicomputers in user areas with connections into larger mainframes.)

Note the striking similarity between the organization of the distributed DP functions (as shown in Figure 9.6) and the early DP organization shown in Figure 9.2. In many ways, it is as if the organization has come full circle regarding the organization of data processing, but Figure 9.6 reflects a more mature installation, one in which full-service data processing has come to be an integral part of the corporation. The combination of centralized and decentralized computer resources recognizes the need for a multilevel approach to satisfying users' needs.

APPLYING THIS INFORMATION TO YOUR DATA CENTER

1. How has your data center organization changed in the past year? In the past three years?

2. When did the last revision to the data center organization chart occur?

3. What were the reasons for the latest changes in the organization chart?

4. When do you anticipate the next change in the data center organization chart?

SUMMARY

In organizing the data center, the DCM must be aware of the diversity of the talents, training, job characteristics, and creativity levels of the personnel in the data center. The range of activities within the data center gives yet another dimension to the task of managing the center's resources. These activities resemble those found in a production line atmosphere, have a similarity to research functions, and involve the physical custodianship of valuable resources—namely, the company's data.

You should expect the data center organization to change as new levels of technology are introduced to the center, as additional workload volumes are placed on the data center, and as data processing becomes a more integral part of the corporation. As the DCM, you must continually evaluate whether the present organizational structure is the most effective for the job that is expected to be performed in the data center. This structure must represent clearly the lines of authority and responsibility, yet it must be streamlined enough to allow people to get their work done. Frequent or capricious changes in an organization are disruptive both to its staff and to those people who have to deal with the organization, but an organization that has no organizational changes over an extended period of time is a stagnant, unresponsive operational entity. The DCM must find a middle ground between these two extremes and construct an organization that serves today's needs and that positions the data center for tomorrow's requirements.

The organizational positions discussed in this chapter must be filled with people who have the talent and qualifications to bring these positions to life. The next chapter explains how to match the skills of the people with the requirements of the positions.

10

Matching People and Positions

The establishment of an organization chart, as described in the previous chapter, and the definition of job characteristics form the basis for finding people to fill data center positions. This chapter looks first at the possible reasons for employee turnover; then we discuss ways to ensure that you find the right candidate for the job and that you establish effective training programs, which will help keep your employees in the right job.

ASSESSING THE TURNOVER RATE

Vacancies, of course, exist in any organization from time to time, and, in fact, employee turnover, when kept to an acceptable level, can actually be healthy for the organization. New people and ideas are beneficial for any group, helping to prevent the "in-breeding" that occurs when a group exists for a long time with no new ideas or changes in its method of doing things. The key for the data center manager, of course, is to determine what vacancy or turnover rate constitutes an "acceptable level."

One must define *turnover* more precisely before concluding whether a given rate is good or bad. If turnover is defined as a change in personnel in a given position and if the change is due to an incumbent being moved up or promoted within the organization, a relatively high turnover rate may be acceptable since knowledge of the installation and of the applications is staying within the organization.

On the other hand, if turnover is defined as a change in personnel in a given position and if the change results in the incumbent leaving the company, a turnover rate in excess of 25 percent is probably unacceptable, especially if it occurs in nonclerical positions. Clerical positions, such as data entry, are more easily filled than technical or management positions, since clerical positions are more amenable to standardized training and orientation. Thus, a higher turnover rate can be accepted for clerical positions than for nonclerical positions.

Pinpointing Why Turnover Occurs

For existing positions, analyze the turnover rate over a period of time, such as one year. First of all, determine if the overall rate within the data center is acceptable (no matter what the overall turnover rate is, however, a vacancy caused by a key individual leaving is usually not acceptable!). Examine how the current rate compares with the rate experienced over the past few years. Look for trends or patterns to the vacancies over the past several years. High velocity turnover in virtually every position within the data center can be symptomatic of:

1. Poor data center management

2. Underpaid personnel

3. Undesirable management or personnel policies throughout the company

4. A technically and professionally stagnant environment

5. A combination of these factors

Poor general management within the center can take place when, for example, a DCM pays inordinate attention to the technical side of managing the center (such as by dedicating large blocks of time to hardware evaluation) while neglecting areas such as personnel interrelationships or user relations.

Underpaid personnel are a frequent problem leading to high turnover rates in companies where the upper management is not attuned to the relatively high pay scales that are prevalent in the data processing industry. Since you must compete in the personnel marketplace for scarce resources (namely, talented individuals), you must keep management advised as to how the company's pay levels for computer personnel compare with the market rate in the area. On the other hand, be aware of the fact that, quite frequently, people who leave an organization give low pay as the reason for their leaving to mask the true reason. You must assess each situation to determine whether pay was, in fact, the reason for quitting.

Undesirable company policies are another source of irritation that can lead to people leaving the company. Examples include stingy vacation plans, niggardly education programs, and poor working conditions, such as a "sweatshop" atmosphere where the assumption is that everyone will work fifty to sixty hours per week with no compensating time off and with no recognition of individual accomplishments. Since the company is competing with all other companies for data processing talent, those policies that might be satisfactory for other positions may not be competitive with the policies and benefits available to data processing people in other companies.

A company whose data processing environment is not stimulating will probably have a high turnover rate. A stimulating environment is created when managers in data processing, user, and upper management areas are mutually committed to providing the most effective service available. This does not necessarily mean that the company must continue to swap hardware and software in and out as a requisite for staying on the leading edge of technology. The most successful companies are those that wisely spend their money (on data processing *and* other disciplines). These companies achieve a balance among interesting applications, reasonably current hardware and software, and a genuine concern for their people to develop a well-managed operation.

Turning a High Turnover Rate Around
(or Avoiding It Altogether)

Data center managers who see an overall turnover pattern throughout all data center positions must take action to stop this trend. *Follow the basic problem-solving steps:*

1. Assess the reasons for the high turnover rate.

2. Identify alternatives.

3. Select a course of action that will correct the situation.

Creating an Action Plan. For each corrective action, the cost, benefit, and risk should be outlined. The *costs* will include the direct cost involved in the solution to the problem, such as the cost of increased salary levels or more education, and may include some indirect costs, such as the increased cost for the company's providing similar benefits to other (that is, non-data processing) personnel in the company.

The *benefit* will be the resulting reduction in the turnover rate, *but the analysis of these results should include several checkpoints to determine progress.* For example, if the turnover rate was 37 percent, 41 percent, and 39 percent, respectively, for the past three years, you may get approval to institute a more generous education program in order to bring the turnover rate down to 25 percent within the next three years. In this case, interim targets should be set to determine whether progress is being made before the three years have elapsed. These targets, for example, might be to achieve turnover rates of 33 percent, 29 percent, and 25 percent in the next three years.

The *risk analysis* portion of the action plan should include a statement as to what the costs or penalties will be if the action plan is not approved. For example, disapproving the education program may carry a risk of continuing the high turnover rate or even of increasing it. The costs to the company in this case include increased orientation costs as more people move through a given position and the lower productivity of the positions with high turnover.

Rotating Assignments.   High turnover and vacancy rates in specific positions can result from poor job conditions, the wrong degree of supervision, or incompatible personalities. In addition, many jobs within the data center are put together without regard for the day-to-day job satisfactions that people need in order to do a good job. Mundane tasks, such as watching a group of printers in order to change the continuous forms when needed, offer little or nothing in the way of personal job satisfaction. *The routine nature and relative simplicity of this type of job suggest that the task should be rotated among several people in the center or made a part of a more varied job.* Then, instead of having one person dedicated to the printer task, several people can be crosstrained in a cluster of jobs that include tape handling, printer monitoring, and job staging (that is, loading card readers or physically positioning work to be done). *These people can rotate responsibilities on a daily or weekly schedule, or the "pool" of jobs can be assigned to a "pool" of people with the individuals agreeing among themselves as to who will do a particular job at a specific time.*

There are several advantages to handling the routine tasks in this way. First, the tedious, boring work has been distributed among several people so that it is a relatively small part of any one person's overall assignment. Second, teamwork within the machine room has been enhanced because the group of people rotating these jobs share the responsibility for how much productive work has been done during an hour, shift, day, or week. And, ideally, this shared responsibility will encourage these people to come up with new ideas for improving the productivity. Third, crosstraining gives the individual a better look at several jobs within the data center and gives you, the DCM, flexibility in assignments when vacations, emergencies, or promotional opportunities arise.

Ensuring Effective Supervision.   Improper supervision can also lead to unacceptably high turnover rates. A supervisor who has come from a "production line" type of job (such as data entry) must adjust his or her supervisory techniques if put in charge of a group of people whose work is more sporadic in nature (such as quality control). The control over the latter group has to be more subtle than that used for the former group; the quality control people, of course, are expected to be productive, but you cannot quantify their productive output as easily as you can with data entry.

Data entry supervision involves organizing and staging the work so that the data entry operators can work at a steady rate with minimal interruptions for questions and instructions. Quality control supervision requires that the supervisor clearly spell out the procedures for the group, encourage teamwork, and keep people informed as to what's going on in the data center and in the company, but then be willing to step back and allow the people to work on their own, since each quality control task will be different from the last. Recognizing these differences can go a long way toward making the work more enjoyable and more rewarding for the individuals, and this, in turn, should reduce the turnover rate in these sections.

If continual turnover occurs for most of the jobs under the control of a specific supervisor, the source of the problem would appear to be with that supervisor rather than with a specific job or with the people who have been working in the job. Perhaps the supervisor is not comfortable with management or supervisory responsibilities, and perhaps some management development programs would remedy the problem. Or, if a supervisor has been trained in supervisory techniques and still has problems in retaining people, this individual may be unsuited for a supervisory position. An inability to relate to others or a tendency to over-supervise are two personality traits that can cause a previously productive employee to become an ineffective supervisor. *As DCM, you must decide whether the supervisor's behavior and attitudes can be changed in order to solve the problem. You should talk with the individual and explore ways of improving supervisory performance.* Often, a "heart-to-heart" talk will reveal that the person is uncomfortable as a supervisor and would prefer a job with less responsibility. In some cases, your only recourse is to remove the individual from supervisory responsibility and reassign him or her to another position.

CREATING ACCURATE JOB DESCRIPTIONS

Job descriptions form the basis for matching individuals' talents with the requirements for a position. Whether a job vacancy is due to employee turnover or to the creation of a new position, a good job description is essential in managing the people resources within the data center. It takes a good deal of time to set up job descriptions properly, but, once established, they are very useful for interviewing candidates and for comparing one position against another for salary and responsibility levels.

The first pass at developing job descriptions should include a survey of the people who currently hold those positions. Ask those people to list the tasks that they perform and the approximate percentage of time spent on each task. This step often reveals that many tasks, which your employees are now doing routinely, were not part of the original concept of the job. *Compare various descriptions to determine the relationships between the jobs in the data center.* For example, look again at Figure 9.1 and then determine how a quality control job compares with and relates to a dispatch job at your installation.

The next step is to formalize these descriptions so that the entire set of job descriptions has a consistent format and so that the jobs properly relate to one another. In writing the descriptions, plan on publishing and distributing them to people in the data center.

Figure 10.1 provides a format for job descriptions. A consistent format like this one helps ensure that all facets of the job have been considered when defining the position. The first sections ("job title" and "general function") describe the job and how it relates to other jobs in the data center; the next two sections ("reports to" and "directs work of") describe at what level the job occurs in the organizational structure. The "major responsibilities" section covers the specific tasks that the employee must fulfill; *you can use this part of the job description for structuring your evaluations of how well the employee is achieving the objectives of the position.* The section entitled "skills and characteristics required" lists the typical background, skills, and attributes that are needed to perform the job. "Working relationships" enumerates the people or positions with which an employee in the given job regularly comes in contact.

To provide additional perspective on the jobs within the data center, you should identify a career path flow for these jobs. This would typically show the skills and qualifications needed for advancement as well as the usual amount of experience necessary to perform each job. For example, the career path for the network monitor/communications controller might lead to the position of machine room supervisor or to the performance monitoring section.

Whether job vacancies are filled from within or from outside of the organization, they should be viewed as an opportunity to improve

Job Title: Network Monitor/Communications Controller

General Function: Monitor on-line computer network using status boards, control panels, and vendor-supplied monitoring equipment

Reports To: Machine Room Supervisor

Directs Work Of: None

Major Responsibilities:

Primary   Evaluate online terminal network response time and service; adjust communications line resources when unbalanced traffic loads occur; maintain service levels to all on-line users.

Secondary   Inform machine room supervisor of demand and service patterns with suggestions for improving service to users.

Skills and Characteristics Required:
Analytical, resourceful, must enjoy troubleshooting, must work well under pressure, must possess good oral and written communication skills

Working Relationships: Other machine room personnel, users, vendors

---

FIGURE 10.1.   *Sample Job Description*

the staff. Thus, it is important that accurate, up-to-date job descriptions exist to reflect the qualifications needed within the center.

TRANSFERRING EMPLOYEES FROM WITHIN YOUR ORGANIZATION

When a data center position is filled by transferring people from other departments in the company, you have the advantage of dealing with "known quantities," and many companies encourage intracompany transfers as a means of providing growth opportunities for their personnel. Presumably, as the DCM, you can talk with the job candidate's current manager and can get a candid evaluation of the individual's strengths and weaknesses, work habits, and attitudes. This should serve as the best type of reference you can hope to get. *In some cases, however, the candidate's manager may give a glowing report in an effort to pass off a poor producer to another department. You can eliminate this pitfall by crosschecking the individual's background with several other managers and with the personnel department.*

On the other hand, intracompany transfers create a touchy situation when the employee is found to be unacceptable in the data center after a fair job trial has been given. The person may find that the data center work was not of the type he or she expected, or the individual may simply not be capable of doing the work. The DCM cannot afford to keep the person if he or she is not measuring up to the task, but there may be a stigma attached to the person's returning to the original department. One of the attractions that data processing positions hold, especially to others in the company, may be the knowledge that data processing jobs are generally higher-paying positions than other jobs in the company. *In-depth interviewing and a candid portrayal of the job should go a long way toward eliminating candidates' misconceptions and thus should help ensure a successful intracompany transfer.*

HIRING PEOPLE FROM OUTSIDE THE COMPANY

People hired from outside the company bring new ideas into the data center and may challenge the status quo. Your problem as data center manager is determining how to verify the claims or credentials of these job candidates with any certainty. Data processing specialists are known for their frequent changes of employers. It is possible for job applicants to misrepresent, accidentally or intentionally, their qualifications and experience. An applicant may want to make the work experience sound more glamorous or meaningful than it really was, for instance. Again, the interview is crucial in helping you avoid this situation. The following section discusses interviewing techniques.

INTERVIEWING JOB CANDIDATES

A good interview involves an exchange of information between the two parties involved. Plan to give the applicant ample opportunity to recap background and experiences as well as to ask questions of you. *To prepare your questions, request the applicant's résumé in advance of the interview.* Here are several items that can be gleaned from a typical résumé and that can form the basis for interview questions:

- Time gaps in the employment history

- Claims of individual accomplishment

- Patterns of increasing responsibility and broader experience

There should be continuity of employment or the applicant should have a plausible explanation for the gaps. Even if time periods in the applicant's work life did not relate to data center assignments, these time periods should be listed and a brief notation made that explains the activity during that time period.

Try to find out specific information about general résumé claims. For example, if the résumé says, "I set up a quality control procedure for the data center," ask the applicant exactly how this was done. How comprehensive was the control procedure? Was it implemented? Is the installation still using it? Did the applicant develop the procedure single-handedly?

A series of jobs with increasing responsibilities or broader job scope indicates that the individual is capable of growing and that the employer has recognized this talent and is willing to assign greater responsibilities to the applicant.

Be prepared to ask a series of open-ended questions. These are questions that are not readily answered with a "yes" or "no" and do not have an expected response built into them. Examples of this type of question are:

- Describe your involvement in setting up the data center quality control procedure mentioned in your résumé.

- What benefits were realized as a result of the new procedure?

The applicant's answer may reveal his or her feelings towards a job situation or attitudes about job environments, but the applicant is not able to structure answers to match your feelings.

It is a good idea to have more than one person talk with the applicant and to have more than one interview with the applicant, especially if the position carries any significant level of authority and responsibility. Following the first interview, recap the interview and note items that were unclear or that should be explained more fully by the applicant. The second interview can include follow-up questions on these items and, perhaps, a more detailed description of the job or the company so that the applicant has better information on which to base a decision if a job offer is extended.

ESTABLISHING AN EFFECTIVE TRAINING PLAN

One way to ensure that your employees' skills match their positions is to establish a training development plan that will bring individual skills and interest areas into line with company requirements. First, ascertain the training needs for each employee and for each position. Evaluating the staff and the job requirements in this manner shows you where you need to correct current deficiencies in the training that has been given to date.

Next, compare the current skill levels with those that are going to be needed in the future. In this way, you can formulate a plan that will provide phased training to your employees in order to yield the correct skills at the time they are needed in the center. For example, if the installation is currently operating in a strictly batch environment but has plans to implement an on-line application within the next eighteen months, the education plan should ensure that one or several people are sent to appropriate classes (such as a course on teleprocessing monitor software) in plenty of time so that they are prepared to operate an on-line application when it becomes productive. (This is yet another reason for the DCM to stay in close touch with users and the systems development area in order to get an early warning as to plans such as a new on-line application). Similarly, if the data center is expected to change the mainframe significantly as a response to increased workloads and company requirements, the training plan should allow enough time and resources so that all of the necessary people are properly trained on the installation and operation of the new equipment.

Choosing Training Tools

A key part of the data center training plan is a set of standards against which the various educational offerings can be measured. To establish these standards, review course outlines, obtain references from others who have used the course, and set up trial periods for evaluating the materials.

A detailed course outline can tell you whether the content and level of presentation is appropriate to your needs. The flyers and brochures for course offerings usually have at least a brief outline of the material to be presented. If this does not give enough information on which to make a decision about the course, don't hesitate to contact the sponsoring organization to get more information. It is especially important to understand the *level of presentation.* The sponsoring organization usually attempts to put together a course that will have broad appeal. If your installation is reasonably advanced or is rather naive in a particular area of data processing, it will pay you to find out how simple or complex the presentation and treatment of material will be. What may be a valuable seminar to some people may have little new information for others.

Of course, one of the best ways to judge the value of a course is to have a reliable assessment from someone who has already attended the course. You should check both with an attendee from outside your company and with your own people after they have returned from the course. Ask about:

- Course content

- The level of presentation

- The mix of people attending the course

- The applicability of the materials to the individual's situation

In these follow-up interviews with your own staff members, don't simply ask one or two general questions and let it go at that. Ask specifically:

- What the person learned
- How he or she would evaluate the installation's progress and methods in the topic area
- What changes might be put into effect as a result of the class
- How the course was of benefit to the individual
- Whether he or she would recommend sending others to the course

As a reference check on a particular course, you can send one person to a class in advance of possibly sending a group of other people from your installation to the same class. In order to do this, however, you must have a good training plan that shows you how much time to allow for sending the one person, evaluating the results, then sending the other people.

It may appear attractive and economical to send one person to a class and then have that person return and teach the rest of your group, instead of sending everybody to an outside class. This is a false economy. Most people who attend classes are not able to teach a group of people effectively. It is too much to ask that a person become an expert on a topic after attending one class. *If there are many people in your installation who should be taught the material, explore the possibility of bringing the course instructor into your facility.* This will cost less money than if you send everybody off to class.

Some training media, notably videotape courses, are available for a trial review period. Again, advance planning is essential if benefits are to be realized from the evaluation period. When no planning is done, the videotape course is usually dropped off by the vendor, a great deal of interest is shown for the first several days (with everyone wanting to watch the tapes at once, it seems), then the novelty wears off, hardly anyone watches the tapes after the first week or so, and then the DCM has to decide whether to purchase the course materials.

Instead of this haphazard method of trying out a videotape course, set up an evaluation plan. The plan should identify specific individuals who will test and rate the materials. These individuals should represent a cross section of experience and talent in your or-

ganization. The materials can then be judged as to suitability for un-
trained people, for those with average experience, and for those with
considerable experience. At the end of the vendor's trial period, you
are in a much better position to make a decision as to the value of the
course.

There are a number of ways to train data center people in addition to formal classes. Task forces, team assignments, brainstorming
sessions, and workshops all have value as training vehicles, but they
should supplement rather than supplant the formal training media.
The *task force* and *team assignments* are especially valuable for training less experienced people when they are teamed with more senior
people from the data center, the user area, or both. In this way, the
junior members gain from the experience of the other team members
while the team as a whole profits from the junior members' fresh perspective, which may lead to a new solution to the problem at hand.

Brainstorming sessions act as training opportunities because of
the free exchange of ideas from participants with a variety of perspec-
tives, specialities, and experience levels. The great lesson to be
learned from brainstorming is that many ideas, which may be so zany
that they would never be mentioned in a more constrained atmosphere, can be slightly modified and turn into effective solutions to a
problem.

The *workshop* allows practical application of concepts and
methods in a controlled setting. Workshops are particularly effective
in training many people at one time, especially after these people
have had some formal education in the topic at hand. For example,
after some formal classes have been given in a new procedure for
setting up an application (such as a month-end accounting cycle) in
the data center, a workshop session is helpful in testing both the procedure and the level of understanding of the people who will be
working with the new procedure. Minor changes in the procedure can
be ironed out during the workshop and questions can be answered on
the spot.

Assessing the Cost/Benefits of Your Training Plan

The training program that is undertaken should be measured in
typical cost/benefit terms. There will be direct and indirect costs and
tangible and intangible benefits. The following items represent some
of the costs and benefits:

- *Costs:*
  - Course fee
  - Transportation
  - Living expenses
  - Lost on-the-job time

- *Benefits:*
  - Additional skills
  - Improved productivity
  - Enhanced morale

Course fees, depending on the duration of the course and the sponsoring institution, can range from $50 to $900 and up. The length of the course may vary from one day to several days to a week or more. Some technical institutions sponsor courses that run for one or two days and are designed for "hands-on" personnel who will be directly involved in using the skills learned. These courses are very practical and may cost $50 to $100. Universities and independent vendors who sponsor higher-level courses usually charge more money (for example, $300 to $900), and these courses may run for two, three, or five days. The content of these courses is usually a combination of conceptual and practical material, or it may include a briefing on some state-of-the-art topic or development.

The transportation and living costs are those expenses that are incurred in the course of getting to and attending the class. These will vary according to the location of the class (local or out-of-town) and the duration. Lost on-the-job time can create an additional cost in the form of overtime pay to the person who covers for the "student."

The additional skills gained by the individual through training represent the prime benefit to the organization. Some skills may be a mandatory part of the progress of the data center; for instance, if a new mainframe is to be installed, the operators must be trained on the new equipment if the center is to realize any benefit from the change. In other cases, the training may develop additional skills that will improve the productivity of the data center. These benefits are less tangible, but they can be measured by comparing productivity levels before and after the training, and then assigning cost savings to the changes in productivity.

As we noted in the discussion on vacancies and turnover, an ongoing training program has a beneficial effect on the morale of the people in the data center. This benefit may not be measurable for several years, but it is clear that the lack of a training program in the data center is costly, at least in terms of employee turnover. The rapid changes in data processing technology make training an integral part of the maintenance and development of individual skills. If this opportunity is not made available to personnel, employees will leave the organization in order to stay current in their skill areas.

APPLYING THIS INFORMATION TO YOUR DATA CENTER

1. What is the vacancy rate for data center positions within the last three years?

2. Are personnel in any specific positions turning over faster or slower than those in other positions?

3. What are the underlying reasons for this faster or slower rate of turnover?

4. Do you have a training plan for the data center?

SUMMARY

Many organizations assert that "people are the most important resource we have." This chapter has given you ideas on how to obtain, nurture, and enhance this valuable resource.

As the DCM, you should analyze the turnover rate in the data center, consider various sources of personnel for the center (both internal transfers and outside hires), develop your interviewing skills, and have an ongoing training plan for your people. Put together a realistic cost/benefit analysis of the training program. Recognize the heavy investment an organization has in its people and give them meaningful work.

When people have been given the responsibility for performing a given job, the DCM and the individual need a regular means of evaluating their performance in that job. Chapter Eleven outlines and discusses ways of measuring professional performance.

11

Measuring Professional Performance

The performance of the people working in the data center directly impacts the efficiency of the center. As DCM, you must find ways to measure this performance in order to achieve optimum productivity and to reward the individuals. This chapter reviews the objective measures that can be used, discusses how you can motivate your employees to perform well, and suggests ways to prepare performance reviews.

USING OBJECTIVE MEASUREMENT TOOLS

The objective performance measurements are those that can be made without interpretation or emotional bias. They are job factors that can be quantified or about which there is little doubt as to whether the task was satisfactorily accomplished. These measures must be mutually agreed upon in advance by the manager and the worker if the objective measures are to be effective.

In order to establish quantitative measures, begin by reviewing the job description write-up, then attempt to assign quantitative targets to each of the primary responsibilities shown in the job description. Note that the job description can describe the responsibilities of a group of people (for instance, the data entry section) and that the performance measurement targets are geared specifically for an individual. Thus, the performance objective for one person in data entry may be to achieve an average rate of 12,800 strokes per hour while the objective for another person may be to achieve a rate of 11,500 per hour. The job description provides a framework for the work of the section; the performance objectives provide a framework for the work of the individual within that section.

Stating Measurement Objectives

In the data center, jobs such as data entry lend themselves easily to quantitative measurement. The objective may be to achieve a specific average gross keying rate, or it may be to reduce the number of keying errors by a specific percentage over the course of the year.

For the jobs associated with the job flow section of the data center, the target may be to improve user or customer service by reducing the average waiting time between work stations by, for example, five percent. It is not appropriate to set an objective such as "increase the number of jobs handled by x percent" because the individual has no direct control over the number of jobs reaching the data center or his or her work station.

The objective for a position such as the tape librarian can also be quantified. Here, the objective may be stated as: "Maintain accurate records of tape location and activity in order to achieve an error rate of less than 1 percent when the tape library records are subjected to a physical inventory and verification." Again, *the objective is stated in a way that gives the individual control over the accomplishment.*

The tape library objective was *not* stated in terms of the number of tapes handled or in terms of pulling accurate tapes for job execution. The number of tapes is dependent upon the volume of jobs and on the type of jobs. If the installation has a tape control software package in use, the accuracy of the tapes will be controlled automatically by the package. Therefore, goals relating to these two factors are neither appropriate nor meaningful.

For jobs in the machine room section, the objectives may be a bit more difficult to quantify on an individual basis. You might create team objectives by "bundling" several jobs within the section and then setting objectives for the team. The console operator, tape handler, and printer attendant can be linked together as a team for these purposes. Their objectives may be stated in terms such as: "Process application work for the accounting group in order to meet the established performance targets."

This type of objective presumes the existence of performance targets, such as those stated in a service agreement (as discussed in Chapter One), that have been established with the user. For example, performance objectives for three financial applications might appear as follows:

Application	Delivery	Cost
Accounts payable	95 percent on time	$1.15 per check
Accounts receivable	92 percent on time	$0.95 per invoice
Financial statements	98 percent on time	$5,000 per month

Using objectives like these takes into account the difficulty of measuring the work of each individual with any certainty, and it fosters a cooperative, teamwork attitude among these individuals.

Determining Types of Objectives

Note the type of objective that has been set in each of these cases:

- Increase average keying rate (data entry)
- Reduce average waiting time (job flow)

- Maintain an error rate of less than 1 percent (tape library)

- Meet user performance targets (machine room)

In each instance, the objective goes toward improving the service and productivity of the data center, which, presumably, is the overall objective of the DCM.

The individual-job objectives should reflect the issues that are currently deemed important. In the case of the tape librarian, for instance, reducing the error rate is the top priority. Once this is done, a subsequent objective for this position may be to improve the handling of the installation's off-site file storage practices. This would reflect a shift in importance from control of on-site library materials to an emphasis on the off-site control. Of course, the on-site control continues to be important; the new objective simply brings another factor into the picture.

The jobs in the operations control section of the data center (that is, the standards and procedures, quality control, user contact, and planning groups) are less amenable to quantitative measures, but some objectives can still be established. The standards and procedures area may have an objective of revising a specific procedure within the next year or by a particular date (this type of objective can be assigned to the group or to a specific individual, depending on the magnitude of the task).

An objective for the user contact group may be that of working with the user on a specific issue to reduce procedural questions about a particular application. This may translate into the user contact group setting up and conducting an application workshop with the user within a desired time period.

Like the objectives for the job flow positions, these objectives reflect the emphasis that you, as DCM, wish to place on various areas, and they contribute to the overall performance of the data center.

MOTIVATING EMPLOYEES TO PERFORM WELL

No discussion of performance review can be complete without looking at how you motivate your employees to meet the performance standards. Positive motivation is the result of a combination of things, not the least of which include the following:

- The work environment
- The level of assignment
- The amount of authority and responsibility
- The feeling of being needed
- The operating style of the manager
- The employee's relationship to the manager

Let us look more closely at the following motivational factors:

- Money
- Recognition
- Participation
- Use of talents
- Career opportunities

Money

Money is undoubtedly an important factor in an individual's job satisfaction; however, as Abraham Maslow points out in his "hierarchy of needs," money satisfies a fairly low-level need and cannot be used as the only or the most important motivational element in the job. The DCM must be able to motivate people by taking into account the other factors listed above.

Job Recognition

Quite often, the slightest bit of recognition by the manager for a job well done pays big dividends in job motivation for the individual. Consider the day-to-day work environment for many of the people in the data center. Much of the work is repetitive, and it is seldom acknowledged when it is done properly. The people doing the work may begin to wonder whether anyone knows they exist. Therefore, *a "pat on the back" from you, as the DCM, can do wonders to help these people regain a sense of accomplishment and importance in the organization. This is particularly important when users have given compliments regarding the work of the section or of a specific person. Don't hesitate to pass on these good words!*

Sense of Participation

It is also important to give people a sense of participation in the workings of the data center. This is not to say that you can relinquish responsibility for management of the center or that management by committee takes hold. Instead, participation means that everyone is given the opportunity to contribute ideas for improving the workings of the center, and they understand where their task fits into the activities of the company.

In Chapter Seven, we pointed out that data center communications with users can be enhanced by briefing the users on the activities of the data center and by giving them occasional tours of the center. Similar techniques work equally well in giving data center workers a sense of belonging to the organization. *Take the time to explain the objectives and workings of the company as well as to explain specifically how the work in the data center relates to the workings of the user departments.* For example, control section workers should be aware of how the work they do impacts the user areas—namely, what difference does meeting or missing a deadline for delivery of a report or for completing the running of a job make in the user area? What exactly happens in the user area if the report is late or if the job is not completed by a certain time? The user may have related deadlines that can only be met if the information from the data center is available on a reliable, timely basis. (When you gather this information for your employees, you may find out that, in fact, the user does nothing with the information for several hours or for days after receiving it from the data center. This reveals a false urgency attached to the deadline, and it should stimulate a conference between you and the user to review the existing due dates.)

It has been said that the best masonry work results when "the bricklayer builds a cathedral." The individual pieces of the job may appear trivial, but they become significant when the individual has a sense of contributing to something larger than the specific task. An individual motivated by a sense of participation will gain more satisfaction from the work and will probably produce a higher caliber of work, thus reducing the quality control problem. In sum, make sure that everyone in the data center knows where his or her "brick" fits into the "cathedral."

Use of Talents

Another motivating factor in job performance stems from the individual's need for his or her talents to be used properly. An individual who works well with people should not be sequestered as a tape librarian with little or no contact with the outside world. Conversely, a person who enjoys the discipline of clerical tasks or working with numbers will probably not be happy in a job that is limited to informal, unstructured tasks such as troubleshooting user problems. You must understand clearly the strong and weak points of each employee in the data center in order to take advantage of his or her strengths.

Career Opportunities

Among the motivating forces in any work situation is the career path associated with the job. This factor is particularly important in data processing positions since a company with no discernible planning for an individual's career path is likely to lose that person to another company or another opportunity. Communicating the company's view on career plans can take place during the performance review.

The career paths for people working in the data center will vary with the level of data processing activity within the company, the relative maturity of the computer function within the organization, and the talent and motivation of the individual. The career path also depends, of course, upon the type of position that is being evaluated. The relatively low-level (that is, nonsupervisory) positions in the data center are stepping stones for positions of more responsibility but that involve basically the same type of work.

At some point, an individual may move from a nonsupervisory job to one involving the supervision of others. The DCM should be particularly aware of these transition points in the careers of the data center people because the migration to more responsible assignments will probably require additional training. Historically, the people working in the data center have high school degrees whereas people working in systems and programming tend to have college degrees. The result is that on-the-job training prevails in the data center, rather than a broad array of outside courses and formal training being available for data center people.

In another contrast with the systems and programming area, the data center usually does not provide people with a *gradual* increase in the level of supervisory responsibility and experience. One is either a supervisor, or one is not. This creates a discontinuity in the individual's career path: one day the employee is a member of a group, and the next day he or she is a supervisor. All of this suggests that the DCM find ways to "groom" people for future positions within the data center in order to ease this transition. This can be done by having people (for instance, lead operators) represent the data center on project teams or having them manage small task forces or committees of short duration in order to gain experience in managing and dealing with people. Another way to "break in" people to more responsibility is to assign them the task of developing standards for the data center. This assignment will require that interrelationships be explored and understood, and it serves to develop writing and communications skills, which will be necessary when the person obtains more responsibilities.

PREPARING THE PERFORMANCE REVIEW

The two main components of a performance appraisal are the review of past performance and the statement of anticipated performances and job assignments. *Take the time to prepare adequately for these reviews.* Note that the review conference may be one of only a few times during the year when the individual has your specific attention.

The review of past performance usually includes a discussion of the positive and negative aspects in the individual's performance. Ideally, this is a give-and-take situation with the reviewer candidly assessing the performance, and the individual frankly voicing his or her feelings toward the job, the organization, and perhaps toward the supervisor or manager. *Ask the employee to think about these things before the review takes place.*

Identify clearly the areas in the person's performance that need improving. Set the standards for the improvement that you expect to take place before the next performance review. Generally speaking, one should not expect a person to make significant improvement in more than one or two major areas during a given time period. *Select one or two areas on which the person can concentrate and look for progress in these specific areas.*

APPLYING THIS INFORMATION TO YOUR DATA CENTER

1. Do people in your data center know the criteria that will be used to measure their performance?

2. Do the data center people know how their work fits into the total corporate picture?

3. Are data center people aware of the possible career paths available to them?

SUMMARY

To measure professional performance, you need to establish specific objectives for data center personnel. You should use the job description as a point of departure for setting individual objectives. Each person's objectives should reinforce and advance the data center's overall objectives (such as improving productivity and reducing costs for services).

Make a point of recognizing good performance by giving someone a "pat on the back" when their work merits praise. At periodic, formal performance evaluations, reevaluate the individual's objectives, review past performance against the objectives, recognize the individual's accomplishments, and set out a plan to correct shortcomings.

III

Getting Results—
Managing the
Information Factory

12

Controlling Production and Inventory

The data center is usually viewed as a technical center, probably because of the complex electronic equipment found in the center. While this view is not incorrect, it has, in some ways, clouded the issue of how to manage the business of pushing work through the center. To give you some perspective on the problem, Chapters Twelve through Fourteen present the data center as a production center, much like a factory.

The data center, in many ways, is an information factory. It uses raw materials (data), machinery (computing equipment), known processes (programs), expendable supplies (paper), and labor (people) to produce a product (information). It is not a center for new-product development. The systems and programming area does that, although the data center should be somewhat involved in that development (much as a manufacturing department stays in touch with the research and development areas of the company). Just as in the manufacturing facility, the data center and its manager do the best job for the company when they are able to produce products with high standards of accuracy and quality, on a timely basis, and as efficiently as possible. This chapter looks at production control and inventory control in order to yield some insights about how to make the data center more productive. The

147

schematic diagram that was introduced in Chapter One is
reproduced here (as Figure 12.1), and we will refer to it frequently
throughout this section of the book.

THE GROWING COMPLEXITY OF ELEMENTS TO BE CONTROLLED

We might call production and inventory control the means that you, the data center manager, have for "marshalling" the center's resources in order to ensure efficient functioning. The specific tools available for accomplishing production and inventory control include shift scheduling, which positions people to do their jobs; production documentation, which allows the work to be positioned for optimum efficiency; operating documentation, which allows data center personnel to report usage of the hardware and software resources; and operations scheduling and inventory control, which bring together the demand for and availability of the center's resources. Each of these tools will be discussed in this chapter, but first it is important to look at the complexity of the control problem that you face.

There has been a marked increase in the complexity of the data center as the equipment configurations have enlarged and as multiple vendors have come into the equipment picture. Operating systems have become immensely complex pieces of software as modules are developed to support the variety of functions and the array of hardware found at the typical installation. Virtual storage systems have allowed the physical processor to be stretched conceptually into a much larger machine. In the process, a need has arisen for the installation manager to be more aware of the interrelationships between hardware and software, within the software itself, and of the key role that qualified staff people play in effectively using the hardware and software resources. The expansion of telecommunications applications has increased the demand for responsive hardware and software and has caused yet another complexity for the DCM to understand and manage. Data base software and discipline have become parts of many installations in response to the increased applications demand.

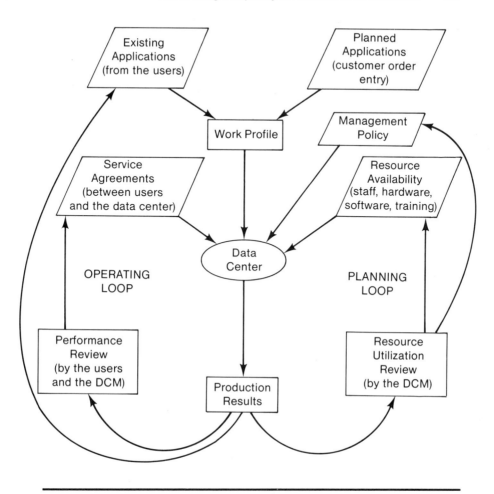

FIGURE 12.1.   Balanced Organizational Structure for a Data Center

With each new element that is introduced into the data center mix, the complexity of the center increases. In trying to control four items, for example, you must set up six separate interfaces. When the number of elements under control reaches ten, forty-five separate interfaces are required (see Figure 12.2). With fifteen elements, the number of interfaces escalates to 105. At a minimum, these increases in complexity introduce a need for more control and management at every step of the way. Whether these elements are generically different (such as storage devices, modems, and software), whether the elements represent different vendors whose equipment is in the data

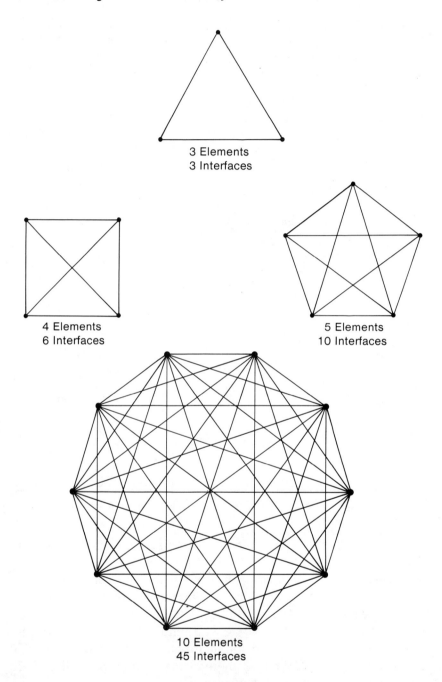

3 Elements
3 Interfaces

4 Elements
6 Interfaces

5 Elements
10 Interfaces

10 Elements
45 Interfaces

FIGURE 12.2.   *The Complexity Problem*

center, or whether they appear as a combination of different devices and different vendors, the control and management problems increase dramatically as each additional element is introduced into the operating environment. The following sections provide suggestions for maintaining control even in the face of this growing complexity.

CONTROLLING PRODUCTION

Before beginning a production run, a factory's production manager must determine how the production resources will be deployed. In the data center, then, the DCM must combine the three basic production resources (people, equipment, and time) for the most effective utilization.

Scheduling Shifts

The DCM is frequently faced with the problem of staffing the center for three shifts each day and for five, six, or seven days each week. The following paragraphs offer suggestions about techniques for handling this task.

Shortening the Work Week. Originally, the eight-hour shift and five-day week of the traditional office and factory were carried over into the data center. Operations on the sixth and seventh days, when necessary, were staffed using overtime. Many installations have recently tried variations on this theme, with four-day weeks and ten-hour shifts or three-day weeks and twelve-hour shifts being most popular. Among the reasons for the popularity of these extended-hour shifts has been the high cost of gasoline and the rush hour traffic in urban areas. Obviously, the three- and four-day weeks reduce the distance traveled and the number of trips that have to be made, and they improve the time at which these trips are made.

There are dozens of variations that can be made on the basic three- or four-day work week schedule. Shown as Figure 12.3 is a typical three-day week, twelve-hour shift schedule. Figure 12.4 depicts an alternate method of setting up a three-day week, twelve-hour shift schedule.

Time	Mo	Tu	We	Th	Fr	Sa	Su	Mo	Tu	We	Th	Fr	Sa	Su
0600	A	A	A	B	B	B		A	A	A	B	B	B	
	:	:	:	:	:	:		:	:	:	:	:	:	
	:	:	:	:	:	:		:	:	:	:	:	:	
	A	A	A	B	B	B		A	A	A	B	B	B	
1800	C	C	C	D	D	D		C	C	C	D	D	D	
	:	:	:	:	:	:		:	:	:	:	:	:	
	:	:	:	:	:	:		:	:	:	:	:	:	
0600	C	C	C	D	D	D		C	C	C	D	D	D	

Note: A and B teams start at 0600 hours; C and D teams start at 1800 hours.

FIGURE 12.3.   Sample Schedule for a Three-Day Week,
Twelve Hours per Shift

Both of these schedules have the same advantages to the employees—fewer trips per week and a commute during off-hours. For the company, there is the advantage of one less shift turnover per day, which many feel is more efficient than the two turnovers needed with a three-shift operation. The alternative shown in Figure 12.4 presents some additional advantages and disadvantages. Along with the twelve-hour shifts, the work days are flip-flopped on alternate weeks. This gives one team a nice seven-day break, while the other team is working six out of seven days during that stretch. Most employees enjoy the additional leisure time (it's like a week's vacation every other week), but some people "complain" that they have too much leisure time. Conversely, working six out of seven days can be quite fatiguing, especially by the fifth or sixth work day.

A random sampling of those using the twelve-hour shifts has given inconclusive results as to its benefits and drawbacks. For those data centers that must operate twenty-four hours a day and six days per week, this method will result in less overtime being paid than if the center operated with three eight-hour shifts for five days and covered the sixth day with overtime. In going to the extended shifts, the DCM may have to negotiate with the personnel office of the company to make an exception to the company policy of days that are seven and one-half or eight hours long. Typically, the people working the twelve-hour shifts are paid for a week of thirty-seven and one-half hours, even though they only work thirty-six hours. Some installations com-

Time	Mo	Tu	We	Th	Fr	Sa	Su	Mo	Tu	We	Th	Fr	Sa	Su
0600	A	A	A	B	B	B		B	B	B	A	A	A	
	:	:	:	:	:	:		:	:	:	:	:	:	
	:	:	:	:	:	:		:	:	:	:	:	:	
	A	A	A	B	B	B		B	B	B	A	A	A	
1800	C	C	C	D	D	D		D	D	D	C	C	C	
	:	:	:	:	:	:		:	:	:	:	:	:	
	:	:	:	:	:	:		:	:	:	:	:	:	
0600	C	C	C	D	D	D		D	D	D	C	C	C	

Note: A and B teams start at 0600 hours; C and D teams start at 1800 hours.

**FIGURE 12.4. Alternate Schedule for a Three-Day Week,
Twelve Hours per Shift**

bine the twelve-hour shifts with several people working eight-hour shifts. The base operating teams work twelve-hour shifts, but eight-hour shift workers are used to supplement the team and provide additional coverage for peak workloads.

Rotating Shifts. The other aspect of personnel scheduling, along with the length of the shifts, is whether the people should rotate across various shifts. As with shift length, there are many ideas, opinions, and variations on the shift rotation concept. Installations running on a seniority basis usually do not rotate the shifts, relying instead on the preference of senior workers to determine who will work which shifts.

Shift rotation also provides advantages in terms of training, auditing, and control. When people move to different shifts periodically, most people in the data center will learn how to operate a great variety of applications; in other words, shift rotation helps to keep the people crosstrained. The audit and control aspects are enhanced with shift rotation because it prevents one person from operating or setting up the same application for months or years at a time.

The mechanics of rotating shifts may vary. The "team" approach is fostered if the workers and supervisors rotate together. Other companies have found benefit in rotating the workers in one direction, such as third shift to second to first, while the supervisors rotate in the opposite direction, such as third shift to first to second. The advantage, it is felt, is that the supervisors is able to work with all of the people on all shifts over a period of time. When salary and promotional recommendations are needed, each of the supervisors is able to contribute to the overall evaluation of the person.

Allowing Flex-time. Flex-time is a modern office management technique that has not proved too successful when tried in the data center. Flex-time allows each person to more or less set his or her own work hours, provided that the employee work a given number of hours within a one- or two-week period and provided that he or she is on the job during a defined "core time" each day. The core time may be defined, for example, as being from 10:00 A.M. until 2:00 P.M. Employees could work from 6:00 A.M. until 2:00 P.M., from 10:00 A.M. until 6:00 P.M., or any other combination as long as they are at work during the core time and work the total required hours. In the data center, this has not worked too well simply because, since you provide a service to the rest of the company, you must be able to serve the "customers" on a reliable basis, which, in turn, requires a staff of people who are available during all hours of the center's operation.

Establishing Good Production Documentation

To run an application efficiently, you must have good production documentation. As DCM, you must have tough documentation standards and must insist on their being met before any application goes into a production status. The standards for the installation should be published and distributed to everyone on the systems and programming staff and should be applied to all software whether it is developed internally or purchased from software vendors or others.

Putting a good documentation procedure into effect requires hard work, tenacity, and the backing of management. An installation that has not enforced documentation standards in the past will find that cracking down and enforcing the standards will result in grumbling, complaints, and threats to take the issue to higher authority. *You should prepare your boss for a confrontation with users, which may result when you refuse to put an inadequately documented application into production. You will need strong management support to withstand the users' complaints about your delay in the implementation of their application. On the other hand, you should expect and welcome this type of reaction. The first several test cases of this type will clear the air and serve notice that the documentation program is backed with authority in the interest of producing both higher volume and higher quality work in the data center.*

Once the documentation standards have been established, the DCM should make a point of regularly checking the progress of new application development in the systems and programming area. A continuing review and involvement in application development will allow you to press for adherence to production standards and will allow the standards to be more easily adopted by the application developers. Look again at Figure 12.1; the application reflected by production documentation is part of the "planned application" load and, as such, becomes an integral part of the workload profile for the installation. This, in turn, affects the resource utilization and availability aspects of the planning loop.

Documentation Checklist. *Among the basic things that should be included in the software documentation are:*

1. System narrative

2. System flowchart

3. Program set-up instructions

4. Time and date deadlines

5. Run frequency

6. Input sources and samples

7. Data entry layout

8. Data file requirements

9. Data file retention cycle

10. File usage matrix

11. Job control language (JCL) list

12. Operating error message list

13. User error message list

14. Restart procedure

15. Control procedure

16. Output destinations and samples

17. Test plan narrative

18. Test data set(s)

19. Test results

20. Systems department sign-off

21. User department sign-off

22. Data center sign-off

Figure 12.5 illustrates a documentation checklist. Note that space is provided for responsible parties to initial each item as it is reviewed, and the distribution is indicated so that copies can readily be sent to those who have a need to know. In the upper right corner of the form, space is provided for the three key sign-offs (that is, the systems and programming manager, the data center manager, and the user manager) and the routing instructions are indicated. This form can also be used for program revisions and maintenance as well as for new work.

Refer again to the twenty-two item checklist above. Many of these are well known or self-explanatory, but several items are worth noting. Item 4, time and date deadlines, is a key item since it documents the expectations of the user and the commitment of the data center in running the application. It is an integral part of the service agreement between the data center and the user area. This item— which indicates when the application results are to be available to the user (in the case of batch applications) or when the system is to be available (in the case of on-line applications)—is the basis for operations' planning and is a starting point for the scheduling of data center resources and delivery arrangements between the user and the center. From this information, the arrival time for input from the user can also be scheduled.

The sixth item, input sources and samples, ties into the fourth item since it specifically identifies the sources of input (such as users or other programs) and illustrates their form and expected volume.

The data file requirements shown as Item 8 should be verified against the file space allocation plan for disk storage and against the tape library management procedure for tape files.

The data file retention cycle, Item 9, must conform to the installation standards for file back-up and recycling and should cause the

SYSTEM NAME

_____

DATE _____

	INITIAL	ROUTE
PROJECT LEADER		
DOC. REVIEWER		
S&P MANAGER		
D.C. MANAGER		
S&P SECRETARY		
S&P		
DATA CENTER		
USER MANAGER		
VAULT		

	TO BE PROVIDED BY:				DISTRIBUTION			
	INITIAL	ANALYST	PRGRMR	USER	S&P	DATA CNT	USER	VAULT
TITLE AND COVER PAGE		X			1	1	1	1
TABLE OF CONTENTS		X			1	1	1	1
I. LIST OF PROGRAMS		X			1	1	1	1
II. REVISIONS		X			1	1		1

III. SYSTEM DOCUMENTATION

	TO BE PROVIDED BY:				DISTRIBUTION			
	INITIAL	ANALYST	PRGRMR	USER	S&P	DATA CNT	USER	VAULT
A. REQUEST FOR... SERVICES				X	1	1	1	1
B. FEASIBILITY STUDY		X			1			
C. DESIGN STUDIES		X			1			
D. CORRESPONDENCE		X			1			
E. SYSTEM FLOWCHARTS		X			1	1	1	1
F. SYSTEM NARRATIVE		X			1	1	1	1
G. DATA ENTRY LAYOUT		X			1	1	1	1
H. FILE LAYOUT		X			1	1	1	1
I. TEST DATA & RESULTS		X			1			1
J. TEST DATA NARRATIVE		X			1			1
K. DATA ELEMENT DEFINITION		X			1	1	1	1
L. DATA ELEMENT CROSS REFERENCE		X			1	1	1	1
M. PROGRAM AND FILE RETENTION CYCLE		X			1	1	1	1

IV. PROGRAM DOCUMENTATION

	TO BE PROVIDED BY:				DISTRIBUTION			
	INITIAL	ANALYST	PRGRMR	USER	S&P	DATA CNT	USER	VAULT
A. PROGRAM CHART			X		1	1		1
B. PROGRAM NARRATIVE			X		1	1	1	1
C. PRINT CHART		X			1			1
D. REPORT SAMPLES		X			1	1	1	1

FIGURE 12.5.   Documentation Checklist (2 pages)

	TO BE PROVIDED BY:				DISTRIBUTION			
	INITIAL	ANALYST	PRGRMR	USER	S&P	DATA CNT	USER	VAULT
E. SOURCE LISTING			X		1			1
F. COMPILATION LISTING			X		1			1
G. LINK MAP			X		1			1
H. PROGRAM INVENTORY CARD			X		1			
I. DELETE CARD			X		1			
J. ERROR HANDLING								
a. DATA CENTER		X			1	1		1
b. USER		X			1		1	1
K. CONTROL INFORMATION		X			1	1	1	1

V. INPUT & OUTPUT

A. INPUT SAMPLES			X		1	1	1	1
B. DATA ENTRY INSTRUCTIONS			X		1	1	1	1
C. OUTPUT SAMPLES			X		1	1	1	1

| VI. USER RUN PROCEDURE | | X | | | 1 | 1 | 1 | 1 |

| VII. JOB CONTROL LANGUAGE LIST | | | X | | 1 | 1 | | 1 |

FIGURE 12.5.   (cont.)

files of this application to be included in the data center's overall retention plan.

The file usage matrix (Item 10) gives a ready source of information as to which programs use a given file and which files are used in a specific program. Additionally, the matrix can indicate whether a file is updated or simply referenced by a program. Figure 12.6 illustrates the file usage matrix. It shows Programs A through E for an application and shows the way in which Files 1 through 5 are used in the programs. For example, File 2 is updated by Program B and Program E and is an input file to Program C.

Item 11, the job control language (JCL) list, serves as a bridge between the system designer's concept of file usage, space allocation, and job streaming, and the center's operational considerations for these same issues.

It is useful to segregate the application's error messages into

	File 1	File 2	File 3	File 4	File 5	
Program A	I		Ø	I		
Program B		U	I			
Program C		I			Ø	
Program D				Ø	I	
Program E		U			I	

I = Input
U = Update
Ø = Output

FIGURE 12.6.   File Usage Matrix

those that impact the operation of the application (Item 12) and those that impact the user (Item 13). An example of an operating error message is one that indicates that an indexed disk record cannot be found. This is a condition that normally should not occur and that needs attention from a systems specialist (not from the user). An example of a user error message is one that points to a problem that the user must solve (such as a validation error on an input transaction).

The center's capability and method for restarting the application is spelled out in Item 14, the restart procedure.

The control procedure (Item 15) gives the data center a set of specifications for verifying that the production work has been run correctly. This procedure spells out which control totals are to be matched and compared, the expected volumes for input and output, the anticipated running time, the planned number of terminals in an on-line network, and the control of sensitive documents within the application.

Items 17 and 18, the test plan narrative and test data set(s), serve two purposes. They indicate the amount of testing that has been done on the application, and they form a benchmark for maintenance and modification to the application. *This is an important aspect of production control in the data center. Any changes that are made to the application after it has been put into production must be run against this test data base to confirm their validity.*

The three sign-offs indicated in Items 20, 21, and 22 reflect a three-way understanding as to what is to be provided to run the application, what is to be delivered from the application, and the timing of both. For the systems department, this sign-off indicates that someone with authority in that department is satisfied that the documentation meets the installation standards and that this person is willing to take responsibility for the documentation's quality and completeness. The user manager signing the documentation cover sheet indicates a clear understanding of the user's obligation to provide data for the application. The DCM's sign-off formalizes the data center commitment to run the application and meet the various delivery and quality standards reflected in the documentation.

Documenting Data Center Procedures

The standard operating procedures for the data center should include documentation for running the center. *The instructions should cover the steps to be taken to start up the computer, to shut down the computer, and the operating indicators under normal conditions. The procedures also include a* profile of applications *that are run normally at specific points during each day of the week.* This profile can later be compared against job logs or console registers to confirm that the planned jobs were run and, as a security measure, to verify that unauthorized jobs were not run. The *console registers* are generally standard output produced as a console log by the operating system. They indicate, at a minimum, job step name, start time, stop time, operator messages, and operator responses.

Shift Reports.   A daily part of the operations documentation is the shift report prepared by the lead operator or the shift supervisor. Shift reports are relatively informal logs of events that occurred during the shift. They do not duplicate or replace the console logs. Instead, they contain information that the DCM can use for following up points with users or others regarding operational difficulties and unusual situations, such as intermittent difficulty with pieces of equipment as well as surprise visitors or extraordinary phone calls during the second and third shifts.

Note that these reports are very informal and are used as "early warning" information to the DCM. The spontaneity of these reports is what makes them most useful, and the operator should be encouraged to report any newsworthy information without worrying about the form, style, and grammar of the report.

Operational Problem Reports. For definite malfunctions in either hardware or software, a more formal report should be filed. An operational problem report, like that shown in Figure 12.7, illustrates the kind of information that should be captured by operating personnel when problems occur. This form reflects the conditions that existed at the time the failure occurred. It can serve as a starting point for problem tracking by the DCM. We will discuss this point in greater detail in Chapter Thirteen.

Problem Control Number: _129_

Application Name: _Order Entry_

Problem Category:

____ Hardware   ____ Operating System

_X_ Network   _X_ Application Program

____ Storage Capacity   ____ Data

Description of problem:

Terminal #3 not getting response on attempted add'l descrip. transact. (screen ØE52)

Program running when problem occurred:

Number: _E 451_ Name: _Daily Order Process._

Restart attempted? _X_ Yes ____ No

Restart successful? _X_ Yes ____ No

Problem occurrence date: _2/14/82_ time: _1410_ hrs

Problem report prepared by: _J. Palmer_

To be completed by data center manager:

Program placed in nonproductive status:

____ Yes _X_ No   Date: _2/14/82_

Systems department notified: (name) _D. P. Jacques_

Date: _2/14/82_ Time: _1505_

User manager notified: (name) _Max Reveneaux_

Date: _2/14/82_ Time: _1505_

FIGURE 12.7. Operational Problem Report

Scheduling the Operations Workload

The scheduling process in the data center usually concentrates specifically on the scheduling of the central processing unit. In fact, all of the resources of the center must be considered. That is, *the scheduling process must ensure that the right resources are in the right place at the right time and in the right amount. To accomplish this, you need to take a methodical approach in analyzing the data center work. The workload must be defined, adjustments to the expected workload must be forecast, the work must be done, the resulting resource utilization must be compared with the expected utilization, and adjustments must be made in the schedule.*

These steps form a control loop for the DCM to monitor the production levels in the data center. The schematic diagram in Figure 12.1 shows this control loop, its major components (such as service agreements, the work profile, and so on), and the functional areas that are involved with each component (such as data center users).

Defining the Workload. The workload definition is based on historical operating data and forecasts of resource utilization for the application. For existing applications, the historical data are readily available. For applications being put into production, operating data from similar applications may have to be used and interpolated. For this task, an *application resource estimate* (a sample of which is shown in Figure 12.8) is very helpful. (This form is discussed in more detail in Chapter Thirteen.)

In addition to estimating the resources for an application, you must also consider such factors as the time and date deadlines, preparation time needed, data sets used, the source of these data, logical dependencies between tasks, resource dependencies or contentions between tasks, application priorities, and the check-out and dispatch time needed. All of these items are essential in defining the workload. You can obtain this information from the systems designer and through conferences with the users.

Analyzing Resource Availability and Utilization. The resource availability component of the planning loop (again, Figure 12.1) is based on historical and anticipated data center resource data. As indicated in the diagram, the resource availability and the resource utilization components form a smaller loop within the larger schema. In order to analyze the availability and utilization of data center resources, you must look at every component within the three resource

```
┌─────────────────────────────────────────────────────────────────────┐
│                    APPLICATION RESOURCE ESTIMATE                      │
│                                                                       │
│  Application Name: _____  │
│                                                                       │
│  Estimated Implementation Date:___/___/___  Run Frequency_____  │
│                                                                       │
│  Approximate Program Size (largest):_____ (K bytes)              │
│                                                                       │
│  Files Used                                                           │
└─────────────────────────────────────────────────────────────────────┘
```

APPLICATION RESOURCE ESTIMATE

Application Name: _____

Estimated Implementation Date:___/___/___   Run Frequency_____

Approximate Program Size (largest):_____ (K bytes)

Files Used

Existing	*New*	*Record Size*	*No. of Records*	*Sequential/ Random*
_____	_____	____	____	____
_____	_____	____	____	____
_____	_____	____	____	____

Input

Name	*Source*	*Volume*
_____	_____	_____
_____	_____	_____
_____	_____	_____
_____	_____	_____

Output

Name	*Disposition*	*Volume*	*Delivery Time*
_____	_____	____	_____
_____	_____	____	_____
_____	_____	____	_____
_____	_____	____	_____

Remarks:

Prepared by:_____   Date: ___/___/___

FIGURE 12.8.   *Application Resource Estimate*

categories—hardware, software, and people. The hardware components, for example, include memory, data channels, devices (by class,
such as sequential, random, unit record, network), and time. Among
the software resources to be reviewed are multiple programming capabilities, memory management, data file handling, space manage-

ment for random access devices, control of magnetic tape usage, network control, and terminal response. The people resource should be looked at with regard to staffing levels by time period during the day or week, workloads within each time period, and the caliber of person assigned to each task.

The utilization of all of these resources should be checked to determine if any unacceptable utilization levels are present, such as markedly overscheduled or underscheduled resources. Indicators of these problems include lengthy service queues or substantial slack time or slack capacity for a given resource. The remedies can take the form of obtaining more resources or of redirecting the workload to relieve overutilization, and cutting back on the resource units in the case of underutilized resources.

Before applying either of these remedies, however, you must test the resource subloop against the work profile portion of the total control loop. This allows you to gain workload information before making a resource decision. For example, if a look at the work profile—especially the information on planned applications—indicates that a substantial application is scheduled to go into production soon, you can expect that underutilized resources will soon be put to use. On the other hand, if there are no planned applications close to production, you may have to cut back on equipment or people in order to bring underutilized resources under control.

Either augmenting or cutting back resources may not be a wise action beyond the short term if the immediate workload is not representative of the expected workload in the longer term. It takes a reasonably long time to obtain any of the resource components (on the order of at least several months); therefore, their use must be carefully planned.

Most job-monitoring software provides at least minimal information regarding hardware resource utilization, including paging rates and central processor utilization. As the installation's resource mix becomes more complex, more sophisticated hardware or software monitors may be needed to yield more detailed resource usage data. There are scores of devices and software products on the market that provide these data.

Involving the User in Scheduling. The service agreement and performance review components form the operating loop within the larger schema of Figure 12.1. Whereas the planning loop involved mainly the data center, the operating loop involves the data center and the users. The service agreement targets (see Figure 12.9) are the "before" part of the picture. These target levels are established when the user and data center people agree as to the delivery and cost expected in connection with running the applications for a given user area. The "actual" figures shown for "On-Time Delivery" and "Cost" are the "after" part of the picture.

On a periodic basis (for example, once a month), the DCM should meet with the user manager to review the actual performance and cost as compared to the target levels. Significant changes that result from these meetings can be taken into account in reviewing and adjusting the data center schedule.

Summing Up Work Scheduling.   The schedule must be a "living" document—one in which changes are to be expected as the supply of and demand for data center resources changes. Too many units of any resource will result in extra costs being incurred. Too few units of any resource will result in customer dissatisfaction. However, at the outset, the DCM must realize that rarely will the resource-versus-workload combination be optimal. The goal is to strike some sort of balance between too many and too few resources, while knowing that there will be peak workloads when resources are short and there will be slack periods when resources will be in excess supply. There are a number of automated schedulers on the market, but the use of these packages does not reduce the hard work that must be done to identify and define scheduling problems. The packages make the mechanics of scheduling easier, but the accumulation and analysis of raw data must still be done.

The previous discussion dealt with scheduling at a macro level within the data center. Figures 12.10 and 12.11 represent scheduling schematic diagrams for batch and on-line operations at an application level. The diagrams illustrate the input, process, and output functions, list the actual events that take place within each function, indicate the user and data center involvement with each event, and show the management issues associated with each activity. Note that, in Figure 12.11, there are fewer actual events in the data center and increased participation by the user for on-line versus batch processing, but many of the same management concerns remain for the DCM (namely, response time, efficient allocation of disk space, and contention between batch and on-line resources). *Thus, while the on-line environment appears to allow more passive involvement from the data center than batch*

Data Center Service Agreement

User: Finance and Accounting

For month ending: March 31, 1982

Application	Frequency	Time Due	On-time Delivery		Volume		Cost		
			Target (1)	Actual (4)	Target (6)	Actual	Target (5)	Actual	Variance
Accounts Payable:									
(2) Transmitted to data center	weekly	3 P.M. Thur.	100%	80%	250	243			
(3) Checks to user	weekly	8 A.M. Fri.	100%	100%	250	243	1.15/check	1.14/check	0.8% (7)
Accounts Receivable:									
On-line cutoff	daily	5 P.M.	100%	100%					
Invoices to user	daily	8 A.M.	100%	95%	125/day	100/day	0.95/invoice	1.10/invoice	−15.8% (9)
Financial Statements:									
Transmitted to data center	monthly	3rd day	100%	100%	200	210			
Report package to user	monthly	4th day	100%	100%			$5,000/month	$5,050/month	−1% (8)

* * * Note: Negative variances are unfavorable. * * *

Reviewed by:

_____ Data Center Manager

User Manager

Date: April 10, 1982

FIGURE 12.9. Data Center Service Agreement

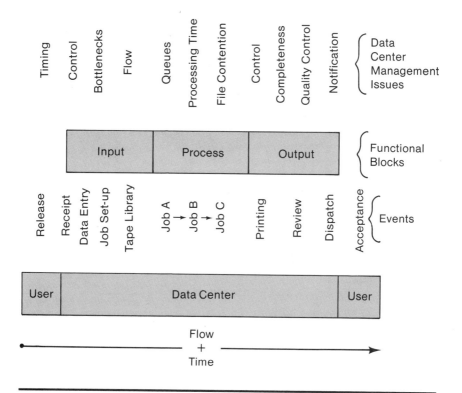

FIGURE 12.10. Batch Application Scheduling

processing does, the thinking, planning, and monitoring that goes into scheduling data center resources for on-line operations requires as much, or more, involvement than the batch environment.

CONTROLLING INVENTORY

Inventory control in the information factory, while a part of the resource availability portion of the planning loop, consists of monitoring those parts of the data center that are subject to frequent physical handling. This includes such items as magnetic tapes and expendable supplies (like continuous form paper and card stock).

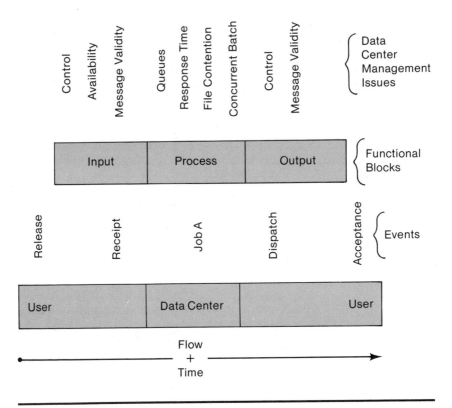

FIGURE 12.11.   On-Line Application Scheduling

Control Procedures for the Tape Library

Good security and control practices require that tape libraries be located in a dedicated, separate room under the control of the tape library staff. In reality, some data centers have their tape libraries in the same room as the mainframe and, in some instances, accessible by anyone in the computer room. This often occurs in the small installation where the same person may remove and return tapes in the tape racks as well as operate the mainframe. While this is understandable, it must be pointed out that these installations are trusting the integrity and record-keeping abilities of the operator and that these installations have security and control vulnerability. Data centers without separately controlled tape libraries are increasingly being written up as deficient by auditors. *This reinforces the notion that data should be recognized as an organizational resource, just as the organization's per-*

*sonnel or physical plant or inventory quantities are resources, and that
data should be handled and protected as a resource.*

As companies put more and more information into a data base
and as applications become more integrated, the information resources of the organization are embodied in the computer data base.
This transition can take place over time and may not take the form of
a single, dramatic event. Separating the location of the tape library
and strictly limiting access to it is imperative in securing this resource.
*For the tape librarian to be responsible for the integrity of the library, ac-
cess to the library must be restricted and control procedures instituted for
signing out and returning tapes in the library. If the workload in the center
does not justify having a librarian during the evening and night shifts, the
day-shift librarian should withdraw and stage the proper tapes for the
other two shifts. The following day, the librarian returns the tapes to the
library area. In the interim, the tapes that have been staged are under the
custody of the shift supervisor or lead operator.*

The use of software packages that provide automated tape library control has helped to reduce improper use of tapes and has
enhanced the prescribed tape rotation for given applications. These
tape control packages can be justified rather easily when they are
evaluated in terms of costs and benefits. Their costs can run to several
thousand dollars on a purchase basis, but the benefits accrue quickly
and substantially. Benefits take the form of better tape control and
reduced numbers of tapes.

Within a few months of installing a tape control package, a data
center often finds that the package has prevented usage of the wrong
tape for an application. If this happens just one time, the installation
has probably recovered the cost of the tape control package because of
the cost and time needed to reconstruct a destroyed data tape (if the
data center is fortunate enough to have the source data available to
reconstruct the tape!).

The second benefit of the tape control package is that it will
probably reduce the total number of tapes needed to support a given
number of applications. Most tape control packages have a built-in
facility to monitor the back-up cycles and rotation of the tapes within
an application. This exact, dependable control mechanism often allows the installation to release tapes that had previously been held in
the library but that were not part of a regular back-up cycle. It is not
unusual to discover that 10 to 15 percent of the installation's tapes

were unnecessarily reserved in the tape library. Releasing these tapes to the available tape pool provides a benefit in the form of cost avoidance.

Controlling Paper Supplies

Continuous form paper is one of the supplies that the DCM must control. In recent years, price and availability have been the main concerns regarding this commodity. Some paper vendors offer annual contracts that guarantee prices and assure availability of the material throughout the year. Under this arrangement, the customer periodically draws stock from the vendor's warehouse and is invoiced based on the contracted price and the quantity drawn.

APPLYING THIS INFORMATION TO YOUR DATA CENTER

1. How "productive" are the resources in the data center?
   Hint: Ask yourself how many people are on the data center staff and how many hours per day is the data center operating today compared with the staff and hours one year ago. What is the relative personnel effort needed to operate the center for one hour in those two time periods?

2. How is the productivity of these resources measured?

3. Would extended-hour shifts (such as ten-hour or twelve-hour days) work in your data center?

4. Does your data center have formal requirements for accepting an application into production?

5. What method is used to notify users of operational problems?
   Example: Refer to Figure 12.7, the operational problem report.

6. What method is used to control use and storage of magnetic tapes in your data center?

7. Is the application documentation adequate? What effort (in cost and time) would be needed to make the documentation better?

SUMMARY

Here is a list of things to do for production and inventory control in your data center:

- Review the balanced data center structure (Figure 12.1) and be sure you can match each of the points in the figure with an action you take in your data center. If there are open spots, institute procedures to fill in these voids.

- Be wary of increasing the complexities and interrelationships in the data center.

- Review your documentation and documentation standards. If you're not satisfied with them, take steps to improve them.

- Use an operational problem report to track problems and to make sure a problem is being promptly resolved.

- Insist on application resource estimates well in advance of an application being put into production. This gives you adequate lead time for deploying your data center resources.

- Have a written service agreement with each of your user areas.

13

Providing the Best Possible Customer Service

To provide the data center's users (or "customers") with the best possible service, the DCM must assign high priorities to quality assurance, reliability, and the realization of performance standards. Many factors can be used to measure customer service, but the key criteria in virtually every data center are:

- On-line response time
- On-time report delivery
- System availability
- Rerun performance
- User satisfaction

This chapter considers the role these items play in the operating loop of the data center schematic (Figure 12.1) in order to provide good customer service from the "information factory."

PROVIDING QUALITY ASSURANCE

It is important to define and distinguish the following terms: quality assurance, data integrity, data security, and auditability. *Data integrity* deals with the ability to access and update data files and elements while maintaining logically correct relationships among these data. *Data security* addresses the problems of determining and signalling proper and improper attempts to access or obtain data within a given area of responsibility. *Auditability* allows you to monitor activity within a program, application, or the data center itself in order to determine whether proper controls are in effect regarding monies, processing volumes, and data integrity.

Quality assurance combines all of these things and reflects the total job being done by the data center and its people. Put another way, quality assurance involves asking the following questions:

- Was the job done correctly?

- Was the job done on time?

- Are authorized people able to depend on the data they receive?

- Are unauthorized people prevented from receiving data?

- Does the work performed meet the standards set for the job?

Setting Standards

Let us look at the last point first. *You must set standards for jobs in the data center in order to know whether the work output meets the standards.* That statement sounds so elementary, yet many data centers go about doing their work day in and day out without knowing what standards they are expected to meet, either as a center, as a work group, or on a job-by-job basis. *The standards must be set at the time the application is being designed, must be verified during application testing, must be met before an application becomes productive within the data center, and must be met on a continuing basis once the application is in production.* The standards that result are the product of joint meetings between the users, systems and programming, and the data center.

The installation should have standard procedures and conventions that are to be followed by the analysts and programmers in developing an application. For example, as DCM, you should be sure that program testing is conducted using file extracts and file copies, not live or production files. There are two main reasons for this. First, the production files should never be used for testing due to the high probability of a test attempt improperly changing the data on the file. Second, extracts of files or short-volume file copies should be used to shorten the run-time for testing and to make it easier to check testing results. A representative set of data on a test file can be very useful, especially in the early stages of testing, to determine whether the program works properly.

When the testing has progressed to its final stages, full-volume files can then be used to verify that record-counting and totaling routines and accumulators are sufficiently large and to determine typical running times. This final testing, however, should only be done on a copy of the file and not on the production file.

Making an Application Resource Estimate

Beyond the programming standards, there should be operational standards for each application that the center processes. One of the keys to user satisfaction is having the user know what to expect from the data center concerning a given job. For this reason, the data center people and the user should get together early in the development stages of an application to set tentative operating standards. Many of the points that have to be covered during such a meeting are found in the application resource estimate introduced in Chapter Twelve and repeated here as Figure 13.1.

You should take note of several items on the estimate form—namely, run frequency, existing files, input sources, output disposition, and output delivery time. Each of these items set a standard for the new application in that they describe certain expectations. When this estimate is completed during the development phase of an application, both the user and the data center know what to expect. If the center does not have sufficient resources to meet the standards, you can take action to obtain the resources or can make the shortage known to the user and a compromise can be reached. This is much preferred to the "surprise" method of implementing an application, in which the user has certain expectations for the application but the

---

APPLICATION RESOURCE ESTIMATE

Application Name: _____

Estimated Implementation Date:___/___/___   Run Frequency_____

Approximate Program Size (largest):_____ (K bytes)

Files Used

Existing	*New*	*Record Size*	*No. of Records*	*Sequential/ Random*
_____	_____	_____	_____	_____
_____	_____	_____	_____	_____
_____	_____	_____	_____	_____
_____	_____	_____	_____	_____

Input

Name	*Source*	*Volume*
_____	_____	_____
_____	_____	_____
_____	_____	_____

Output

Name	*Disposition*	*Volume*	*Delivery Time*
_____	_____	_____	_____
_____	_____	_____	_____
_____	_____	_____	_____
_____	_____	_____	_____

Remarks:

Prepared by:_____   Date: ___/___/___

FIGURE 13.1.   *Application Resource Estimate*

data center is surprised by the run frequency or delivery time and does not have the resources to adequately process the application.

The run frequency, obviously, can indicate the number of times an application is run within a given time period, but it can also indicate the hours of operation for an on-line application. The *existing files* portion of the form is important in identifying the source for certain data and should force the planners to verify that these data actually exist, that they exist in a usable form, and that there are no security problems involved in the new application accessing the existing file or data.

In order to complete the entries for *input sources,* you must talk with the user and reach an agreement on what materials are to be sent to the data center (such as source documents, punched cards, or online transactions), and what input time deadlines are needed for the balance of the processing to be completed on schedule. Similarly, the *output disposition* and *output delivery time* entries are important because they show that you and the user agree on what is to be delivered from the application and at what time the delivery is to be completed.

All of these elements will be used in shaping the service agreement with the user, and they are the key to the data center's ability to meet user expectations and in the user's perception of the job the data center is doing.

ENSURING RELIABILITY AND HIGH PERFORMANCE

Setting performance standards and getting user agreement is only the first part of providing good customer service. The second and more obvious part is that of actually providing the service that the customers expect. In attempting to build credibility and good user relations, nothing speaks as loudly and as convincingly as solid, reliable performance. You, as data center manager, will have to continually monitor data center performance, meet with users to get their reactions to the service, and make necessary adjustments to data center resources.

To do this, you must clearly understand the data center objective regarding customer service. For some data centers, this objective will be that of optimizing throughput for all jobs. This objective is typical of a batch processing installation. For other centers, the objective will be to provide maximum availability of the computing resources to the on-line users. In still other centers, the objective will be to strike a balance between throughput and availability. This last goal is most prevalent in installations that are in a transition period between a total batch operation and a heavy on-line environment. It must be recognized that these two goals tend to conflict with each other. You must, therefore, understand the trade-offs between the two and communicate with the users as to the final orientation of the data center.

Writing the Data Center Service Agreement

We looked briefly at a data center service agreement in Chapter Twelve. The agreement is very useful as a basis for meeting with users to discuss and improve customer service from the data center. Let us look more closely at the sample service agreement (repeated in Figure 13.2); numbers shown in parentheses here are keyed to the same numbers in parentheses on the figure.

The service agreement is a top-level picture of the mutual agreement needed between users and the center. To arrive at the on-time delivery targets (1), the user must understand clearly when input or transactions from the user department must reach the data center (2) in order for the center to, in turn, meet the delivery deadlines (3). Determining these deadlines helps to force many issues into the open, such as the user's ability to deliver materials on schedule, the volume of work expected, and the commitment by the data center to deliver the information to the user. In other words, the agreement helps eliminate the invalid assumptions and misinformation that often occur regarding the expected (1) versus the actual (4) performance.

The target costs (5) are based on anticipated work volumes (6) and the cost of data center resources to provide the services. Note that the costs are expressed in terms that the user understands, using units of measure such as "check," "invoice," and "dollars per month." This type of measurement lets the user relate directly to the work being done and to the cost of doing the work. In contrast, a data center that expresses its service charges in terms such as "memory increments" or "thousands of bytes of storage" tends to leave the user feeling powerless to understand what's going on, to sense problems, or to take action to correct problems.

The DCM and the user manager, in reviewing the data center performance on a periodic basis, can decide which of the service levels needs corrective attention. In the example shown in Figure 13.2, the service for the accounts payable and financial statements applications appear to be quite acceptable. The delivery has met or exceeded

Data Center Service Agreement

User: Finance and Accounting

For month ending: March 31, 1982

Application	Frequency	Time Due	On-time Delivery		Volume		Cost		
			Target (1)	Actual (4)	Target (6)	Actual	Target (5)	Actual	Variance
Accounts Payable:									
(2) Transmitted to data center	weekly	3 P.M. Thur.	100%	80%	250	243			
(3) Checks to user	weekly	8 A.M. Fri.	100%	100%	250	243	1.15/check	1.14/check	0.8% (7)
Accounts Receivable:									
On-line cutoff	daily	5 P.M.	100%	100%					
Invoices to user	daily	8 A.M.	100%	95%	125/day	100/day	0.95/invoice	1.10/invoice	−15.8% (9)
Financial Statements:									
Transmitted to data center	monthly	3rd day	100%	100%	200	210			
Report package to user	monthly	4th day	100%	100%			$5,000/month	$5,050/month	−1% (8)

* * * Note: Negative variances are unfavorable. * * *

Reviewed by:

User Manager _____ Data Center Manager _____

Date: April 10, 1982

FIGURE 13.2. Data Center Service Agreement

the targets and the actual costs are within 1 percent of the target costs
(7 and 8). The accounts receivable application, however, should be
discussed in order to identify operating problems between the user
and the data center. Note that the delivery is 5 percent below the target and that the actual cost is 15.8 percent higher (9) than the target
cost.

Again, the advantage of the service agreement lies in its presentation of facts that can be used to correct problems and improve customer service. Rather than trade opinions as to what actually
happened, the user manager and the DCM can use the performance
data to take action, then compare the results during the next service
review.

Using Problem Reports to Improve Customer Relations

Chapter Twelve introduced the operational problem report as an
aid to production control. Let us look at it again here, since it can have
a direct bearing on good customer relations. Figure 13.3 provides a
sample operational problem report.

A source of great frustration to users (customers) is the feeling
that nothing is being done to solve their problems. Rightly or wrongly,
if the users hear nothing from the data center after a problem occurs,
they assume that they and their problem have been forgotten. The
problem report documents who in the user area has been informed of
the problem and at what time they were informed.

*The DCM should have a procedure that formally turns the problem
over to a specific person for resolution. That person should also be responsible for keeping the user informed as to the progress, or lack of
progress, on solving the problem.* This procedure lets the user know
that some attention is being given to the problem, and it forces the
data center people to stay on top of the problem until it can be solved
or until it is formally turned over to somebody else (such as a systems
specialist or technician) for resolution.

*When the problem has been solved, the system or program that was
in error should be reintroduced as a production item by testing it thoroughly and documenting the test properly. Just as when new work is
being put into production, the corrected work should be accepted (or
"signed off") by the data center, the systems and programming department, and by the user.* In this way, the user is kept informed of the
status of the application at every step along the way. *It is this type of*

Problem Control Number: _129_

Application Name: _Order Entry_

Problem Category:

 ___ Hardware   ___ Operating System

 _X_ Network   _X_ Application Program

 ___ Storage Capacity   ___ Data

Description of problem:

 Terminal #3 not getting response on attempted

 add'l descrip. transact. (screen ØE52)

Program running when problem occurred:

 Number:_E 451_ Name: _Daily Order Process._

 Restart attempted? _X_ Yes ___ No

 Restart successful? _X_ Yes ___No

Problem occurrence date: _2/14/82_ time: _1410_ hrs

Problem report prepared by: _J. Palmer_

To be completed by data center manager:

Program placed in nonproductive status:

 ___ Yes _X_ No   Date: _2/14/82_

Systems department notified: (name) _D. P. Jacques_

 Date: _2/14/82_   Time: _1505_

User manager notified: (name) _Max Reveneaux_

 Date: _2/14/82_   Time: _1505_

FIGURE 13.3. Sample Operational Problem Report

---

communication and involvement that makes for good user or customer relations.

 On a daily basis, the DCM and others from the data center staff should meet to review the status of all operational problem reports. This review includes matching open reports against a problem report log (to make sure none of the reports have been lost or are aging on someone's desk) and ascertaining exactly what is being done to correct the problem. *As a DCM, don't accept a statement such as "We're still working on it" as a status report. Find out exactly what avenues are being pursued, what is holding up progress, what additional help is needed, and when a solution is expected.* You can then determine when a problem should be escalated in terms of urgency or management and vendor involvement. Following the review meeting, the user manager should be notified as to the status of the problem.

APPLYING THIS INFORMATION TO YOUR DATA CENTER

1. Does your data center use an application resource estimate during the development stage of an application?

2. Do users clearly understand their obligation to meet input deadlines for their applications in the data center?

3. Does your data center use service agreements with users?

4. How do the data center's actual cost and delivery compare with the target costs and delivery?

SUMMARY

High quality work and reliable performance are the key ingredients in providing good customer service. To achieve consistent quality and reliability, you should:

- Set standards for the data center and for people in the data center in order to have "yardsticks" for measuring actual performance.

- Meet with users to get agreement on data center resources that are needed in new applications, and review service agreements with users on a monthly basis to monitor data center performance and to maintain contact with user management.

- When operational problems occur, use a formal mechanism to report the problem to the user, then stay in contact with the user until the problem has been resolved or turned over to another area for solution.

Excellent customer service is the best way to "sell" users and management on the job being done in the data center.

14

Using Industrial Engineering to Manage the Information Factory

Industrial engineers are continually measuring the performance of factory processes, looking for ways to improve the productivity, and recommending when resources should be changed in order to increase the productive output of the factory. The DCM, likewise, must monitor the usage of the data center resources, look for ways to increase productivity, and identify points at which more or fewer resources must be made available. This chapter, then, discusses the industrial engineering aspects of managing the data center; these are the same elements that go into the resource utilization review (see Figure 12.1): measuring the usage of the center's resources, looking for ways to smooth the processing paths that work takes through the center, and gathering sufficient information to make decisions concerning the addition or replacement of specific resources.

OPTIMIZING THE WORKFLOW

A time-consuming but useful exercise for the DCM is to sketch the workflow that jobs take while being processed within the data center. The workflow should be evaluated with an eye toward reducing the waiting time and eliminating bottlenecks in the center. Figure 14.1 illustrates this type of conceptual sketch.

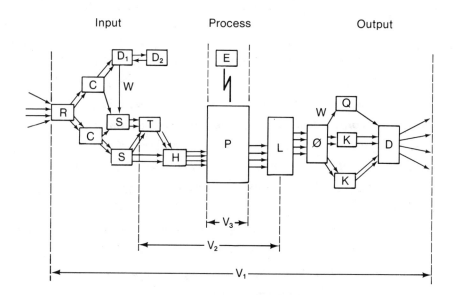

V_1 = Batch turnaround
V_2 = Remote job turnaround
V_3 = On-line turnaround or response time

R = Receiving
C = Classification
D_1 = Data Entry Supervision
D_2 = Data Entry
S = Job Set-up
T = Tape Library
H = Staging Area
P = Process

E = On-line
L = Spooling
Ø = Output
Q = Quality Control
K = Check-out
D = Dispatch
W = Wait Time

FIGURE 14.1. Data Center Workflow

Reducing Wait Time

From a mechanical standpoint, note that the figure shows a series of stations, or events, linked by a series of paths. Associated with each path is some amount of waiting time, indicated by the *w* next to the path. Every time work moves from one station to another, there is some slack time or wait time incurred before the work is taken up at the next station. Obviously, the total of all of the slack times represents the total waiting time for a job while it is in the data center.

Reducing the waiting time on any of the paths will reduce the total waiting time. The best way to reduce the wait time on a path is to eliminate the path entirely, but, usually, any progress that is made toward reducing the wait time is likely to be achieved by finding small increments rather than by discovering one or two large, wasteful steps. Therefore, the analysis of the waiting time can be a somewhat tedious process.

The workflow diagram illustrates the flow for a typical job and serves as a standard for measuring workflow in the center. For example, a job involving batch updating of a master file is initiated when the user submits transactions (on some sort of document) and a job request to the data center. This work is received (R), classified (C) as to the type of work needed in the center, sent to the data entry supervisor (D_1), then assigned to someone in data entry (D_2). After the transactions have been keyed, the data entry supervisor (D_1) checks the work, logs the job out of data entry and sends it on to the job set-up section (S). After the job has been set up, the necessary tape files are drawn from the tape library (T) and the job is sent to the staging area (H) before being processed on the mainframe processor (P). Reports produced by the job are spooled (L), printed, and sent to the output (O) area. From this station, the results are sent to a check-out (K) station (a set of the results could also go to the quality control (Q) station), then on to the dispatch (D) area for release to the user. At any point along this path, the wait time can be reduced if everyone in the data center is sensitive to the amount of time a job spends in the wait queue just ahead of his or her station and if everyone attempts to reduce this time.

Eliminating Bottlenecks

The second way to improve overall productivity in the data center is to eliminate workflow bottlenecks. *While you are analyzing the wait time, you should also study the intersections of workflow paths at each station to see if some of the paths can be directed to other stations or if multiple, similar stations should be set up.*

Figure 14.2 illustrates a modification to the workflow shown in the previous figure. Notice that multiple stations have been set up for the functions C and K in order to reduce the paths that had converged on a single station. Redirecting the flow like this can often reduce the wait time because the bottlenecks are being reduced or eliminated.

Figure 14.3 is another variation on the same sketch, but this one reduces the number of stations. In doing this, however, the contention or bottlenecks at several stations (such as S, H, and K) may have been increased. Thus, there are trade-offs to be made between eliminating flow paths and increasing bottlenecks at a given station.

Educating Users About Turnaround Time

It is interesting to look at various perceptions that users have concerning data center turnaround time. Many users have an impression that the entire workings of the data center consist of what happens in the processor (function P in the diagrams). To these users, turnaround time is imagined to be that represented by the V_3 line of Figure 14.1. For batch users, the turnaround time is more correctly shown as line V_1 since the batch work requires the full interaction of the data center people on that particular job. It is clear that the user who expects turnaround time to be V_3 but who receives turnaround time V_1 will be dissatisfied.

When the work comes into the data center via remote job entry and is returned to the user via some remote printing operation, the

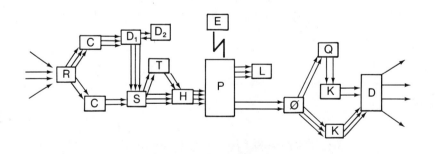

FIGURE 14.2.   Alternate Data Center Workflow

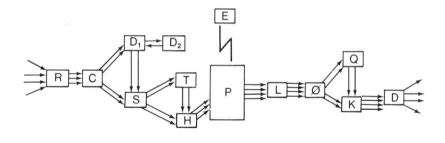

FIGURE 14.3.   *Modified Data Center Workflow*

turnaround time is that shown as V_2 in the figure. It is only when the applications are on-line that the turnaround time is that shown as the V_3 line. At that point, the turnaround time is usually referred to as "response time."

The key issues for the DCM are the reduction of the turnaround lines (V_1, V_2, and V_3) and the continuing education of the users so that their expectations are not out of line with what the data center or the characteristics of the user's application can deliver.

IDENTIFYING CONTROL POINTS IN THE WORKFLOW

The monitoring of work through the data center involves tracking jobs through various control points within the center. The following sections discuss the attributes of each control point and identify the relationships among the control points.

The Job Input Control Point

The input and receiving station in the data center is the point at which batch jobs start their path through the data center. People assigned to the receiving station should have a sense of urgency in promptly receiving, classifying, logging in, and passing on jobs.

The logging of jobs provides a good starting point for tracing work and responding to user inquiries. It also can be used as a checkpoint to determine whether work has been received from given user departments. *If the input has not been received at its expected time, the receiving personnel should contact the user, find out why the work is late, and when the work is now expected to arrive. Word of the late input should be passed to the shift supervisor or DCM since the absence of this input will cause adjustments in the balance of the schedule and may result in missing the on-time delivery targets stated in the service agreement.*

The Data Entry Control Point

Although many companies are disbursing the data entry functions to user areas in the form of remote batch work or are reducing these functions with the advent of more on-line applications, data entry remains a substantial part of the data center activities. It is a labor-intensive area with an emphasis on high throughput and low error rates. Typical productivity rates for data entry range from 10,000 to 18,000 strokes per hour and above with a national average of 10,600 strokes per hour (Rhodes, 1980). Over the course of one day, approximately 75,000 strokes can be expected as productive output.

The cost for data entry can average $0.04 per sixty-character record. This is calculated by adding the following costs:

- Operator wages
- Operator benefits
- Supervisor wages
- Supervisor benefits
- Equipment costs

The sum of these costs is then divided by the total keystroke rate to arrive at the cost per keystroke.

There is an apparent discrepancy between an hourly production rate of, for example, 15,000 strokes and a daily rate of 75,000 strokes. As it turns out, the high rate cannot be sustained over a seven- or eight-hour period, due to interruptions, job set-up time, and the tedium of the work itself. On the other hand, it has been found that *the data entry section is more productive when it has a modest backlog of work. Therefore, data entry sections are usually staffed to handle about 90 percent of anticipated peak workloads.* Most data center managers prefer to have the backlog and achieve higher productivity rates than to have idle labor capacity and lower productivity rates.

Incentive systems have been used in the data entry area, generally with success. Companies that have been surveyed report that incentive systems yielded an effective productive day of 7.3 hours compared to 6.7 hours before the incentive was established (Rhodes, 1980). These companies also reported concern on the part of the data entry operators that the incentives were designed to weed out the less productive people and that the incentive levels would gradually rise, making it more difficult to keep up with them. You can help reduce these anxieties by explaining clearly to the data entry staff the goals and objectives of the data center (in this case, cost and productivity issues), the reasons for the incentives, and the likely results of meeting or missing the objectives. (For example, low producers will be released, excess people will be transferred to other sections or departments, or the continued high cost of data entry will result eventually in all data entry being sent outside the company.)

As an alternative to data entry done internally, data entry service bureaus are available. The cost for this service generally runs from six cents to twelve cents per record. For specific jobs, the cost can be substantially higher if the source documents are difficult to understand or are illegible. A lower rate may result if the service bureau takes the work on a low-priority basis or if the service bureau is looking to fill excess capacity.

You should compare periodically the internal rates with those of a data entry service bureau. In general, the internal rates should be lower. If they are not, the service bureau represents a competitive alternative for the company, an alternative that should be seriously considered if the internal rates cannot be reduced below those of the service bureau.

The service bureau has been a good alternative for those companies that are in a transition period from batch data entry to on-line systems and that have vacancies in the data entry section. Rather than fill these vacancies (knowing that in a few months the on-line application will be in production and there will be excess capacity in the data entry section), the company chooses the service bureau as a way of doing the work for the short term.

If service bureaus are used, complete job specifications must be provided. It is advisable to have the bureau furnish a work sample and cus-

tomer references. Prices and deadlines for pick-up and delivery should be clearly understood by both parties.

The Mainframe Control Point

The heart of the data center, in terms of productivity, is the central processing unit (CPU) or mainframe. Those outside of the center often think only of the CPU when they think of the data center. Those working in the center are consciously or unconsciously directing their work efforts from the user areas toward the CPU or are performing tasks that flow away from the CPU toward the user areas. It is appropriate, therefore, to give some thought to the way in which the mainframe assignments are structured.

To begin, consider several activities associated with the console operator's job; then think about whether these activities work positively or negatively toward increasing mainframe productivity. In other words, which activities involved with the mainframe should the console operator be allowed to do? Each installation's circumstances will lead to slightly different answers. You can use the following typical standard operating procedure for operators as a jumping-off point:

Item	*Operator activity*
1. Patch software	Prohibited
2. Interact with programs	Prohibited
3. Set up jobs	Discouraged
4. Report status	Yes
5. Report trouble	Yes
6. Adhere to schedules	Yes
7. Emphasize throughput	Yes
8. Emphasize availability	Yes
9. Troubleshoot	Yes
10. Analyze problems	Yes
11. Repair hardware	Possibly

Patch Software. Console operators patch software when they have complete confidence in their ability to program. There is little doubt in the minds of many operators that they really should be programming rather than some of the people who are in the programming area. As a result, when a program malfunctions (especially on the evening or night shift), an operator may decide to "fix" the program by changing the source code, recompiling the program, and rerunning the job.

This scenario is *not* grossly exaggerated, and it is loaded with trouble for the DCM. The problems include the lack of program change control, improper testing of the production changes, lack of documentation for the changes, breaches of good security practice, preempting of a responsibility that belongs in the programming area, and misuse of the operator's time. *The operator should operate the system, not do bootleg programming. If the operator is bent on programming, arrange for transferring the person to the programming department. Establish data center standards that prohibit operators from patching software.*

Interact with Programs. Interaction between the operator and programs occurs frequently with older programs. The interaction requires the operator to respond to console messages issued by the program, with the response having a bearing on the logical outcome of the program. For instance, a program that issues the message: "ENTER x IF REPORT 1, y IF REPORT 2" or one that directs the operator to: "ENTER THE CHECK PAYMENT DATE" will yield different results depending on the operator's response.

There are two major problems with having operators interact with programs in this way. First, the operator is expected to know the logical possibilities inherent in the program and be able to select correctly from among the logical alternatives. *Having the operator make decisions or enter decisions that affect the outcome of the program is a practice that should be avoided.* The users, in such a situation, do not have control of their own applications and, further, are not likely to appreciate the work of the data center. In the examples cited above, the wrong decision on the part of the operator would give the user the wrong results. *Instead of giving the operator the responsibility for making the correct decision, have programs such as this modified to eliminate these messages and have the user take responsibility for the logical decisions in the program.*

Secondly, letting the mainframe stand idle while the operator responds to the message cuts into the efficiency of the data center. This type of programmed halt usually is found in programs that were written when the practice of operator intervention was more common, before the advent of extensive, multiple-program execution. While this was tolerable in a simplified operating environment, it is wasteful in an environment where the emphasis is on the productive use of the mainframe.

Observe that this prohibition does not apply to operator messages that are issued by the operating system and that deal directly with the operating environment at the time. These messages are necessary for the operator to communicate with the operating system. They also provide all the more reason to eliminate the logical program messages so that the operator can concentrate on responding effectively to the system messages.

Set Up Jobs.   Having the operator set up production jobs by organizing the job control language and withdrawing tape files detracts from the productivity of the operator and the mainframe. In a strict sense, therefore, it should be discouraged, but we must add that whether it should be prohibited will depend on the size of the installation.

In smaller data centers, the operator often must do multiple duties, including the setting up of jobs. In many instances, the evening and night shifts in the computer room are marked by long-running jobs that leave the operator with little to do in terms of interacting with the computing environment. In these situations, using the operator to set up jobs makes good use of the operator's time. *In any case, using the operator to set up jobs can present some security problems; that is, since only one person is handling the transactions, the job request, and the setting of parameters for the job, the operator could run the job several times, doctoring files and output along the way. Better control results when someone other than the operator sets up the jobs to be run on the mainframe.*

Report Status; Report Trouble.   Having the operator report on the operating status and report any troubles with the equipment makes good use of the operator's unique perspective. *Intermittent problems with hardware or software and unusual operating conditions within a production application should be noted by the operator and reported to the appropriate people if immediate corrective action is not taken. In the case of unusual conditions within a production application, the operator should be instructed to document any status readings, settings, and key indicators that would be useful to pass on to those who are going to work on fixing the problem.*

***Adhere to Schedules; Emphasize Throughput; Emphasize Avail-
ability.*** These three items, taken together, make up the main objective of the mainframe operator—namely, to keep the mainframe
(which is the "production line" in our information factory) running at
top efficiency. Resources of this type operate most efficiently when
they are properly scheduled, loaded, and operated.

There are subtle differences in emphasis among a batch mainframe, an on-line mainframe, and a mainframe that runs a concurrent
combination of both. With a batch mainframe, schedules must be followed if the total workload is to be completed in the expected time.
This orientation leads to the emphasis on the second factor,
throughput. Proper job preparation, efficient scheduling, smooth tran-
sitions between tasks, and prompt release of programs that malfunction go together to improve throughput in the batch system.

In the mainframe that supports on-line applications, the schedule is still followed, but the greater emphasis is placed on the availability of the system to the on-line users. The schedule dictates the
hours of operation for the on-line network, and the operator is responsible for making the network resource available to the users at those
times. With the emphasis on on-line availability, there is an implicit
willingness to use the mainframe at something less than its full computing capability. Response time and total availability receive a higher
priority than maximum usage.

In the combination batch/on-line environment, a balance must
be struck between pure throughput and availability. A heavy emphasis on either will detract from the achievement of the other. The corporate steering committee should help determine the degree of
emphasis placed on each of these seemingly conflicting objectives.
The committee should not say, "The data center manager should emphasize availability rather than throughput"; rather, the direction
should be given as, "During the day, applications A, B, and C (on-line
applications) should receive highest priority in the data center."
Clearly, the steering committee is not going to tell the DCM exactly
how to achieve the balance, but the committee should provide guidelines as to the relative importance to the organization of the on-line
applications as compared to the batch applications.

Troubleshoot; Analyze Problems. The operator is in a good
position to perform first-level observation of operating situations, and
this vantage point can be used to advantage in the areas of trouble-

shooting and problem analysis. The key to using the operator in this way is the clear identification of the limits to which the operator can go before the analysis must be turned over to others.

Operator involvement in troubleshooting is beneficial, but it cannot be done at the expense of the primary operator objective of optimizing computer performance by emphasizing throughput and availability. An on-line environment, for instance, gives the operator the opportunity to watch things such as line traffic, numbers of terminals active, and mainframe channel activity without impairing the throughput and availability of the system. Experienced operators are able to make minimal adjustments that help the performance of the system, such as carefully changing the program mix that is running or modifying the priorities of tasks being executed, but more far-reaching adjustments of the environment should be made in a more studied, off-line atmosphere. *By all means, use the operator's perspective to observe, inspect, and document operating problems and to do a basic analysis of conditions, but have a cut-off point where the operator formally turns the problem over to others to pursue the solution.*

Repair Hardware. Most hardware repairs done by operators have been confined to basic, mechanical repairing and maintenance. Changing printer ribbons, clearing card jams, and perhaps changing drive belts have always been considered part of the operator's duties, but most mainframe vendors have maintenance contracts that prohibit anyone but their own repair personnel from repairing their equipment beyond these limits.

This brings to mind a word of caution to the DCM. *If the vendor's personnel ever give your people permission to attempt to correct a malfunction, be sure that the situation is documented and made part of your vendor file.* Verbal authorization by the vendor can come back to haunt the DCM if the vendor later insists that the customer is liable for the cost of parts and corrective maintenance because someone other than the vendor's people repaired the equipment.

There have been recent developments in hardware technology that are beginning to change this traditional situation where only the vendor repairs the hardware. More compact electronics, modular circuit boards, improved diagnostic information, and the vendor's continuing efforts to reduce their repair costs have resulted in some vendors allowing data center personnel to perform first-line equipment troubleshooting and repair. This work usually involves the operator swapping circuit boards to get the equipment operational, then sending the failed module to the vendor for further analysis. Operator repairing of hardware is likely to become more prevalent in the future.

The Control Points at Peripherals and Terminals

Peripheral equipment can be categorized, from the data center point of view, as *attended* or *unattended*. Attended equipment requires regular attention or intervention in order to make the resource usable. Examples of attended equipment are card readers, punches, printers, and tape drives. Unattended equipment requires little attention and is ready to be used (rather than being a resource that needs attention before it can be used). Examples of unattended equipment are disk drives, mass storage units, modems, and remote terminals. From the viewpoint of the DCM and in terms of managing efficiently the information factory, the attended devices are more labor-intensive; the unattended devices need subtler control mechanisms.

The attended devices generally use some form of expendable supplies, such as cards, tapes, or continuous forms. Therefore, effective use of these devices depends on the combination of adequate physical supplies and the proper amount of available labor. *In structuring the data center jobs and physically locating the equipment within the center, pay attention to the placement of the devices so as to minimize travel distances between devices monitored by one person, between the equipment and the source of supplies, and between the devices and the input/receiving areas and output/dispatch areas of the data center.*

The unattended devices need controls, and their usage must be regularly monitored. Devices such as disks and terminals are more passive than the attended devices, but their availability, in both form and amount, is generally taken for granted by those who use them. Users assume that terminals, for example, are available and working when the users want to use them. These assumptions are widespread where disks and data bases are involved. Once the data base has been established on the disks, this resource is quietly available to the users until the allotted space is filled up or until an operating problem occurs. To reduce the chances that either of these occurrences will become catastrophic, the data center must monitor the conditions surrounding the data base.

Managing the data base resource requires some preventive measures and some means of recovering and resuming production after a problem occurs. *File volumes, transaction volumes, and control totals for both records and other key indicators (such as dollar totals) should be checked each day.* For example, if an on-line application that has regularly had between 1,500 and 1,800 transactions per day has a day with 3,000 transactions—or with 400 transactions—this condition should be pointed out to the user manager. There should be a logical explanation for the change in volume (such as a one-time influx of work already known to the user manager, or such as 80 percent of the on-line operators out sick on the same day). If the reason is not obvious, the DCM and the user manager can investigate further.

In addition, any unusual conditions and discrepancies should be promptly resolved. *The users must be educated to the sensitivity of data base integrity and should clearly understand the need to follow controls for accessibility and daily auditability.* For example, it is essential that users know how to use their passwords and that they understand why their password must be kept secure (compared to writing it on their calendar or taping a note to their telephone with their password on it). This must be coupled with information about the penalties for compromising security (such as probation, transfer, or dismissal).

COMPILING THE TOTAL RESOURCE REVIEW

The DCM is expected to have just enough resources available to do the job at hand—just like Goldilocks's dilemma, the amount of resources should be not too much and not too little, but "just right." The DCM's problem, of course, is how to resolve two conflicting objectives: providing the best service to all users while reducing the cost of operating the data center. Periodic conferences and meetings with users help you to forecast what the major future applications will be, but you must also continually monitor resource usage within the data center.

Recall that what is being managed is a *total* computer resource consisting of hardware, software, and people. This means that the critical point in this resource mix will be continually shifting. In addition, each major resource will have its own critical point. For example, operators may be in short supply at the same time that job set-up clerks are abundant. The channel capacity on the central processor may be quite adequate while the main memory is critically short. Relieving either of these pressure points can shift the critical point to another area within the major resource. Adding main memory to the processor may relieve the memory bottleneck, only to find that the internal speed of the machine is not adequate to handle the increased processing load.

To compile a review of the total resource usage, you need to follow several basic steps in order to identify any problem areas and take corrective action. These steps can be shown as a closed control loop:

1. Measure

↓

2. Evaluate

↓

3. Adjust

↓

4. Return to Step 1.

In somewhat more detail, the following steps are needed:

- Set performance and service goals.
- Measure the existing levels of performance and service.
- Evaluate the existing levels against the target levels.
- Identify areas where the two levels do not coincide.
- Develop tentative plans for correction.
- Test the tentative corrections.
- Implement the corrections that move the actual performance and service levels toward the target levels.

Measuring the Resources

The measurement step includes the definition of what services are being provided and the cost of these services. This measuring is a type of inventory of the resources available to the DCM. *The number, type, and skills of the data center people should be documented. Similarly, the software capabilities should be noted, such as the general characteristics, resources needed by the software, and the constraints imposed by the software (for example, the number of terminals versus the memory needed). In like manner, the hardware resource must be measured and cataloged. Look at the following variables:*

- Available processor cycles
- Memory size
- Processor instruction rate
- Processor usage
- Paging rates
- Data channel capacity
- Data channel usage
- Disk space capacity
- Disk space usage
- Batch/on-line mix, by shift
- On-line work profile:
  - During busy hours
  - During average hours
  - Transaction volume
  - Processor usage
  - Disk usage

The above data with all their details can form a stepping-off point for constructing a model of existing data center activity (usually via the use of simulation software or writing a program to correlate the above variables and to allow changes in the values of these variables).

Evaluating the Measurements

Following the measurement, the results can be checked or evaluated against the service objectives that were set for the center. The service objectives are directly tied to the service agreements discussed earlier.

The actual usage of data center resources must be evaluated against the originally forecast usage of these resources. Did the users submit more or less units of work than forecast? If so, this is a volume variance and may account for deviations (plus or minus) from delivery-time and cost targets. Was there a change in the composition of the workload? If a given task was run more than expected and another job run less than expected, this will result in a different resource utilization than predicted, given that the two jobs have different resource usage profiles. Finally, if the level of work and the make-up of the work materialized as forecast, but the delivery and cost targets were not met, a variance has occurred in the level of efficiency within the data center. (This, of course, could be a positive or negative variance.) Your job as DCM is to determine what changes will be made to improve the data center's performance and increase its productivity.

The levels and frequency at which the performance data are examined will vary and will depend somewhat on the specific conditions within your data center. *You can look at several broad indicators on a weekly or monthly basis and be alert for significant changes in these indicators; response time, turnaround time, and user feedback are three broad indicators that should be watched for signals of impending trouble.* Once such a signal appears, more detailed information is needed. For example, if response time for terminals has increased, more detailed data are needed that show the application mix during various times of the day, the numbers of terminals concurrently on-line, and so on.

If any one of these pieces of information points toward the problem, the same type of information gathered on a more frequent cycle will be helpful. If the response time measurement was made on a weekly basis, for instance, you should step up the frequency of obtaining that information to have it available on a daily or hourly basis.

Much of this type of information can be presented graphically in order to aid in the understanding of it. Moving averages, time-lines, bar charts, and pie charts are all useful graphic devices for the measurement and evaluation steps. Figures 14.4, 14.5, 14.6, and 14.7 provide examples of this type of presentation.

Figure 14.4 reflects the *amount* of the processor capacity that is being consumed. It is expressed in terms of a percentage scale on the left of the chart (the absolute amount of instruction cycles consumed

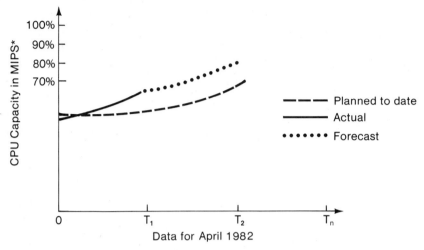

*Millions of instructions per second

FIGURE 14.4.   *Time-Line Graph for Capacity Utilization*

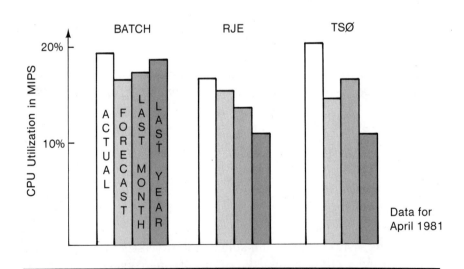

FIGURE 14.5.   *Bar Graph for Capacity Utilization*

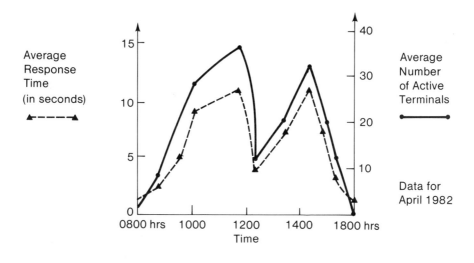

FIGURE 14.6. *Average On-Line Activity by Time of Day*

will, of course, depend on the size and type of processor you have). As part of your planning process, this capacity consumption is forecast for a series of time periods: T_1, T_2, ... T_n. These time periods can be months, quarters, or years. In the figure, this planned consumption is shown by a dashed line. The actual consumption is plotted periodically, shown by a solid line. When the actual line has been plotted, you should evaluate the actual versus planned and forecast the expected consumption for the remaining time periods. The expected consumption is shown with a dotted line. The forecast line allows you to make necessary adjustments to your processor resources.

Figure 14.5 shows actual processor utilization for a specific time period, shows the forecasted usage, the usage one month earlier, and one year earlier. This is further broken down by basic types of usage (batch, remote job entry, and time sharing are shown here, but choose categories that are meaningful to you). Again, this graph allows you to compare what has happened, what is happening, and what was forecast.

Figure 14.6 indicates average on-line activity by time of day, shows the average response time (in seconds) and the average number of active terminals. (Forecast lines could be added to this graph or kept separately.)

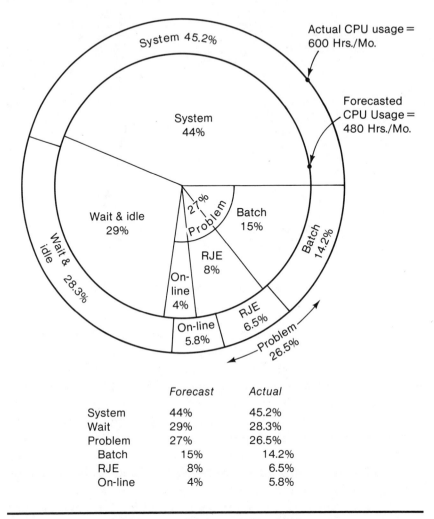

	Forecast	Actual
System	44%	45.2%
Wait	29%	28.3%
Problem	27%	26.5%
Batch	15%	14.2%
RJE	8%	6.5%
On-line	4%	5.8%

FIGURE 14.7.   Hardware Utilization Report

Figure 14.7 shows *how* the processor capacity was utilized in terms of problem, wait/idle, and system states. The forecasted CPU usage could be preprinted and the actual usage plotted on a periodic basis (of course, the actual circle can fall inside, outside, or right on the forecasted circle).

It is also helpful if the performance standard levels can be super-imposed on the charts along with the actual results.

Assessing Various Measurement Tools

There are a number of tools available to assist in the measurement of data center resource characteristics. Among these are hardware monitors, software monitors, job accounting packages, benchmarks, and simulation packages. Each of these has its own strengths and weaknesses:

- *Hardware monitors* have little or no machine overhead, are very accurate in their measurement, and are very expensive.

- *Software monitors* take a variable amount of overhead resources depending on the frequency of the sample data taken, are reasonably accurate, and are less expensive than hardware monitors.

- *Job accounting packages* yield general results about the duration of a job, but they do not give specific information about the job characteristics while the job was running (because these packages were not originally designed to do that type of measurement). The job accounting packages run efficiently, taking little machine overhead, and are relatively inexpensive.

- *Benchmarks* and *simulations* can be quite useful, but they each take a long time to set up properly and to run so that objective information results.

The effective use of existing resources, both the evaluation tool resources and the total data center resources of people, hardware, and software, will allow the data center manager to try to reconcile the dual objectives of providing the best service at the least cost. Accurate prediction of future resource needs will allow the DCM to improve the productivity of the data center.

The use of simulation and models will allow the present workload and resource utilization mix to be simulated, evaluated, and future workload/resource combinations to be simulated, evaluated, and varied. This work represents the resource availability portion of the planning loop within the data center schematic diagram (Figure 12.1). Thus, the planning loop has been closed, and it has been integrated with the production line (workload, processing, and the resulting productive output) and with the operating loop in that the resource usage is tested against existing and forecasted service levels.

APPLYING THIS INFORMATION TO YOUR DATA CENTER

1. What can be done to streamline the workflow in your data center?

2. When were the console operator activities last evaluated?

3. What activities are the console operators doing that could be done more efficiently by somebody else?

4. What aids do you use to plan and control flow? Performance? *Examples:* Schematic diagrams, walk-throughs, interviews with data center personnel

SUMMARY

The following closed loop lists the steps recommended in this chapter for streamlining the data center's operations through the use of industrial engineering techniques:

1. Identify your performance and service goals.

2. Diagram the data center workflow.

3. Assign time values for typical job flow in the data center. Consider both:
   • The wait time prior to each station
   • The time spent in each station

4. Compare these time values against goals.

5. Study backlog at each station.

6. Study bottlenecks at stations where flow converges.

7. Adjust flow to reduce backlog, eliminate bottlenecks.

8. Test adjusted flow on reduced volume of work.

9. Fine-tune the adjustments; implement a new flow pattern.

10. Return to Step 1.

IV

Handling the Business Details of Data Processing

15

Budgeting for the Data Center

Budgets are the means by which organizations forecast their revenues and expenses for a given period of time, with the hope that the revenues will meet or exceed the expenses. The health of the organization will dictate the overall budget amounts, strategy of expenditures, and the operations that can or cannot be carried out during the time period represented by the budget. Thus, as DCM, you must be attuned to the prevailing atmosphere within the company in order to prepare a budget that is consonant with the corporate strategy. Projects and expenditures that may be approved with little resistance or questioning during prosperous or expansionary times can be disapproved or subjected to rigorous examination during rough times for the corporation. This chapter discusses how to prepare and present the data center budget.

PREPARING THE BUDGET

The time period or horizon covered by a budget will vary from one company to another and is somewhat dependent on the size of the organization. A twelve-month horizon is fairly common, but many companies use a horizon of fifteen, eighteen, or twenty-four months. The longer time frame is common in larger companies simply because there are more budget pieces that must be put together to form the corporate budget than there are in smaller companies.

Defining Two Types of Budgets

There are generally two types of budgets: operating budgets and capital budgets. The *operating budget* takes into account the projected workload and the resources needed to service these workload levels. The *capital expenditure budget* forecasts the corporate capital needed to fund major projects. The capital budget frequently covers time periods of three, five, eight, or more years, regardless of the time horizon used for the operating budgets. For reasons of corporate planning, capital budgets, like operating budgets, are put together to form a composite picture of the funds needed by the corporation over the next several years.

The DCM should consult with the controller or with the financial department within the company to get a precise definition of what the company considers to be a capital expenditure. The usual definition of a *capital asset* (that is, an asset whose cost can be capitalized and depreciated) is one that has a reasonable expected life (for example, two years or more) and one whose cost is significant to the company (for example, $300 or more). An asset must pass *both* tests in order to be capitalized—that is, the asset cost must be above the given dollar amount and must have an expected life of some given duration.

Identifying Budget Components

A budget, at the most elementary level, is made up of income elements and expense elements. Each of these, in turn, is comprised of fixed items and variable items. For our purposes, the fixed elements are those items that can be forecast with some degree of certainty for the period covered by the budget. A typical list of budget elements is shown in Figure 15.1.

Fixed income amounts are the result of a corporate allocation of funds with which to run the data center. More will be said about this in the following chapter during the discussion of the allocation method of accounting for data center services. Briefly stated, the allocation of money for the data center can be viewed, for budget purposes, as a type of income to the center. It is fixed in the sense that the amount is known at the start of the year and the amount is generally not subject to change during the year.

A second type of fixed income to the center is the income that comes to the corporation as a result of a contractual commitment that the corporation may have with clients. To the extent that these commitments may result in work being done in the data center, we can consider that some portion of this contract income is a fixed income to the data center. In practice, these arrangements are not too common, and the more prevalent type of fixed income is in the form of the corporate allocation.

Income Items	*Expense Items*
Fixed:	*Fixed:*
• Corporate allocation	• Salaries
• Contract income	• Benefits
	• Hardware
	• Maintenance
	• Services
	• Program products
	• Supplies
Variable:	*Variable:*
• Internal users	• Overtime
• Outside users	• Agency fees
	• Training
	• Travel
	• Contracted services

FIGURE 15.1. Budget Elements

Variable income is income that results from a chargeback system of accounting for data center services. This method, like the allocation method, is discussed in more detail in Chapter Sixteen. This income is classified as variable since the level of "income" to the data center is directly dependent upon the amount of data center services that are consumed by the users.

Another form of variable income is the revenue produced by the sale of data center resources to outside parties. This is not a common source of income except, of course, in the case of service bureaus, whose main reason for existing is to generate funds by selling services to outside parties. The typical "inside" data center will only realize revenues from outside parties in cases where a significant amount of excess capacity exists and where some effort is made to sell this surplus capacity (in the form of machine time, data entry work, or technical consulting, for instance) to people outside of the company. Since this income is generally unpredictable in terms of the timing and amount, it is classified as a variable income element.

Salaries are fixed expense items. *A salary plan should be developed as one of the worksheets in the budget preparation process.* This plan indicates the individual wages or salaries for people in the data center at the start of the year and the total payroll amount as of the start of the year. To this, anticipated changes in staffing levels are added along with expected increases in payroll amounts and the timing of these increases. This information allows the calculation of the total payroll amount for the year and a payroll level as of the end of the year.

The budgeted amount for benefits is usually a function of the budgeted amount for the wages and salaries. Most controllers will provide a percentage factor that the company expects to use in budgeting for benefit amounts. This amount represents the cost to the organization for funding benefits such as vacation pay, health insurance, life insurance, pension funds, and the like. Depending upon the scope of the company's benefit program, the benefit percentage can range from 20 to 35 percent or beyond.

Expense items such as hardware, maintenance, outside services, program products, and supplies are budgeted based on contractual commitments or on expected usage. Hardware and maintenance can be budgeted based on contractual terms, although there may be provision for periodic changes in these rates. If this is the case, of course, the anticipated changes in the rates should become a part of the budget amounts. Services and supplies can be budgeted based on prior years' usage and then adjusted for expected changes in the usage levels. For example, if a major on-line system is expected to be put into production during the coming year, the supply budget should be reduced to take into account the reduced use of paper. On the other hand, if one of the primary applications is expected to increase substantially in volume of work during the coming year, the paper budget may have to be increased.

Expense items that cannot be forecast accurately as to the degree of usage or that may be more discretionary in nature are classified as *variable expense* items. Items such as overtime, agency fees, training, and travel can be increased or discontinued depending on the conditions that materialize during the operating year. If workloads in the data center turn out to be exactly as forecast, the overtime may not have to be incurred. If vacancies in the data center positions can be filled by internal transfers or by advertising in the newspapers, the agency fees will not have to be spent. If a budget crunch occurs during the year, discretionary spending on things such as training and travel can be curtailed. Significant increases in the data center workload can require that large sums of money be spent on overtime or in the hiring of additional people. While, ideally, such variations in the workload should be anticipated and therefore should be a part of the budget, an unexpected rise in the business level of the company will have to be handled by the data center. In this case, the additional revenue to the company will, it is hoped, offset the additional cost to the data center. Conversely, a dramatic drop in business levels will require cutting back in the expenditures of the data center in order to conserve funds. The likely areas in which to begin the cutbacks will be in the discretionary or variable expense areas.

PRESENTING THE BUDGET

The specific format and media for presenting the data center budget will vary depending upon the method preferred by the company. Most budget presentations will include, of course, the expected income and expense levels and a comparison of these levels with

Data Center Budget
(in thousands of dollars)

Item	1980 (actual)		1981 (estimated)		1982 (budget)
Salaries	$ 900	+ 9%	$ 981	+ 9%	$1,069
Benefits	270	+ 9%	294	+ 9%	321
Overtime	100	+15%	115	+ 3%	118
Hardware	1,000	+12%	1,120	+18%	1,322
Supplies	240	+16%	278	+18%	328
...	...	..	...	..	...
...	...	..	...	..	...
...	...	..	...	..	...
...	...	..	...	..	...
TOTAL	$3,200	+13%	$3,616	+15%	$4,158

FIGURE 15.2.   Budget Presentation

those of previous years. Figure 15.2 shows a prototype layout for these presentations.

Justifying the Budget

The format shown in this illustration presents a good picture of the absolute amounts for each budget item, the relationship of each item to the total budget figure, the trend of each item, and the trend of the overall budget amount for the past several years. In presenting or "defending" the data center budget, the DCM must be prepared to explain these relationships and to put the various items into perspective.

For example, note that the overtime amount is expected to increase by only 3 percent for 1982, compared to the 15 percent rise in the previous year. This may be explained by the concurrent increase in the hardware amount, rising by 18 percent compared to 12 percent. If the hardware increase is because of a planned expansion in the configuration, the rate of change in the overtime expense may be expected to decrease since the increased capacity would presumably require less overtime. The opposing argument can be made that, at least during the year when the change is made, the overtime expense will continue to grow since parallel running and conversion to the new equipment could require more, rather than less, overtime.

The rate of increase in the salary budget is shown as a constant 9 percent for both years. This rate of change, however, could exceed the corporate guideline for salary budgets. The rationale for this amount may lie in the fact that competition for talent in the local market requires that these rates be paid, even though they are relatively higher than the salary budget rates for other parts of the company. The DCM must be prepared for these types of questions and will be expected to explain the reasoning behind the various budget items.

Zero-Base Budgeting

The budget presentation discussed above centers on explaining the incremental differences between the two budget years. Some companies insist on a *zero-base* approach to budgeting. Using this approach, all items are scrutinized as if they had not existed on previous budgets; that is, the new budget starts from a base of zero dollars. Each item must be justified as to its presence and its amount, whereas the incremental approach focuses on the change in the amount for each item and has the underlying assumption that the item is necessary in the first place. Regardless of the approach taken, the DCM should be prepared to defend and explain each item.

Whether or not the zero-base approach is used, the DCM should periodically review each item on the data center budget and question its need and amount. Given the rapid rate of change in most data centers, you should expect that new items will have replaced other items that have outlived their usefulness over the course of a few years. Be alert for these situations in order to minimize the total dollar resources needed to run the center and to make the best use of those dollars that you are given.

Quantifying the Benefits from the Data Center

In justifying the data center budget, make sure that the benefits that are derived from the work done by the data center are presented to users and to management. On many of the applications, you may need to enlist the support of the user area manager in developing an analysis of the benefits. Wherever possible, these benefits should be quantified and specifically identified. Look for specific examples where costs have been reduced or avoided or where service has been improved through the use of the data center facilities. To accomplish this, compare the present volume levels, service levels, and cost levels with previous levels for these items. The service agreement is a good source of this information. It is concise and has been reviewed and agreed to by the user manager. Use the delivery, volume, and cost portions of the agreement, then list the service patterns over a number of months. Figure 15.3 shows a sample format for presenting this information.

Make sure that you take into account the costs and benefits that are present in the user areas as well as those in the data center, since a modest increase in cost in the data center may result in significant reductions in cost in the user area. Note that these cost/benefit relationships are continually changing. It should not be assumed that an application or a piece of equipment continues to justify itself. By reviewing and questioning the payoff of various expenditures, the DCM is in a strong position to explain these situations to users and management and can often make recommendations for eliminating activities that do not return good value to the organization.

APPLYING THIS INFORMATION TO YOUR DATA CENTER

1. What capital expenditures are forecast for the data center in the next three years?
   Examples: The purchase of new equipment, the cost of adding or improving workspace in the data center (furniture, carpeting, and so on)

2. What trends are observable by comparing the data center budgets for the past five years?

3. What reasons can be given for these trends?

DATA CENTER SERVICE HISTORY

User: Finance and Accounting
Application: Accounts Receivable
Period: Jan. through Dec. 1981

| | On-time Delivery | | Volume | | Cost | | |
	Target	Actual	Target	Actual	Target	Actual	Variance
Jan*							
Feb*							
Mar	100%	95%	125/day	100/day	0.95/inv	1.10	−15.8%
Apr	100%	96%	125/day	95/day	0.95/inv	1.02	− 7.4%
May	100%	94%	125/day	100/day	0.95/inv	0.97	− 2.1%
Jun	100%	97%	125/day	115/day	0.95/inv	0.96	− 1.1%
Jul	100%	100%	125/day	120/day	0.95/inv	0.95	
Aug	100%	100%	125/day	130/day	0.95/inv	0.95	
Sep	100%	99%	125/day	135/day	0.95/inv	0.93	2.1%
Oct	100%	100%	125/day	140/day	0.95/inv	0.91	4.2%
Nov	100%	100%	125/day	135/day	0.95/inv	0.92	3.2%
Dec	100%	100%	125/day	125/day	0.95/inv	0.93	2.1%

Note: Application was placed in production on Feb. 20th.

	1980	1981
Average daily invoices	121.3	119.5

Average cost/invoice

	1980	1981
User costs	$2.754	$1.25
Data center costs	0.00	0.958
Total average cost per invoice	$2.754	$2.208

FIGURE 15.3 Data Center Service History

SUMMARY

When putting together the data center budget, do your homework!

- Understand the format and definition of terms that your company uses in constructing a budget.

- Be aware of what's happening (good and bad) with the corporation's economics.

- Put together a picture of data center expenditures over the past several years that can be compared to your budget request for the next year. Be able to explain trends and variances in these data.

- Don't be afraid to present data center success stories—cases where you have helped to reduce overall corporate costs for an application.

16

Accounting for Data Center Services

The budget is a look ahead, a planning vehicle for expenditures in the data center. On a day-to-day basis, the DCM must have a method of accounting for the use of data center services; this chapter describes accounting methods that you can use.

EXCEPTION REPORTING

Operating expense reports are generally provided by the company's accounting or controller's office. These reports, issued on a monthly or periodic basis, reflect the actual expenses incurred in running the data center and are often structured to compare the actual expenses to the budget amounts. The reports are, of course, a means of tracking the operation of the data center from a financial point of view and, as such, are useful as an early warning device for impending problems.

The DCM should establish some type of exception reporting *mechanism, whether or not the controller's office provides that type of report. The exception reports center on the identification of revenue, expense, or workload activity that is substantially different from what was forecast. A tolerance level of plus or minus 5 percent might be used as a guideline for potential trouble spots in the operation.*

Figure 16.1 illustrates a sample graph for this type of information. If income, expenditures, or work volumes go beyond the tolerance range, the item should command more intensive management attention. Anticipate questions in these areas and be prepared to respond with background information about these operating situations. For instance, the controller may question you as to why the data center expenses are 8 percent over budget (year to date) and 12 percent over budget for the month of June. Your explanation might be that a planned purchase of paper stock for the data center was moved up two months in anticipation of a price increase from the vendor. Costs are expected to be back within budget by the end of August.

The more that can be done to explain radical changes in volumes, expenses, and the like, the stronger will be your position with upper management because you will appear to know what's happening in the data center. *Rather than wait for these questions, you should confront the situations and resolve problems or formulate a sound plan to deal with the exception conditions.*

Any significant exceptions to the planned levels of activity signal potential problems in the operation of the data center—either in terms of falling short of performance goals or in terms of having more work than can be handled with the given resources. In either case, the direct effect is a change in the balance that exists between costs in-

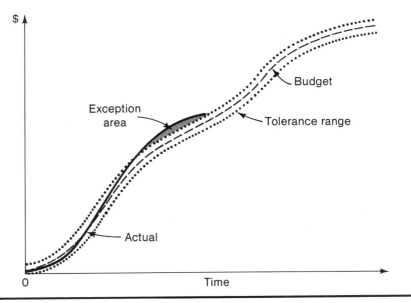

FIGURE 16.1.   Budget Versus Actual Expense

curred and the dollar resources that have been provided to the data center for its operation. This imbalance, in turn, shows up when accounting for the services performed by the data center. There are two primary methods of accounting for data center services: the allocation method and the chargeback method.

THE ALLOCATION METHOD OF ACCOUNTING

The allocation method of accounting for data center services is sometimes referred to as the "Big Pot" method of accounting. Under this method, the organization allocates a lump sum of money (hence, the "big pot") for the operation of the data center. (The same method may or may not be used for the systems and programming area within the same company.) The amount of money in the pot is roughly based on the amount of money spent in previous years with some very rough adjustments for anticipated changes in the level of activity in the data center. The DCM is expected to provide service to various users by converting these dollar resources into hardware, software, and people resources within the center. In theory, the center is to serve any user who requests service from the data center, regardless of whether that user had used the center previously.

The allocation method tends to encourage the use of the data center resource by the users. To the user, the data center appears to be a "free good" in that, no matter how much or how little of the center's resource that user consumes, the amount of direct cost to the user is exactly the same: zero. Instead, the cost of running the data center appears as corporate overhead.

Among the advantages and disadvantages of the allocation method are:

- Advantages:
  - Low administrative overhead
  - Costs treated as utilities
  - Few accounting records

- Disadvantages:
  - Costs not allocated by application
  - Few accounting records
  - Limited accountability

The advantages are those factors that encourage the use of the computing facility by the users. Since the cost of running the center appears as a corporate expense, much like a utility, the user can use any amount of the resources of the center at no direct cost. This results in very low administrative overhead and requires the keeping of relatively few accounting records by the DCM. The records that are kept reflect resource usage in very general terms and are used by the DCM to formulate next year's budget in equally general terms.

While the allocation method does not *require* a great deal of record keeping, it is good policy for the DCM to keep fairly detailed usage records. There is a tendency for an installation to move from the allocation method to the chargeback method over some amount of time (Nolan, 1979). When this transition occurs, the records that have been kept during the allocation era will serve as the basis for constructing chargeback algorithms.

The disadvantages of the allocation method include the lack of a formal requirement for keeping accounting records and the limited accountability for the use of data center resources since the costs are not distributed to specific application areas. Since there is limited accountability on the part of the users, they may expend little effort in planning and in communicating their plans for computer usage. This can leave the DCM in the position of having to second-guess the intentions of the users or to provide excessive capacity for sudden, unexpected demands.

THE CHARGEBACK METHOD OF ACCOUNTING

The chargeback method of accounting for data center services is based on the notion of directly charging, on some kind of cost per unit, those who use the resources of the center. This method ostensibly gives tighter control over the use of the center. There are several advantages and disadvantages to the chargeback method:

- Advantages:
  - Money appears on user budget
  - Users help justify expenditures
  - Users help data center to get funds
  - Data center must "earn" money from users

- Disadvantage:
  - Incurs significant administrative overhead

The primary disadvantage of the chargeback system lies in the need to keep and monitor large volumes of operating statistics in order to establish and maintain the system and to respond to frequent user inquiries concerning the amount of money being charged to them. With the disappearance of the "free good" that the users enjoyed under the allocation method of accounting, the users will begin to question the charges that they receive for data center services. This is especially true during the early stages of installing a chargeback system while the users are becoming accustomed to it.

If the advantages of the chargeback system seem to outweigh the disadvantages, it is not necessarily true that the chargeback system should be installed at every installation. To be successful, the chargeback theory must be understood thoroughly by the users, management, and those running the data center. In the early stages of an installation's development in data processing, the allocation method may be better suited than the chargeback system, since the allocation system will encourage the use of the computer center whereas the costs charged back to the user may inhibit the development of computer-based applications. Further, there is significant overhead associated with chargeback systems, and they do require data center resources to monitor and account for the resulting charges. (It must be noted that the "money" in these cases is generally an internal transfer of funds rather than the hard dollars that would be generated by selling the data center services to outside parties.)

To illustrate how the chargeback system works, let us compare sample budgets for the data center and for a user department:

User Budget		Data Center Budget	
Income	Expense	Income	Expense
•	•	•	•
•	$1,000 Data center	$1,000	$ 500 Hardware
•	•	•	350 Salary
•	•	•	150 Other
•	•	•	•
	_____	_____	_____
	$1,000	$1,000	$1,000

Assuming that the data center is operating as a cost center rather than a profit center, the chargeback algorithm will be structured to recover the cost of providing the data center resources. (Lest anyone mistakenly think that, because the cost of running the data center is recovered from the users, it costs the corporation nothing to have the data center, note that in the above example there are two expense totals offset by one income total. Thus, it still ends up costing the corporation $1,000 to operate this data center.)

Under this system, a kind of check-and-balance equilibrium exists between the amount charged to the users and the amount that users are willing to justify on their budgets for obtaining the services. In other words, the data center must "earn" the money set aside on the user's budget for data processing, since the user is theoretically free to spend this money with the internal data center or could spend the money with another facility to obtain the same or better service. In practice, the user manager may be constrained by corporate policy and required to do the data processing on internal facilities, but the visibility of the data center expense on the user's budget serves to keep the DCM in line as far as service levels and cost of services is concerned. The chargeback system brings into sharp focus the notion of the competitive alternatives available to users, and these, in turn, provide a direct incentive to the DCM to do the most efficient, effective job possible with the given resources.

APPLYING THIS INFORMATION TO YOUR DATA CENTER

1. Are you able to anticipate significant deviations between actual and budgeted operation expenses?

2. Does your data center use the allocation method or the chargeback method to account for data center services?

3. Do the users understand what the data center services cost them?

4. Do the users feel they get fair value for the data center costs?

SUMMARY

The following activities summarize the recommendations presented in this chapter:

- Set up an exception reporting system to help you manage expenses in the data center. Be able to explain significant deviations from budgeted expense amounts.

- If your installation uses the allocation method of accounting for data center costs, you should still be able to identify the costs of serving each of your major users (based on people, hardware, and software resources needed for the particular application area).

- If you use a chargeback method, be able to explain the cost components to your users.

17

Pricing Data Center Services

Operating the data center with a chargeback system requires that the elements of the chargeback mechanism and the pricing of these elements be clearly understood. In this chapter, the elements will be identified, discussed, and put into the context of setting rates and establishing chargeback algorithms for data center services.

THINKING IN TERMS OF APPLICATION RATES

The *application rate* is a means of expressing data center costs in terms that the user can understand—namely, in terms of the cost of the application being run. Rather than billing for data center services in terms of data processing technical measurements (such as in numbers of input/output starts or in memory increments), you should use these technical measurements as a basis for building up an application rate. Thus, the user is able to deal with data center costs on a per-unit basis where the units are familiar to the user, in such terms as "cost per invoice produced" or "cost per report copy." The algorithms you develop must support the billing units that are communicated to the users.

SETTING RATES

The basic expense elements that go to make up a chargeback system are: hardware, software, labor, supplies, overhead, and miscellaneous other expenses. You should take the following steps in order to set up a chargeback system:

1. Classify data center expense items into the categories noted above.

2. Select units of measure for each of the items.

3. Calculate the total usage of each of the items over a given time period.

4. Determine the respective cost for each item over a given time period.

5. Calculate a rate per unit of usage for each item.

6. Establish an application charge unit based on the resource mix used for a given volume of application work.

The following sections provide a closer look at this process.

Categorizing and Measuring Data Center Expenses

Figure 17.1 lists typical data center expense categories. These are, for the most part, self-explanatory; the "other" category could include such items as subscription fees and education costs.

Next, the unit of measure for each item should be selected. Typical units for hardware include the increments of memory used, amount of central processor cycles used, number of tape drives used, amount of disk space used, number of cards read or punched, and number of lines printed. Labor is usually measured in terms of the cost per hour used, although in cases such as the console operator, the labor cost may be expressed as a part of the cost of using the machine since it is difficult to keep track of exactly how much of the operator's time is used on a specific task.

Software utility costs (such as compilers, sorts, and library routines) are generally expressed in terms of the specific cost per year for providing the resource. While this assumes equal usage of the software by all who use the data center, it is a practical approach since the effort needed to identify usage more specifically would outweigh the benefit of knowing the exact level of usage.

Supplies such as continuous form paper are measured in terms of the number of pages used and are charged directly to those who consume this resource. This has the beneficial effect of reducing or eliminating high-cost, custom-printed continuous forms for all but the most necessary circumstances. In similar fashion, the cost of magnetic tapes is charged directly to the application that uses the tapes.

Charging by Application

When all of the resource elements have been identified, their usage and units of measure determined, the cost for that usage calculated, and a rate per unit established, you can then multiply the rate per unit times the number of units used for a given application to obtain an application cost for a specific volume of work. *It is this application cost that should be used when you discuss data center costs with users, and it is this cost that should be used to bill services to the users on a periodic basis.*

To repeat, the DCM must determine the unit cost of each resource item (labor, processor cycles, disk space) and must understand the proportionate distribution of the resources within the application.

Hardware	Software	Labor	Supplies	Overhead	Other
Central processor	Operating system	Operators	Paper	Data center manager	Subscription fees
Tape drives	Compilers	Tape library	Tapes	Quality control	Education costs
Disk drives	Sorts/utilities	Control clerk	Disks		
Control devices	Tape management	Data entry	Expendables		
Reader/printer	Line control	Dispatch			
Communications controller	Performance monitor				
Modems					
Terminals					
Performance monitor					

FIGURE 17.1.   *Data Center Expense Categories*

The application cost, therefore, is built up from a series of unit costs, and the application cost is the item that is relayed to the user. The user must be advised that the application cost will, of course, vary depending upon the volume of work processed.

Using the application cost not only expresses resource utilization in terms that the user understands but it also shows the data center's activities and expenses in relationship to the traditional business units of the organization. For example, billing the sales department at the rate of $400 for every 1,000 new orders entered and $650 for every 1,000 invoices produced puts the issue of charging for services in everyday terms that are understood by the user. This contrasts with data center rates that are expressed in data processing terms such as $0.0001 per 1,000 disk accesses plus $15 for every 1,000 bytes of memory used.

Deriving an application cost requires more work from the DCM, but it makes dealing with users much easier. Users who do not understand what they are paying for are likely to lose interest in the chargeback system yet continue to be frustrated until this frustration finally begins to undermine good user/data center relations.

The following is an example of a chargeback algorithm that makes sense to the user:

- *Assumptions:* Three user terminals are on-line eight hours per day for the accounts receivable application. The application uses thirty-seven dollars' worth of CPU resources and thirteen dollars' worth of operator and network controller time to support the on-line functions and the batch processing associated with producing 140 invoices per day. These costs are a combination of CPU cycles and memory used (in the case of the $37) and personnel salaries and benefits (in the case of the $13). Further, there are 320 operating hours in the data center each month (derived by multiplying sixteen hours per day times twenty days per month) for the CPU and 160 on-line hours per month (eight hours times twenty days).

- The daily costs, therefore, are:
  1. CPU & operating personnel $ 50.00
  2. Disk storage   12.50

$$\frac{(\$5,000 \text{ month}) (5 \text{ percent usage})}{(20 \text{ days per month})}$$

3. Communications controller   10.00
   ($1,600 month) (12.5 percent usage)
         (20 days per month)
4. Terminals   12.00
   ($80 month) (3 terminals)
         (20 days per month)
5. Data center overhead
   • Utilities, supplies   38.00
     ($4.75) (8 hours)
   • Management & administration   10.85
     ($5,208 per month) (8 hours)
         (12 tasks) (320 hours)

                              Total $133.35
                        (Say $140 per day)

$$\frac{\$133.35}{140 \text{ invoice}} = \$0.95 \text{ per invoice}$$

Cost/ Invoice	Volume	Cost	Cost Variance
$0.95	154	$146.30	− 9.7%
0.95	140	133.00	0%
0.95	126	119.70	10.2%

With the estimated cost of $133.35 for processing 140 invoices per day, you may want to quote a rate of $1.00 per invoice, since this gives about a 5 percent cost leeway over the $133.35 figure. Even if the volume varied by 10 percent, this cost estimate would be reasonably safe because the CPU resource is the only factor that will be immediately affected by deviations in the invoice volumes. (Notice that all the other factors are fairly "fixed"—at least in the short term.) Thus, the user could be quoted a cost estimate of $1.00 per invoice for a daily invoice volume of 126 to 154 invoices (which is plus or minus 10 percent from the 140-invoice volume used to develop the cost estimate).

DEVELOPING THE CHARGEBACK ALGORITHM

A chargeback algorithm should have the following characteristics:

- Revenue must equal expense plus profit.
- The results are reproducible.
- The algorithm reflects comparative unit costs.
- The algorithm recognizes competitive alternatives.

The revenues generated by the chargeback system should meet the expenses of the data center plus any profit factor that the center is expected to generate. Centers that are operated as cost centers rather than profit centers are, by charter, expected to generate no profit and, therefore, the algorithm should be constructed so as to recover just the cost of running the data center. This notion underscores the need for a clear understanding among management, users, and the data center—there should be no mistake as to the "mission" of the center. If the center is established as a cost center, nobody should complain later that the center doesn't "pay its way" or contribute to the earnings of the company. Conversely, if the center is chartered as a profit center, users should not be surprised that the center's services are "marked up" in order to generate a profit.

The algorithm that is set up should yield reproducible costs when running the same workload through the same application multiple times. This is particularly important in a multiprogramming environment. The user should expect similar billings for running a given volume of work against a given application; billing should not be concerned with any other activity that may or may not be taking place in the computing environment at the time the work is being run. To accomplish this, use available data from the running of previous jobs in the data center, and separate the data into two parts: the data used to structure the algorithm and the data used to test the algorithm. Set up initial rates by examining relationships among the cost elements in the data center. For instance, in our earlier example of a chargeback algorithm, historical costs were used to identify the relative costs of the various elements (disk, communications controller, overhead).

After these tentative rates have been established, the algorithm should be tested using the data that were set aside for this purpose. Doing the algorithm exercise in these two steps avoids the pitfall of using one set of data to establish the rates, then using these same data to test the rates, which is sort of like saying, "If a equals b, then b equals a."

Once the chargeback mechanism has been checked out and put into use, you must monitor the charges that are generated (by reviewing application volumes, resource utilization, and resource costs) while, at the same time, being very careful about changing the algorithm. If the aggregate amount of money recovered from the chargeback system is substantially over or under the cost of running the data center, the algorithm should be changed. You must then review how the costs relate to each other, how the algorithm was constructed, look for discrepancies between the actual costs and the algorithm, adjust the algorithm, test it, and then inform the users of the new rates.

Recall that the essence of the chargeback system is to have the users budget and be charged for the data center resources that they use. The budgeting will be done based on the expected rates published by the DCM; therefore, the rates should be changed only with great care and after proper deliberation. *Make sure that the respective components of the chargeback algorithm bear a reasonable relationship to the costs of providing those resources. If the central processor costs more than the card reader, for example, it should cost relatively more to use one unit of processor resource than to use one unit of reader resource.*

Finally, the chargeback algorithm should recognize the presence of competitive alternatives to the data center. If your data center's charges exceed the cost of obtaining the same type of resources from another source, you will probably find that your management and users seriously question the operation of the data center, to say the least. As we pointed out in Chapter Sixteen, the use of a chargeback system gives the users the alternative of spending the data processing money in their budget at the internal data center or at another data center. Again, this check-and-balance feature of the chargeback system should ensure that you, as DCM, continually keep an eye on the cost of providing services to users and strive to bring the company the best data center capability at the lowest cost.

APPLYING THIS INFORMATION TO YOUR DATA CENTER

1. When were your data center prices last reviewed?

2. If a chargeback algorithm is used, are the unit prices related to the overall cost of these resources?

3. Is the chargeback algorithm able to reproduce costs for the same level of work processed through the same application?

SUMMARY

Set your data center's rates based on technical measurements, but express them in terms of application units, which make data center charges easier for users to understand.

Recall that a chargeback algorithm must have the following characteristics:

- Revenue must equal expense plus profit.

- Results are reproducible.

- Reflects accurate unit cost relationships.

- Recognizes presence of competitive alternatives.

Set rates that allow some variance in your costs and in the user's workload volumes so that you don't have to reset the rates for the slightest variations in these factors. Change the rate structure only after careful analysis, and thoroughly test the revised algorithm before putting it to use.

18

Analyzing the Data Center's Major Expenditures

The ability to put together a tight, well-reasoned cost/benefit analysis of existing or proposed environments is a necessary skill for the DCM. This is especially true when major expenditures, such as equipment acquisitions, are under consideration. In this chapter, we discuss two basic analysis methods and provide a comparison of alternative ways of looking at an expenditure.

In many companies, detailed financial analyses and presentations are the responsibility of people such as the controller or the financial vice-president rather than of the DCM. Nonetheless, you need at least a passing understanding of the type of analysis that is being performed, since the results of these analyses can have a profound effect on the directions that are or are not taken in the data center.

USING THE PAYBACK PERIOD TO EVALUATE AN EXPENDITURE

A relatively straightforward method of evaluating projects is to determine the payback period for the project or for various alternatives to the same project. The payback period is the length of time necessary for the sum of the annual net cash inflow to equal the initial investment. Stated in terms of a formula, this becomes:

$$C = (I_1 + I_2 \ldots + I_n)$$
where
C = Initial cost
I = Net inflow per year
n = Number of time periods

The payback approach is a relatively quick method for getting a rough idea as to the viability of a project, and it is often used to determine whether a project will produce a quick return on the investment. It is well suited for high technology projects since this type of analysis typically does not deal with projections beyond two or three years.

There are, however, several drawbacks to the payback method. It does not take into account the timing of the income flow and, thus, it ignores the time value of money. It does not consider any income beyond the payback period; therefore it favors projects with high early returns even though those returns may decrease sharply after the payback period. Finally, this method does not consider differences in the level of investment for given projects. For instance, an outlay of $120,000 for a project with annual inflows of $40,000 has a payback period of three years while a project with an initial cost of $12,000 with inflows of $4,000/year also has a three-year payback period. The investment level between these two projects is substantially different.

The following is an example of the payback approach. Suppose that two equipment options are being considered, each with a payback period of three years, and that they have the following characteristics:

Item	Option A	Option B
Cost	$10,000	$12,000
Inflow/year	$ 2,500	$ 4,000
Payback period	3 years	3 years
Unrecovered amount	$ 2,500	$ 0

In this case, Option B appears to be the better choice since it will "pay for itself" within the three-year period. While Option A has a lower initial cost, the smaller inflow amount leaves an unrecovered amount at the end of the third year, thus making this option less attractive.

Consider another set of alternatives with a three-year payback period:

Item	Option M	Option N
Cost	$10,000	$10,000
Inflow: Year 1	2,000	3,000
Year 2	4,000	3,000
Year 3	4,000	3,000
Year 4	3,000	5,000
Unrecovered amount after third year	0	1,000
Total inflow after fourth year	13,000	14,000

In this example, Option M is more attractive in the three-year time frame, but Option N would be relatively better over a four-year period when one looks strictly at the total income flow with no regard for the time value of money. If a three-year hurdle has been established for data center capital expenditures, Option M would be chosen on the basis of the payback period approach.

In these examples, note that the cost and inflow items have been presented as lump sums of money. In practice, a great deal of effort may have to go into deriving these numbers. The initial cost is comprised of expenses such as equipment, site preparation, one-time costs for cutover, and the like. Similarly, arriving at the net inflow number can require the aggregation of several items such as labor cost, other operating expenses, and depreciation expense, offset by the benefits that result from obtaining the equipment.

EVALUATING AN EXPENDITURE ON NET PRESENT VALUE

The net present value (NPV) method of evaluating expenditures yields different and, perhaps, more valuable information than the payback period method. The NPV approach takes into account the time value of money—that is, this method puts into perspective the fact that differences in the timing of either spending or receiving given funds results in differences in the overall present value for a given outlay. The NPV calculation uses the following formula:

$$NPV = C_0/(1+r)^0 + C_1/(1+r)^1$$
$$\ldots + C_n/(1+r)^n$$

where

NPV = Net present value
C = Cost per time period
r = Rate of the cost of capital
n = Number of time periods

To use this formula, algebraically add the total cost for a given time period. This becomes the variable C in the formula. Year "0" is the point at which the project begins; therefore it is the point when the initial outlay is made. This amount, C_0, will be divided by $(1+r)^0$. Subsequent values for C_1, C_2, and so on reflect the net cash flow for time periods 1 through n (usually a time period is one year for these purposes). These values of C are divided, respectively, by $(1+r)^1$, $(1+r)^2, \ldots (1+r)^n$. In the examples in this chapter, a cost of capital rate of 15 percent is used, giving $(1+r)$ values of 1.15, 1.3225, 1.5209, and 1.7490 for years 1 through 4 respectively.

This method is based on the notion that a dollar available today is worth more than a dollar available tomorrow. Put another way, a dollar available today can be invested and can earn money; a dollar that is not available until some future time cannot be put to work until that time. In the meantime, the opportunity to put that dollar to work has been lost. The term *opportunity cost* is often used to describe those earnings that have been lost because the money was not available to invest until a later time period.

Figure 18.1 shows a net present value analysis using the data in Options M and N from the previous section. At the end of Year 3 (the target payback period), Option M appears better because it has a smaller negative cumulative cash flow. By the end of Year 4, Option N looks preferable for the same reason. (Note, however, that there is only a $600 difference in the cumulative discounted cash flow compared to the $1,000 difference in inflow under the straight payback analysis, due to the time value of money for these flows.)

COMPARING ALTERNATIVES USING NET PRESENT VALUE

The methods described above are very useful for evaluating (1) the attractiveness of a specific expenditure, (2) alternative courses of action for the same expenditure, or (3) multiple capital outlays. Either of these evaluation methods provides a means for normalizing seemingly dissimilar pieces of information. Figure 18.2 illustrates this point.

In this example, we use the net present value method to outline three options for solving the same application problem. Note that the initial costs, annual maintenance costs, and operating costs vary from one option to another. The benefit stream is the same for all options. The net present value method helps you to look at these options from a common perspective.

At the end of Year 2, Option C has not paid back the initial investment, while the cumulative streams for Options A and B have gone from negative to positive.

Looking at the data for the end of the four-year period, Option A now has the greatest cumulative discounted net (+36,239). Option C has the smallest cumulative discounted net (+25,626).

As we mentioned before, a good deal of work is involved in de-

Item	Year 0	Year 1	Year 2	Year 3	Year 4
Discount factor—15%	1.0000	1.1500	1.3225	1.5209	1.7490
Option M					
Initial cost	$−10,000				
Inflow	0	2,000	4,000	4,000	3,000
Annual net flow	−10,000	2,000	4,000	4,000	3,000
Discounted net flow	−10,000	1,739	3,025	2,630	1,715
Cumulative discounted net	−10,000	−8,261	−5,236	−2,606	−891
Option N					
Initial cost	$−10,000				
Inflow	0	3,000	3,000	3,000	5,000
Annual net flow	−10,000	3,000	3,000	3,000	5,000
Discounted net flow	−10,000	2,609	2,268	1,973	2,859
Cumulative discounted net	−10,000	−7,391	−5,123	−3,150	−291

FIGURE 18.1.   Sample Net Present Value Analysis

riving seemingly simple numbers such as initial cost, operating cost, and benefits. For the purpose of these examples, the following assumptions are made: *initial cost* is comprised of equipment cost, site preparation cost, and training cost; *annual maintenance* is based on vendor information and the expectation that this cost will rise in future years; *operating costs* are based on expected pro-rata labor costs from various departments; *benefits* are made up of an anticipated lower cost of producing the product or service, and the intangible benefit of improved customer service. The impact of this latter benefit is expected to be greatest in the first two years; therefore, the value of the benefit is shown as decreasing in later years.

Which of these options should be selected? The answer is not inherent in the data shown in the example. The selection will depend somewhat on the strategy being employed by the organization regarding data center expenditures. Looking at the near term (that is, two years), Option B is favorable because it has the smallest initial cost ($77,000) and has the best cumulative discounted net after two years ($4,076). Looking at the four-year projection, Options A and B appear better than Option C in terms of cumulative discounted net, even though Option C has the strongest annual net flow in years 4 and 5.

Item	Year 0	Year 1	Year 2	Year 3	Year 4
Discount factor—15%	1.0000	1.1500	1.3225	1.5209	1.7490
Option A					
Initial cost	$−80,000				
Annual maintenance cost	0	−7,000	−7,490	−8,015	−8,575
Operating cost	0	−1,500	−1,500	−1,500	−1,500
Benefits	0	+59,400	+60,300	+36,270	+37,340
Annual net flow	−80,000	+50,900	+51,310	+26,755	+27,265
Discounted net	−80,000	+44,260	+38,798	+17,592	+15,589
Cumulative discounted net	−80,000	−35,740	+3,058	+20,650	+36,239
Option B					
Initial cost	$−77,000				
Annual maintenance cost	0	−8,000	−8,800	−9,680	−10,650
Operating cost	0	−1,575	−1,575	−1,575	−1,575
Benefits	0	+59,400	+60,300	+36,270	+37,340
Annual net flow	−77,000	+49,825	+49,925	+25,015	+25,115
Discounted net	−77,000	+43,326	+37,750	+16,447	+14,360
Cumulative discounted net	−77,000	−33,674	+4,076	+20,523	+34,883
Option C					
Initial cost	$−96,000				
Annual maintenance cost	0	−10,000	−5,000	−5,000	0
Operating cost	0	−1,770	−1,770	−1,770	−1,770
Benefits	0	+59,400	+60,300	+36,270	+37,340
Annual net flow	−96,000	+47,630	+53,530	+29,500	+35,570
Discounted net	−96,000	+41,417	+40,476	+19,396	+20,337
Cumulative discounted net	−96,000	−54,583	−14,107	+5,289	+25,626

FIGURE 18.2.   Net Present Value Worksheet

If the company is looking at a short-term (say two-year) situation, Option B would be a good choice; after two years, that equipment might be replaced. On the other hand, if the organization is hoping to keep the equipment for five years, Option A appears to be the best choice. Again, the selection will depend on a number of factors, but these analysis methods enable one to put many variables into a common perspective, a perspective that allows the options to be evaluated using criteria recognized by every level of business management.

APPLYING THIS INFORMATION TO YOUR DATA CENTER

1. Has a payback period been calculated for data center expenditures?

2. Has a net present value calculation been made for data center expenditures?

3. Are you able to present a solid business case for major capital outlays in the data center?

4. What intangible benefits enter into the decision?
   Examples: A vendor's service reputation, or the background and training of your personnel on a particular vendor's equipment

SUMMARY

As DCM, you should develop your ability to present a well-reasoned cost/benefit analysis for data center projects. The payback approach and the net present value method are two ways of evaluating and presenting financial data for projects, and they can also be used to compare alternatives.

V

Living With Change

19

Developing Procedures for Security and Disaster Planning

The security of data processing resources is an issue that is receiving grudging recognition at all levels of an organization. The advent of several notorious breaches of security surrounding data resources has highlighted the need for sound security programs and given the DCM an important leverage point in the move to institute a good security program. This chapter deals with the issues that must be considered in organizing and putting into practice security plans and disaster recovery plans.

DEFINING THE FUNDAMENTAL PRINCIPLES OF SECURITY

At its core, a data security program is a classic example of risk assessment, postulation of deterrent measures, costing out the deterrent measures, and weighing the benefit of the deterrent against its cost. Two factors, however, immediately change the simple model into an extremely complex model: (1) the pervasiveness of the risks and (2) the interactions among the various risks.

The risks with which you must deal are dispersed across the organization. They can be classified in terms of physical, logical, and human risks. As such, these risks are found throughout the organization within individual, departmental, divisional, and top management areas. The dispersal of the problem has been accelerated with the advent of distributed computing, smaller physical computing devices, more people making use of computers, and increased use of data base technology.

The interactions among various parts of the data resources subjected to the security measures are constantly becoming more complex and thus magnifying the security problem. Yet the security measures themselves often discourage providing computing resources to more people within the organization. These conflicts must be resolved without abandoning either the need to expand data resources or the need to secure the data. For example, each new terminal user on a system causes a new set of interactions. The security program must address the issues of the physical security of the terminal, the accessibility of data through the terminal, and the segregation of those functions that should be performed via the new terminal from those functions that should not be accessible.

The security program that is implemented must be based on the following fundamental principles:

- Identify and reduce risks

- Recognize limits of measures

- Recognize limits of program

- Balance security measure against security exposure

- Allow monitoring

- Provide for periodic measuring

- Address the total computer resource mix

Identifying Risks and Recognizing Limits

Identifying and reducing risks involves a thorough study of the data resource environment, followed by the development of an action plan and the implementation of that plan to actually reduce the risks. Note that throughout this discussion, the phrase *data resource environment* is used rather than the term *data center* or something similar. This is done intentionally in recognition of the fact that the data resources (and the accompanying security problems) go beyond the bounds of the data center and are present throughout the organization.

Your first step in developing a security program is to review the physical and logical aspects of each data resource in order to identify potential risk areas. The people using these resources must be considered as part of the risk identification. The actions taken to reduce or eliminate the risks should have a material impact on reducing the risks; the security plan should not merely result in a series of token actions that do nothing to reduce the exposure of the organization.

The second step in developing a security program is to recognize the limits of the actions or measures taken within the program. A comprehensive security program will involve many actions, measures, and countermeasures, and each of these will have its own limitations. You must recognize these limits in order to avoid total dependence upon one or two security measures. *Due to the wide range of possible security exposures, you must take a wide range of protective measures if you are to achieve a solid security program.*

Since a broad combination of measures must be instituted to protect the organization, you should also recognize that every program, taken as a whole, has limitations. It is axiomatic that no amount of protective measures will deter an irrational person from at least attempting to compromise the system. This limitation must be admitted and the security system constructed so as to deter *rational* people from attempting to encroach on the system. This is an important limitation: it indicates that there is an upper bound beyond which additional measures will not "buy" a greater level of protection, and it indicates that all security systems have an inherent weakness. You must make this inherent weakness clear to management—that no amount of expenditure will absolutely protect the installation from intrusion. The key, therefore, to implementing a security program lies in the conscientious placement of deterrents that, taken together, significantly reduce the risk to the organization given a rational set of circumstances.

Balancing Security Measures Against Security Exposure

Balancing the security exposure that exists against the measures taken to overcome the exposure is, in some ways, an extension of performing a cost/benefit analysis. It goes beyond such an analysis, however, in the sense that it calls for putting the money and the deterrent measures where they will provide the most benefit. Put another way, if the physical aspects of the data resource, for instance, are causing relatively little exposure when compared to the logical vulnerability, it makes more sense to apply deterrent measures that reduce the logical exposure rather than instituting another physical deterrent. For example, you should put your security efforts into tightening up password control rather than put yet another lock on the data center door.

A balance must also be achieved within each of the measures. The "scale" of the deterrent should match the scale of the exposure. For example, encryption of data may, eventually, be a desirable measure to put into effect at the installation, but if the immediate problem is one of logically separating application data, the situation calls for a remedy (such as logical access control) that will cure the data encroachment problem.

Monitoring the Program and Measuring Its Effectiveness

A good security program allows for monitoring of the program and provides for periodic measuring of the effectiveness of the program. In other words, a security system must be continually observed, nurtured, corrected, adjusted, tested, and measured. You should periodically look at various parts of the total system in order to identify the weakest link and take steps to correct that weakness.

Security measures should alert the proper parties when an attempt has been made to compromise the system. If the system has been operating for some period of time and none of these alerts has been signaled, do not assume that all is well. *Whether or not the alerts materialize, those who monitor the system should attempt periodically to compromise the system, then observe and measure the effectiveness of the system.* These "dry runs" against the data resource will involve a combination of physical and logical techniques. Each attempt should be recorded or reported by the system. A security review should then evaluate the exposure and, again, take measures to reduce or eliminate the risk.

Securing the Total Computer Resource

All aspects of the total computer resource must be taken into account in an installation security program—that is, the hardware, software, and people that constitute the data resource should all be subjected to the risk identification and should be affected by the security measures instituted by the organization. The security program, therefore, will tend to focus on each of the three major elements in the data resource mix in turn. For example, security on the hardware may be relatively strong at one point, while protection of the software and people aspects of the mix may be lagging behind. The next security measure that is implemented should reduce the risk in either the software or people area. This, in turn, may put the hardware part of the mix in the least secure position, causing yet another evaluation of the risks and assets.

This evaluation process is an unending task since some part of the data resource is constantly changing. People are coming and going from the organization—in the data center, the systems and programming area, and in the user area. Hardware and software components are changing or the way in which they are used is changing. Those charged with the security of the data resource must always be aware of these changes and be prepared to adjust the security program to adapt to the changes.

PLOTTING A GENERAL SECURITY PROGRAM

An installation's security program starts with top management involvement. *There must be management recognition that security is an important issue to the organization and a commitment by management to endorse a security program. The program must be viewed as and understood to be an organizational program, not just a data processing or a data center program.* As we have stated, the issues with which a security program is concerned pervade the organization and the measures that are taken to overcome the security risk have an impact on the entire organization.

Once you have obtained top management's assent to undertake a security program, the next step is to conduct a methodical inventory of the data resource assets and their associated security measures. This step should take into consideration all types of assets: hardware, software, data, people, and physical facilities. These general groupings can be further broken down into sublevels of assets. The hardware, for instance, should be identified by its specific parts, such as central processors, storage units, communications gear, modems, terminals, and the like.

Software should be itemized in terms of operating system software, utility or support software, and applications programs. Data should be identified by its use, frequency of updating, frequency of access, and the area responsible for its contents. The people of the organization should be classified by their home department and by their position in the organization; this breakdown, for example, might indicate clerical personnel, support personnel, first-level management, upper-level management, top management, and outside personnel. Physical facilities should be identified by name, type of function, and location.

The initial identification of assets provides the framework for the balance of the security review. *Next, each asset must be thoroughly examined for any security risks that are associated with it.* The basic types of risks that you should consider are: fraud, sabotage, theft, physical destruction, and honest mistakes. The hardware assets, for example, are vulnerable to sabotage, theft, and physical destruction.

For each asset, the possible risks must be listed, along with an assessment of the likelihood that the risk will become an actual problem. Two aspects of the security problem should be considered: first, consider the possibility of an event occurring that would present a risk to the asset, and, second, determine whether or not the event will be detected. *Take particular care in assessing the risks associated with hardware that is located outside of the actual data center.* This includes terminals in user areas and satellite processing units that may be located in data processing subcenters.

The software is vulnerable to fraud, sabotage, theft, physical destruction, and honest mistakes. Of these, physical destruction would be accompanied by some type of hardware destruction, but the other types of risks are particularly insidious in that their occurrence may go undetected for a long time. Again, the risk assessment should determine the possibilities of these threats to the software asset actually materializing, then identify ways in which the event can be monitored.

The data resource is the most underestimated resource in many organizations. Data processing has slowly but surely found its way into many parts of the organization, but many people in the organization do not realize how dependent their operation is on the data that have come under the custody of the data processing group. Many organizations labor under the false impression that, if need be, they could revert to a manual way of doing their work; they do not recognize the substantial commitment that they have made to the computerized applications. Those organizations that do recognize their dependence on the computer often do not recognize the sorry state of their company's security program. The data resource is subject to attack by fraud, sabotage, theft, physical destruction, and honest mistakes. Like the software, all but the physical destruction can take place easily with no outward signs.

Many companies correctly note that people are an important asset to the operation, but they do not consider the people as a possible security threat. People are vulnerable to all of the basic types of security risks: fraud, sabotage, theft, physical harm, and honest mistakes. In addition, people are vulnerable to a variation on these risks—namely, collusion. *The possibility that people within the organization can work together or with people outside of the organization to compromise the assets must be taken into account as part of the security assessment.*

The physical facilities involved with the data resource are subject mainly to physical destruction. The security analysis should be sure to identify all possible physical facilities since, with the proliferation of computing power and activity, some facilities may easily be overlooked.

After you have inventoried the data resource assets and evaluated their relative exposure to risks, you can assemble a composite security picture for the installation. The level of risk should be roughly categorized as to high, medium, and low exposure. The corrective action needed to reduce or eliminate the risk should be proposed and the cost of these corrective actions estimated.

You now have a framework for putting the security plan into action. The composite picture, the risk ratings, and the costs for reducing the risk level can be presented to management for their review and approval. This step is important; in this way, you place the security picture before management for action. Those parts of the risk reduction program that are approved become a set of objectives that the task force concerned with data resource security and you, as DCM, can work toward achieving. Those parts of the program that are not approved have been deemed by management to be of less importance than other issues. By not approving parts of the security program, management is signaling that they are willing to tolerate and live with the risks and exposures associated with certain data assets.

This general security program provides a background for the next section, which offers suggestions for implementing and maintaining a security program.

COMPILING THE SECURITY CHECKLIST

There are an extensive number of items that should be considered during a security evaluation and on a day-to-day basis after a security program has been put into effect. Figure 19.1 classifies some of these items in terms of physical, logical, and personnel aspects of security. *These are procedures that you should incorporate in your security program.*

Instituting and maintaining a data resource security program is difficult and requires continual vigilance. Few, if any, data center managers are totally satisfied with their security program. For one thing, management rarely approves the complete security program the first time it is presented, especially if the installation has not had any security problems. Thus, the implementation of the program is an incremental process, with parts being added to the picture as time goes by, always with the hope that the data resource is not compromised in the meantime. Secondly, the risk/exposure mix is continually changing, and thus a security program almost constantly needs adjustment. A periodic review of the program is the only solution to this problem.

Most DCMs today recognize the need for a thorough security program. Yet a security program is one of those tasks that tend to re-

Securing Physical Assets

- Minimize the number of entrances to the data center.
- Emergency exits should have alarms to indicate unauthorized use.
- Reduce the amount of traffic through the data center (doors can be kept locked, for example).
- Stop people from outside the data center from penetrating data center areas.
- Install magnetic strips on glass and doors to the data center.
- Institute strict accountability procedures (such as sign-out sheets or logs) for movement, copying, and any removal of data and files.
- Conduct unannounced inspections and inventories of data libraries and sensitive forms.
- Require data center personnel to carry and use identification cards.

Securing Logical Assets

- Follow good audit procedures for post-run control and check-out. Verify file usage, record counts, dollar totals, and transaction volumes.
- Review console logs for unauthorized usage.
- Monitor file and transaction volumes; follow-up on any significant changes in either.
- Require strict adherence to control procedures for changing programs and systems.
- Make user areas part of security program with on-going education and information that increases their awareness of security risks.
- Have all on-line applications use password and verification systems for access and use.
- Change passwords often, perhaps at irregular intervals.

Securing Personnel Assets

- Collect all identification cards and access authorization materials from people leaving company.
- Insist on immediate dismissal of personnel fired from sensitive positions in the user and data center areas, such as a tape librarian or computer operator.
- Be attuned to personal and financial problems (such as indebtedness) encountered by data center personnel.
- Rotate personnel assignments.

FIGURE 19.1.   *Security Checklist*

ceive low priority on the installation's list of "things to do"—until something happens. When data security is compromised, there is ample hand-wringing on every organizational level as well as concerted attempts to find a scapegoat for the lack of an adequate program. *It is in the DCM's best interest to make security an installation issue* before *the lack of it becomes an installation regret.*

PLANNING FOR DISASTER RECOVERY

Disaster recovery planning has a great deal in common with security programs, especially the relatively low priority that disaster planning receives until a disaster actually strikes the installation. As with security, it is in the DCM's best interest to develop and maintain a disaster recovery plan, even though developing the plan is tedious work and will receive little appreciation until the plan is put to use in an emergency.

A disaster recovery plan should describe what to do in the face of physical forces that can wreak havoc on the data center or on other components of the data resource. Sometimes these forces are manmade; sometimes they are natural events. The disasters are things like explosions, fires, tornadoes, floods, earthquakes, and hurricanes.

Three Concerns of Disaster Recovery

With any disaster, the primary concern is the safety of personnel. Secondary concerns are the security and integrity of data and equipment and the ability to resume operation. Consider these items one at a time.

The *safety of personnel* requires that regular educational sessions be held. *Fire and evacuation drills should be held periodically, at random times, and on an unannounced basis. People should be informed of the location of emergency equipment and exits, and they should be aware of emergency telephone numbers to be used if a disaster occurs. Battery-powered safety lights should be installed in the data center. Exits should be accessible, well marked, and usable without electric power. Many data centers have electrically operated doors; you should be able to open these doors manually if the power has been cut off. The location of emergency shut-off switches should be plainly marked and known to people in the data center.*

An action plan for *the security of data and equipment* following a disaster should be developed. Clearly, a disaster such as a fire or explosion in the immediate data center area leaves no time for an orderly shutdown of the facility, but other types of disasters frequently allow employees time to take several protective measures. Thus, the disaster plan should list what to do during a catastrophic disaster, such as a fire or explosion, and it should also spell out the steps to be taken during an orderly shutdown. Disasters such as floods and hurricanes usually provide enough advance warning so that at least some of the facility can be secured or equipment moved to a safer location. You must also recognize the need to cover the center in case you receive a "bogus" disaster threat, like the bomb threats that plagued offices and factories in the past. An installation is exposed to a security risk if it is evacuated hastily and no steps are taken to protect or secure the area.

The third concern of disaster recovery is the problem of *getting back in business* as quickly as possible. The amount of time needed to recover varies greatly depending on the type of disaster. It is reasonably safe to say that obtaining replacement hardware is not a great problem. Virtually every hardware vendor will respond impressively, even to the point of preempting other delivery commitments, in order to provide hardware following a disaster that knocks out a data center. Therefore, while provision for replacing the hardware is obviously an item to be included in the disaster recovery plan, there are other items that must be considered in the plan. The amount of money spent on providing alternate facilities and back-up equipment will largely be justified by the relative importance that data processing has within the organization. A less mature installation will spend less money on back-up than a more mature data center, since (1) the less mature installation will have fewer critical applications on the computer, (2) these applications will tend to be independent of each other rather than integrated, and (3) they are relatively easier to transport and put into production at another site than the applications from a more mature data processing installation.

Listing the Components for Disaster Recovery

Setting up a disaster recovery plan involves a step-by-step examination of all resources used by the data center, followed by a detailed plan for either replacing the resource or operating without it, at least in the short term:

1. Itemize the various hardware components, then indicate how each component will be replaced or what equipment will be used until the component can be replaced.

2. List the software components and indicate how they will be replaced or done without. Make sure you distinguish between operating software, such as operating systems and utilities, and application software, namely programs.

3. Data files should also be listed, along with the source of their replacement.

4. In determining the replacement procedure for applications, obtain a consensus from management as to which applications will receive priority when operating from temporary quarters following a disaster. It is not realistic to think that all applications will be operational immediately at the alternate site; it will take some time to organize and bring into production the key applications, and the alternate site may not have the capacity to handle the entire workload.

5. Make sure that all users understand the priorities that will be used to run applications in an interim mode. Some parts of applications, such as "nice-to-have" reports, may not be run, or lower-priority applications may not be run at all until the full facility can be reconstructed. These priorities must be based on the agreement of users, management, and the DCM; they should not be a unilateral decision on the part of the data center manager.

Using an Alternate Site During Recovery

The way in which the installation gets back into production at an alternate site will depend on the size of the installation and whether the organization has a single processing site or multiple locations. Three methods are typically used to provide alternate sites: mutual aid agreements, "empty shell" back-up sites, and "full floor" back-up sites.

The *mutual aid agreement* is an arrangement between two companies that they will help each other out if either of their data centers is damaged or out of business for prolonged periods of time. These can be formal agreements, but, quite often, they are informal. In either case, these arrangements may show good intentions, but they have some inherent problems. The other installation may not be able to make enough time available when the damaged center needs it. Understandably, a company will give priority to its own work before it releases data center time for another company to use. Therefore, one cannot depend on getting large blocks of time at the alternate site (reinforcing the idea that priorities must be set, in advance, as part of the disaster plan).

A second problem with mutual aid agreements is that the equipment configurations between the sites will probably be incompatible. The agreement usually sounds like a good idea when it is first set up, but the capacities, features, and models of equipment tend to change, and these changes are made without consulting the other company. As a result, when the back-up site is needed, these incompatibilities may mean that much of the work cannot be done.

The *"empty shell" back-up* method involves several companies pooling money in order to lease space that could serve as an alternate processing center for any one of the companies. The facility is equipped with sufficient air-conditioning and power to support a computer configuration, but the actual equipment is not brought in until it is needed. Thus, the "shell" of the data center exists, waiting for the equipment. This plan is basically a type of insurance policy in that the companies are spending money each month (perhaps in the area of $2,000 to $5,000 each) for protection against an event that they hope will not occur.

The *"full floor" back-up* method provides a physical site and compatible computing equipment at the site. As with the empty shell plan, several companies contribute to the cost of supporting the full floor facility. The cost is higher than the cost of the shell facility and will vary depending on the level of response desired. For example, if accessibility to the back-up site is wanted within twelve hours' notice, the cost will be higher than if accessibility is needed within twenty-four hours' notice. Often, a low-priority user (such as a service bureau) operates from the alternate site on most days but must relinquish the facility when one of the subscribing members gives notice of the need to use the site.

Whether mutual aid agreements, shell plans, or full floor plans are used for disaster recovery, special attention must be given to the communications and remote processing work done by the center.

These factors add special complications to the disaster recovery process since they are more difficult to relocate in a short period of time. Many companies disperse their risks in this area by placing reasonably compatible equipment in various physical locations of the company. With geographically separated equipment, if one center is disabled, the other centers can each absorb a part of the workload until the disabled center is fully functional again. If data processing has become an integral part of the company, then computer applications will be so essential to the functioning of the company that disbursing the risk is a sensible way of dealing with the problem. This approach is more costly than an approach like the mutual aid agreement because some redundant equipment and capacity will usually exist at each location, but the extra cost is justified in terms of keeping the business running.

The best way to recover data and programs following a disaster is to make use of the off-site back-up copies of data files and programs. The regular operating procedures should spell out the frequency of backing up files, the disposition of these files, and the method for cycling the files back into the center. Conscientious verification that these procedures are being followed provides the best insurance against disaster and gives the DCM a solid method for getting back in business following a disaster.

The Importance of Total Involvement

The involvement of data center, user, and vendor personnel in disaster recovery is a key factor in the success of the recovery. The disaster plan should clearly spell out the duties of each person involved.

Hardware must be checked out, operating procedures set up, processing results verified, and interim delivery methods put into effect. The users must be brought into the picture to ensure their cooperation in submitting work and their understanding while the data center operates under less than ideal conditions. Vendor assistance is needed to bring the replacement hardware efficiently into production and to help make the makeshift configuration as productive as possible.

The disaster planning exercise contains little glamour, but the resulting plan is indispensable when a disaster strikes. Management support, user and vendor involvement, and hard work are necessary to put together a plan that will work when it is needed. The creation, review, and updating of a disaster recovery plan should receive a high priority on the data center manager's task list.

APPLYING THIS INFORMATION TO YOUR DATA CENTER

1. Are you satisfied with your installation's data security program?

2. What steps have been taken to identify security risks at your installation?

3. How has management been made aware of the installation's security risks?

4. Does the management of your company view the data base as a corporate resource?

5. Do you have a disaster recovery plan for the data center?

6. When was the plan last tested?

SUMMARY

The following is a checklist for security and disaster planning:

- Identify and classify risks in your data center into physical, logical, or personnel categories.

- Put together a balanced security plan, one that addresses the three categories above.

- Periodically attempt to compromise or "break" your security system. You should be detected by measures within the system.

- Outline the existing security program and identify its weak spots for top management; obtain their commitment for improving the security.

- Establish a thorough disaster recovery plan for your data center.

- Make management aware of the business risk involved in an incomplete disaster recovery plan.

20

Upgrading and Converting

Upgrading existing equipment and converting to new equipment occurs in the life of every installation. Some of the upgrades and changes are rather simple, as in the case of adding disk or tape storage units to an existing string of similar units. A somewhat more complicated change occurs when the existing equipment is replaced by a larger, but compatible, model within the same vendor "family." The planning that goes into these changes is simpler than, but no different from, the planning that must be done for a comprehensive change in configuration, vendor, and site. This chapter describes comprehensive change and how to manage it.

Whether the actual cutover is smooth or rough depends on the preliminary work that you do. This work consists of specifying clearly the equipment or software needed, conducting a disciplined search and evaluation, and having a thorough plan to accomplish the transition to the new equipment. Each of these steps is discussed in this chapter.

WRITING THE REQUEST FOR PROPOSAL

The request for proposal (RFP) begins with a thorough definition of the requirements that are to be satisfied by the new equipment or software. This definition of needs can draw on the input of quite a variety of people, depending on the scope of the change being considered. User managers and personnel, systems and programming, data center steering committee members, and various people from the data center can be involved. Your goal at this point is to document and weigh the needs of every area that may be affected by the change in processing capabilities.

Each discipline that is involved should list the processing requirements that it considers to be important and determine the relative importance of each item. When all of the lists have been made, the items are consolidated into one master list, which serves as the requirements list for the organization. In developing the master list, you will find that some items are redundant or overlap; these should be combined into one item. Other items may conflict, and these conflicts should be resolved among those making up the lists.

For simplicity, you can establish three categories for the requirements: mandatory, desirable, and optional. As the names indicate, the mandatory requirements are those that are absolutely necessary, the desirable items are those that would be nice to have but that are not absolutely necessary to fulfill the operational requirements, and the optional items are "extras" that would enhance the attractiveness of the proposed operation but that are neither mandatory nor strongly desired. *The items should further be given a numerical weighting factor, which designates the item's importance within the category.* Each item, therefore, will emerge from the requirements-definition phase with two attributes: a category assignment and a numerical weight factor. A sample requirements list is shown in Figure 20.1.

Two important things happen when the requirements list is developed in this manner: (1) the items are identified, and (2) the relative importance of each item is established. All of those who are involved in the definition phase have a chance to lobby for or defend the items they feel are important, and the complete list results from these consultations. The requirements list puts the installation in the strong position of knowing exactly what to look for during the RFP stage. In

Item	Category	Weight
*Local support office	MAN	8
*File compatibility with existing files	MAN	7
*Support twenty-five on-line terminals	MAN	9
*Terminal response time under five seconds	MAN	8
•		
•		
*On-site training classes	DES	6
*Lease/purchase contract available	DES	4
•		
•		
*Active user group	OPT	2

MAN = Mandatory
DES = Desirable
OPT = Optional

FIGURE 20.1.   Sample Requirements List

contrast to this approach, an unstructured look at various vendor offer-ings will usually result in a good deal of confusion and may result in the installation obtaining equipment that they do not need, that does not solve the operational problem, or both. The time needed to put together a solid requirements list is time well spent.

EVALUATING RESPONSES TO THE RFP

When the requirements list has been solidified, a request for pro-posal can be sent out to vendors that details the items on which the vendor's response will be judged. The initial response to the RFP can be evaluated against the requirements list, and the two or three ven-dors that satisfy the largest number of requirements (or the most important ones) can be set aside for further examination. Observe that, once again, the preparatory work that went into making the list serves as a consistent base against which all of the responses can be tested.

The two or three vendors that appear strongest after the cursory evaluation should then be given closer scrutiny. This can be done by a combination of techniques including vendor presentations, customer reference checks, site visits, discussions with specialists on the vendor's technical staff, and benchmarks (tests run with sample data on the vendor's product). The requirements list is again useful because, at this point, it can be used as a type of scorecard for each vendor. Each vendor can be rated on each item on the requirements list in order to develop a total score. Figure 20.2 shows what our sample requirements list looks like after the scoring is complete.

			Vendor A		Vendor B	
Item	Cat.	Wgt.	Rating	Score	Rating	Score
*Local office	MAN	8	9	72	7	56
*File compatibility	MAN	7	4	28	8	56
*25 on-line terminals	MAN	9	7	63	8	72
*Five-second response	MAN	8	6	48	8	64
•						
•						
*On-site training	DES	6	9	54	3	18
*Lease/ purchase	DES	4	9	36	4	16
•						
•						
*User group	OPT	2	8	16	6	12
Total score				317		294
Total mandatory				211		248

MAN = Mandatory
DES = Desirable
OPT = Optional

FIGURE 20.2   Completed Requirements List

The results of this rating and scoring exercise put the competing vendor offerings into perspective. Since the requirements were debated and refined before the vendors were contacted, the chances of the installation being "talked into" a requirement by a vendor are greatly reduced.

It is clear from the above sample scorecard that Vendor A has the better total score. The scorecard has another useful purpose: by isolating the scores for just the mandatory items, a sharper focus is brought to bear on those items that were deemed absolutely necessary in the new equipment. Looking at the scorecard in this way, you can see that Vendor B has the stronger offering with a mandatory score of 248 compared to a mandatory score of 211 for Vendor A. On the assumption that the requirements definition accurately reflects the needs of the installation, it appears that Vendor B provides a better alternative because it does a better job of satisfying the mandatory items.

DEVELOPING A CONVERSION PLAN

The selection of the new equipment paves the way for the next step in the cutover process—developing the conversion plan. On the surface, the preparation of a conversion plan appears to be commonplace and nothing more than common sense. In a way, there can be no argument with this viewpoint. All too often, the conversion effort appears to be so simple that a workplan is not developed or one is developed that is so general that the conversion effort is poorly organized and doomed to failure. *The need to involve users in the planning for conversions cannot be overemphasized. The timing of the conversion must be carefully scheduled to minimize disruption of the users' work and to allow the user to schedule extra time for checking out conversion results.*

Putting together the workplan requires the efforts of people from various disciplines. People from the data center, systems and programming, user areas, building services, technical specialists, and vendors should be involved in the workplan. The plan should identify tasks that have to be done and assign responsibility for completing the tasks. (Critical path or PERT techniques are very useful in putting together a conversion plan and identifying event dependencies.) *You can use the following checklist to define the tasks that must be part of the conversion plan:*

1. Analysis of items to be converted:
   - Data
   - Files
   - Documentation
   - Primary equipment
   - Ancillary equipment

2. Estimates of work effort:
   - Time needed
   - Skills needed
   - Prerequisite events
   - Dependent events

3. Description of conversion:
   - Sequence of events
   - Dependencies
   - Checkpoints by dates
   - Checkpoints by events
   - Verification requirements

4. Events that must take place:
   - Site preparation
   - Data transfer
   - Equipment check-out
   - Equipment overlap period
   - Cutover: one-time versus phased
   - Documentation
   - Training

    The conversion responsibilities should be assigned to specific individuals rather than to a general area. Indicating departmental responsibility makes it difficult to pin down whether a task has been completed. If an individual's name appears next to a task assignment, the monitoring of progress is easier.

    The plan should take into account the state of the art and the technology of the equipment involved in the conversion and the skills of the people involved. Converting to a technology that is in its infancy will very likely result in several false starts and missed due dates due to unfamiliarity with the equipment or unavailability of components or major parts of the conversion equipment. All of these factors should be taken into account in the conversion plan and extra time allowed when dealing with advanced state of the art. *This also suggests that a phased cutover is preferable to a one-time cutover in cases where new technology equipment is being installed, since this method allows for several fallback positions in case the various conversion phases don't work exactly as planned.*

Along with the technical problems, you should anticipate personnel and operational problems in the conversion plan. Some people may resist the changes that are taking place around them and, consciously or unconsciously, create barriers and slow down the conversion and installing process.

Security must be maintained during the cutover. With many more people coming and going through the data center and more equipment present on the data center floor, there is a natural tendency to relax normal security measures. *Security efforts must be redoubled during conversion, especially if it involves a relocation of equipment to a new data center.*

The output and performance from the new equipment should be audited to make sure that all applications that ran on the old equipment run on the new equipment. *The efficiency of the new equipment should be measured after it has been installed for two or three months. These results should be compared to the results that were forecast during the requirement definition and equipment search. Significant differences between the expected and actual performance should be investigated and resolved as part of a good, postinstallation audit.*

APPLYING THIS INFORMATION TO YOUR DATA CENTER

1. Are the installation's requirements thoroughly defined and weighted prior to contacting vendors with a request for proposal?

2. Are all conversions and cutovers subjected to a detailed planning process to identify all contingencies?

3. Is the user adequately informed and prepared for the conversion?

4. Has time been allotted for user checking of conversion results?

SUMMARY

This chapter offers the following recommendations:

- Be sure to spend enough time on defining requirements prior to beginning a search for hardware or software. Obtain a consensus on these requirements, defining those that are mandatory, desirable, and optional.

- Evaluate vendor responses to the RFP on an overall basis and on just the mandatory points.

- Put together a thorough conversion plan, one that assigns specific responsibility for each item in the plan.

21

Preparing Data Center Contracts

The "paperwork" that you must handle as data center manager is usually one of the least appealing parts of the job, yet certain administrative tasks—such as dealing with vendors for contracting and for support—must be done well to avoid spending money unnecessarily or to avoid giving the company more legal risk and exposure on an issue than the company is willing to take. This chapter outlines some of the issues that you should consider in your contractual dealings with vendors.

DEFINING THE KEY TERMS IN A CONTRACTUAL AGREEMENT

A DCM must be aware of the key issues involved in coming to a contractual agreement with a vendor. This does not mean that you need to become a paralegal, but it does mean that you should understand each issue and exactly how important that issue is to the overall position the company wishes to take with the vendor. Each company will have some issues that are negotiable between the company and the vendor. Quite often, it is your job to identify for the attorney the significance of these issues. The sections that follow describe some of the typical items that must be resolved when negotiating a contract. Figure 21.1 illustrates a contract checklist, which is useful in the review and internal routing of the contract to make sure that all interested parties have had a chance to evaluate it.

Contract Term

The length of time that the contract will be in force must be clearly defined. The starting date and expiration date or the starting date and the length of the term must be spelled out in the contract.

Confidentiality Agreement

The contract should include a clause that protects the buying company from any breach of confidentiality by the vendor's personnel. For instance, this clause might read as follows:

Confidentiality. (vendor), its officers, its employees, and its agents, will treat all information and data relating to the Licensee, including but not limited to, its operations, policies, procedures, techniques, accounts, and personnel, obtained by (vendor), its officers, employees, or agents, as confidential and will not disclose any such information or data to any third party or to any of (vendor's) officers, employees, or agents not involved in, or responsible for, the negotiations with respect to this Agreement.

The essence of this clause states that, since the vendor's people will come in contact with or have a need to access the buyer's internal information, the vendor's people will keep this information confidential. This is particularly important when a vendor is being contracted to do a complete system installation. To check out the system, the vendor will have to conduct tests and verify results using company data, which, in some cases, include confidential information. By including this type of clause, you ensure that the vendor agrees to hold this information in confidence.

CONTRACT CHECKLIST

Routing	Approve	Date
1. Data Cen 2. Sys&Prog 3. Legal 4. Managemt		

		*** REVIEW ***		*** ITEM ***
Data Center	Systems & Programming	Legal		
				Contract terms Confidentiality agreement Delivery dates Specific deliverables Reference technical specifications Training commitment Vendor support commitment Repair call response Spare equipment Performance levels Renewal provisions Upgrade provisions Prices Payment terms Acceptance tests Remedies Signing authority

FIGURE 21.1.   Contract Checklist

Delivery Date

If a specific delivery date is important to the data center, it should be included in the contract, possibly with provision for penalties if the date is not met. Often, a precise delivery date is not critical to the buyer as long as the equipment arrives within a reasonable time period after it is due. The equipment arrival *is* critical, however, when the delivery is one step in a tightly planned schedule; in these cases, specify the delivery date in the contract.

Specific Deliverables

The contract should spell out exactly what the vendor is to deliver. A deliverable may be hardware, software, a report, documentation, a training commitment, or combinations of these and other items. The deliverable should be clearly described so that all parties (including unbiased third parties) understand what is meant.

Reference Technical Specifications

Any material that had an important bearing on the decision to select the particular vendor should be included, at least by reference, in the contract. This material can include documentation, letters, benchmark results, technical specification data, and similar items. In this way, you ensure that the factors that caused you to incline toward the vendor will be delivered under the terms of the contract.

Training Commitment

Any commitment made by the vendor for training the buyer's personnel should be made a part of the contract. The commitment can include the type and length of training, the number of people who will be trained, and whether the training cost is included in the contract price or is extra. In some cases, the commitment also states whether the training will be conducted at the buyer's site (or sites) or at the vendor's site (or sites).

Vendor Support Commitment

The vendor's ongoing support commitment, if any, should be made a part of the contract. For example, the number of on-site people provided by the vendor, the location of the vendor's support office, of its parts depot, and so on can be included in this section of the contract.

Repair Call Response

If you are located in a remote area, you should include a contract clause that spells out the vendor's commitment to respond to emergency repair calls within a prescribed amount of time. This is usually stated as a given number of hours between the time the buyer places a repair call and the time the vendor's people arrive at the buyer's site.

Spare Equipment

Spare pieces of equipment available to the buyer should be designated in the contract. This practice is becoming common in installations that have quite a few terminals, for example. Their contracts state that, for every n terminals, the vendor will provide the buyer with a spare terminal. This spare is used as a "floating" terminal and put to use when another terminal fails and until the vendor's maintenance personnel can fix the disabled terminal. This type of clause is used most often by buyers in remote areas or when an on-line application is heavily used and demands maximum operational time.

Performance Levels

Expected performance levels should be spelled out in the contract if this is a key issue to the buyer. The specification, for example, may be stated in terms of the desired "up time" for a system or of the expected response time for an on-line configuration. If you require that the system be available a certain percentage of the time, make sure you spell out the conditions for measuring and defining the available time so that there is no room for doubt by either party as to what constitutes "up time." Make sure the clause defines what is meant by response time, how it will be measured, whether variations in response time are allowed depending on the load present on the system, and what constitutes a load on the system.

Renewal Provisions

You should clearly understand the renewal provisions of the contract. Some contracts that are originally written for an extended term (such as two to three years) will automatically revert to a one-year contract at the end of the original term. Other contracts will automatically renew themselves unless the buyer specifically notifies the vendor of an intent to discontinue the contract or to change the length of the term. There is nothing inherently wrong with any of these variations, but it is important that the buyer understand the possibilities surrounding contract renewal.

Upgrade Provisions

Each vendor generally makes provisions for the buyer to upgrade the equipment configuration within the context of the original contract. *The caution here is that you should be aware of whether the upgraded configuration is subject to the original term of the contract or to some other term.* Some contracts call for an equipment upgrade to "restart" the contract term for those pieces of the configuration that have been upgraded. This could result in part of the configuration having one expiration date and another part of the configuration having a different expiration date.

Prices

The contract should include a price list that details all costs for each deliverable covered by the contract. Any extra cost items, such as transportation or handling charges, should be identified. The buyer should understand which items are ongoing costs and which are one-time expenses.

Payment Terms

The manner in which the expenses must be paid, especially the timing of payments, should be clearly stated in the contract. Of particular importance are any partial or progress payments that are a part of the installation process. As an example, if 85 percent of the purchase price of a deliverable is to be paid on delivery, with the balance to be paid following successful completion of acceptance tests, these provisions should be in the contract.

Acceptance Tests

The buyer may want to include a provision for conducting acceptance tests, using the buyer's data, before final acceptance of a deliverable. *The parameters of the acceptance test should be clearly identified as to what will be tested, what volumes of data will be used, and what results are expected from the new deliverable. Make sure that you include a statement that specifies the time period within which you must conduct the acceptance test following installation.*

Remedies

A realistic remedy must be specified for each item at issue in the contract. The remedy *indicates the recourse that the buyer or the vendor has in the event that one of the provisions of the contract is violated or is not met.* Among the remedies are: monetary daily penalties, the vendor's right to return the buyer's purchase price, the buyer's right to return the deliverable and to recover the purchase price.

Signing Authority

The contract must be signed by someone who has the authority to sign for and bind the parties involved in the contract. This holds true for both the buyer and the vendor. This generally means that the person who signs the contract must be an officer of the respective company.

APPLYING THIS INFORMATION TO YOUR DATA CENTER

1. Are all data center contracts reviewed by legal counsel before being signed by an officer of your company?

2. Have all supporting materials, such as documentation and technical specifications, been included in the contract language?

3. Do all provisions of the contract have remedies to your company in the event that the contract items are not delivered?

SUMMARY

Under ideal conditions, the contract can be put away and forgotten while the buyer and the vendor operate under a relationship that is the envy of anyone who ever installed data processing equipment. While this is to be hoped for, you must be prepared for some rough spots, misunderstandings, and downright problems on both the buyer's side and on the vendor's side. If any of these occur, look to the contract for relief. The axiom "if it's not written down, it doesn't exist" is unfortunately true at that point.

The DCM should carefully review every contract before signing it or before recommending that someone else in the company sign it.

22

Managing the Data Center in the Face of Change—A Case Study

Nowhere is the impact of data center change more evident than in the areas of data base and distributed computing. The case study that follows illustrates some of the conflicts that arise between data processing professionals and the users and management when an installation considers data base technology and when users clamor for distributed computing hardware. The case provides a management perspective on these issues and is meant to encourage users, management, and data center people to view the problems through the eyes of the other parties in the situation. The names of the company and all persons are, of course, disguised. This case was prepared as a basis for discussion rather than to illustrate either effective or ineffective handling of an administrative situation.

DESCRIBING THE CASE

The Riverknoll Corporation is a multidivision organization that had sales of $400 million in 19n5 and net earnings of $17,200,000. The company is comprised of seven divisions and was created through the acquisition of several small- to medium-size companies in loosely related industries. The general manager of each division is responsible for day-to-day operations and for the profitability of the division. Corporate staff services are provided to the divisions in the areas of finance, accounting, and data processing. Data processing costs are recovered from the divisions by means of a chargeback system. An excerpt of the organization chart is shown in Figure 22.1.

A Picture of the Kingsford Division

The Kingsford Division of Riverknoll has had good growth in sales and profits over the past five years. Historical sales and profit figures, in millions of dollars, and a projection for the coming year are:

	19n1	19n2	19n3	19n4	19n5	19n6 (estimated)
Gross sales	$31	$33	$36	$40	$46	$54
Net earnings	$1.4	$1.6	$1.9	$2.3	$2.7	$3.2

These data are further illustrated in Figure 22.2 and reflect an enviable performance record by Jim Collins since he took over the division. Collins took over Kingsford in 19n2 and has won the respect of corporate management and employees within the division as an energetic, innovative manager who gets results, although his management style tends to be rather freewheeling.

The division manufactures consumer products that are assembled at the Kingsford plant and sold to wholesalers for eventual distribution and sale through department and hardware stores. Inventory control and accounting transactions are sent to the Riverknoll data processing center at the end of each day, the data are processed overnight, and the results returned to Kingsford before the start of the

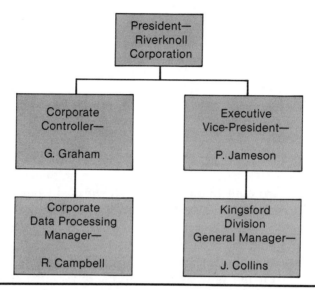

FIGURE 22.1. *Organization Chart for the Riverknoll Corporation*

The Kingsford Division

	19n1	19n2	19n3	19n4	19n5	19n6 (est.)
Gross sales	$31	$33	$36	$40	$46	$54
Sales growth		+6.5%	+9.1%	+11.1%	+15%	+17.4%
Net earnings	$1.4	$1.6	$1.9	$2.3	$2.7	$3.2
Earnings growth		+14.3%	+18.8%	+21.1%	+17.4%	+18.5%
Earnings as percent of sales	4.5%	4.8%	5.3%	5.8%	5.9%	5.9%

Riverknoll Corporation

$$\frac{\text{Net earnings}}{\text{Gross sales}} = \frac{\$17,200,000}{\$400,000,000} = 4.3\%$$

Sales

$$\frac{\text{Kingsford}}{\text{Riverknoll}} = \frac{\$46,000,000}{\$400,000,000} = 11.5\%$$

Earnings

$$\frac{\$2,700,000}{\$17,200,000} = 15.7\%$$

FIGURE 22.2. *Performance Analysis*

next business day. Messenger service is used for the pick-ups and deliveries between Kingsford and the Riverknoll headquarters.

Since assuming responsibility for the division, Collins has streamlined the existing manual procedures for order entry and customer service, but he realizes that the increased volume of business in recent years has put severe strains on these procedures. He is anxious to automate this phase of his operations to provide better customer service.

The Kingsford Division is in a highly competitive business, and customer loyalty to the product is relatively perishable. That is, the wholesalers to whom Kingsford sells put a premium on timely responses to their orders. Suppliers are distinguished from one another by their ability to provide service to the wholesalers and, when this service deteriorates, the wholesalers can easily switch their allegiance to another supplier. In his business forecast for 19n6, Collins has noted the increased competitive pressures and stated that Kingsford will be emphasizing customer services as a means of differentiating Kingsford from its competitors. He would like to put the order entry application on a "real-time" basis in order that the wholesalers could place phone orders with the Kingsford sales administration department and could also determine the status of their existing orders. Under the present manual system, order inquiries are handled by a group of clerks who use customer order status cards (one five-by-eight-inch card for each of Kingsford's 50,000 customers, containing order history and estimated shipment data) to provide wholesalers with information. The posting of these cards is tedious, time consuming, somewhat inaccurate, and typically lags actual events by two to three days.

The First Push Toward Distributed Computing

The idea of installing a minicomputer in his division has always appealed to Collins, and the concept has become even more intriguing in light of the planned emphasis on customer service. Collins, who has attended several data processing seminars for executives and who bought himself a "hobby" computer for his home, sees the mini as a quick way to achieve an operational order entry and inquiry system for Kingsford.

Collins has been discussing the idea with Ron Jackson, a salesman for a computer hardware company. Jackson has estimated that, for $3,000 to $4,000 per month, a minicomputer with three cathode ray terminals (CRTs) could be installed at Kingsford, including an order entry software package. Their current thinking would have Kingsford's mini linked to Riverknoll's corporate data center via a dial-up telephone line. Each morning, a copy of Kingsford's order file would be transmitted from the large Riverknoll data files to the Kingsford mini for the daily order processing and inquiries. At the end of the day, new orders and changes to existing orders would be transmitted to Riverknoll to be merged with other transactions (such as cash receipts and inventories) for updating and batch reporting during the night. Collins has informally discussed his plan with his boss, Pete Jameson, who is Riverknoll's executive vice-president.

"Installing the mini will give me better control of order entry and it'll be cheaper than if I have to pay Riverknoll's rates for an on-line system," said Collins.

Anticipating Collins's request for budget approval for the mini project, Jameson talked to Bob Campbell, Riverknoll's data processing manager.

"Bob," said Jameson, "I'd like to have you review Collins's plan. I know he's got a problem with customer service, but I'm also concerned that we don't just jump into this mini situation without understanding all of its implications."

The Data Processing Picture

The Riverknoll corporate data center has been managed by Bob Campbell for the past four years, during which time the center has experienced rapid changes in the hardware configuration and an increase in processing capacity. These changes have generally been accomplished smoothly with little or no detrimental impact on the users. Increases in hardware capacity have been approved rather routinely by the corporate data processing steering committee, but Campbell's boss, George Graham (who recently joined Riverknoll as corporate controller), has insisted that all future expenditures be rigorously cost-justified.

The data processing function receives mixed reviews from the user divisions. The accounting applications have been installed on schedule and operate without difficulty, while the traditional manufacturing systems (bills of materials, inventory control, and production control) have been implemented with some problems. From a production standpoint, Bob Campbell is proud of the fact that 91 percent of the jobs run in his department are completed on time and that his rerun rate is slightly over 2 percent.

Several corporate divisions, other than Kingsford, have remote job entry capability, and significant progress has been made toward conversion to a large, shared data base system. A data base software package has been installed for one and one-half years and is used in a batch environment to control divisional files for engineering, inventory, routings, and labor reporting as well as corporate accounting and budgeting data. The integrating of order entry into the data base and the conversion of the data base software to on-line processing has been tabled pending a corporate-wide study of divisional needs in these areas. A preliminary report from a task force working on the study is due within eight months.

Campbell, who is a member of the task force, feels that there is sufficient processor capacity available to put Collins's application on-line, but that additional disk capacity and an on-line inquiry control software package would be needed if the Kingsford order entry system were run on-line at Riverknoll. He has reviewed the cost information assembled by Ron Jackson. The cost estimates for the distributed approach (Collins's and Jackson's idea) and for the on-line approach (Campbell's plan) are shown in Figure 22.3. Campbell's study also reveals that neither the hardware nor the software is compatible with anything currently installed at Riverknoll, except that the mini supports a subset on ANS-COBOL.

DISCUSSING THE CASE

The Kingsford Division case illustrates a number of interesting issues, but the major ones appear to be:

- User communications
- Corporate data resource plan
- Managing resources to serve users

Distributed Approach

Item	Monthly	One-time
Minicomputer, including printer, three CRTs, disk storage	$4,000	
Telephone line, Riverknoll to Kingsford, low speed	200	
Modems (two at $200 each)		$400
Operator salary at Kingsford	800	
Total	$5,000	$400

On-line/Riverknoll Approach

Item	Monthly	One-time
Disk storage	$1,000	
Telephone line, Riverknoll to Kingsford, medium speed	500	
Terminals with remote controller	1,800	
Processing charge	1,500	
On-line control software		$15,000
Modems (two at $500 each)		1,000
Total	$4,800	$16,000

FIGURE 22.3.   Cost Estimates

The Issue of User Communications

It is apparent that Mr. Collins and Mr. Campbell have not kept in touch with each other. Collins is determined to put a minicomputer into Kingsford and has virtually given up hope for any help from the Riverknoll staff. Campbell, on the other hand, shows no indication of recognizing or understanding the urgency of Collins's situation.

Collins has had some exposure and minimal experience with data processing. While he is not a DP expert, he is representative of an emerging type of line manager—the person who is informed enough about data processing so as not to be mystified by the jargon and technology, who is not inclined to accept the "stock" DP answer as to the feasibility of an idea, and who legitimately questions why new, bold approaches cannot be tried in order to provide needed service to users. Armed with a bit of knowledge, Collins is likely to go off on his own approach if he is not satisfied that Campbell and Riverknoll are willing to help him. *Campbell must move swiftly to establish a rapport and spirit of cooperation with Collins in order to prevent such a chasm from developing between the headquarters and Kingsford.*

The Issue of the Data Resource Plan

The corporate data resource plan is continuing to emerge with the movement to a large, shared data base in a batch environment. The amount of time needed for the task force to complete its report, much less to implement its recommendations, is unacceptably long in Collins's view. This highlights the dramatic difference in time scales between Kingsford and Riverknoll. Collins, as a line manager, works in terms of days, weeks, and months. Campbell and the task force, as staff personnel, are working in terms of months and years. In this case, the corporate data resource plan, searching for an all-encompassing solution to corporate needs, is not responsive to the more urgent needs of the Kingsford Division.

The Issue of Serving the User

Early on, and throughout this book, we have noted that the primary function of data processing and of the data center is to serve its users. With the Kingsford Division, it appears that data processing resources must be managed better in order to serve users such as Collins.

Figure 22.4 is a modified version of the data center schematic introduced in Chapter One. The service demand (improved customer service and information availability) of Kingsford represents a planned or future workload to be absorbed by the computer resources (whether the resources are centralized, decentralized, or some combination of the two). Since this demand is part of the planning loop, top management, Collins, and Campbell must agree on which resources are needed and which should be made available. If Kingsford is to have its own minicomputer, management must endorse this scheme and provide appropriate resources (personnel skilled in distributed computing techniques may have to be hired or existing per-

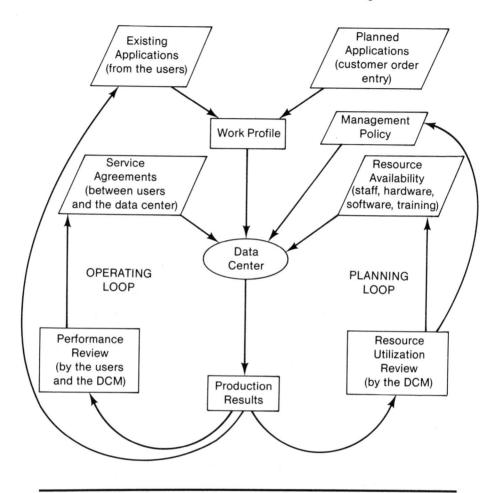

FIGURE 22.4. *Kingsford Data Center Schematic Diagram*

sonnel trained, and special software and hardware would have to be obtained). If the minicomputer idea is rejected and Collins is directed to do all processing at the central site, Campbell must be given sufficient resources to respond to Kingsford's service demands.

Solutions to the Problem

While there has been a breakdown in the dialogue between Collins and Campbell, the situation may still be salvageable. One strategy that Campbell could employ would be to join forces with Collins and use Kingsford as a pilot site for exploring the realm of distributed computing. By providing staff and other resources, Campbell can work with Collins in solving the customer service problem. In the process, the corporate DP staff can gain experience in distributed computing, which may be useful in shaping the final corporate policy regarding data base, on-line inquiry, and autonomous divisional processing. Perhaps the Kingsford application can be put on the mini as a type of interim system, with full recognition of the possibility that it will have to be reworked substantially in a year or two when the corporate approach is more clearly defined. The latter idea will be unpopular with data processing purists striving for the ultimate technical approach to solving the problem, but it is realistic in that it provides responsive service to the user and clearly recognizes the perishable competitive position of Kingsford.

APPLYING THIS INFORMATION TO YOUR DATA CENTER

1. What issues favor Mr. Collins's position?

2. Are Mr. Campbell's concerns justified regarding the data base, distributed computing, and compatibility?

3. Is Mr. Campbell trying to protect his "empire"?

4. What is likely to happen if Kingsford doesn't get the minicomputer and Mr. Collins doesn't meet the divisional sales and profit goals?

5. What strategy can Mr. Campbell employ to reconcile the differences between his position on the minicomputer issue and that of Mr. Collins?

Summary

The message that should be clear from the preceding chapters is that there is rarely a single, correct answer to the myriad problems and situations facing a data center manager. *Instead, the DCM should develop a knack for seeking out as much information as possible about a situation, learn to make an educated cost/benefit analysis, then make a decision, carry it out, and review the results.*

At the beginning of this book, we noted that the DCM has to have the talents of a combination of people, such as a personnel director, industrial engineer, production control manager, computer specialist, and general manager. Stated another way, the data center manager must strive continually to keep in balance the delicate combination of resources represented by hardware, software, and people. The data center is a living, changing entity, and the astute DCM will learn to anticipate and identify the critical resource at any point in the development of the data center. The successful DCM will know the value of planning for contingencies surrounding each of these parts of the resource mix and will recognize that the "pressure point" is continually shifting among these factors.

PREDICTING THE FUTURE

The rapidly changing environment that surrounds the high-technology field of data processing and the data center makes any kind of detailed forecasting difficult. However, there appear to be several very general trends that bear directly on the job of the data center manager:

- Rapidly shifting cost curves
- Increased user involvement
- Increased demand for services
- Higher caliber of data center personnel
- Continued scarcity of dollar resources

Shifting Cost Curves

The rapidly shifting cost curves should surprise no one who has been observing the hardware cost trends of recent years. Perhaps the most dramatic shift occurred in about 1980, when hardware costs became less than 50 percent of many data center budgets. In a visible example of the shifting pressure point within the data center resource mix, hardware was replaced by personnel as the dominant expense item.

Increased User Involvement and Demand for Services

User involvement can be expected to increase as more applications are put into production, as these applications are linked together logically, and as the user community becomes better informed about data processing. These factors, working together with the descending cost of hardware, will also increase the demand for service from the data center. The DCM should be prepared for these developments and should be prepared to bring an open mind to the solution of the problems that these situations create. Traditional centralized-versus-decentralized configurations may have to yield to an operating environment in which various processing and organizational modes coexist. *The DCM should be prepared to lend solid, professional assistance to these opportunities in order to come up with a solution that makes sense, from a business and a capacity point of view, for the organization at that time.*

Higher Caliber of Data Center Personnel

The dispersal of processing functions into user areas and the need to consider a wider range of options when analyzing a situation will result in the data center having a higher overall caliber of personnel. You can expect that the more routine tasks will be converted to automated routines (the tape librarian is an example), and the more labor-intensive jobs will be located in the user areas for source entry of information into the system. This will reduce the need for clerical people in the data center. Concurrently, the increased complexity of the application environment and a broader spectrum of technological choices will lead to data center people with higher qualifications than those generally found in the center today.

Scarcity of Dollar Resources

In the face of all other changes, the DCM will continue to vie with other managers in the organization for scarce dollar resources. The increased demand for services and the higher visibility of the data center within the organization will result in higher spending levels in the former case and more intense scrutiny of data center expenditures in the latter case. The DCM will be expected to return higher levels of productivity for the dollars that the organization invests in the data center.

The entrepreneurial attitude is one that combines experience, an open mind, a willingness to question the way things have been done, a healthy dose of skepticism, a high amount of energy, a talent for negotiating uncharted waters, a dedication to the pursuit of success, and a deep reservoir of optimism. As the data processing future unfolds, this attitude will serve you well.

Selected Bibliography

Allen, B. "Embezzler's Guide to the Computer." *Harvard Business Review*, July–Aug. 1975, 79–89.

Axelrod, C. W. "How Effective is Your Computer?" *Infosystems*, Feb. 1979, 50–54.

Beizer, B. *Micro-Analysis of Computer System Performance.* New York: Van Nostrand Reinhold, 1978.

Bigelow, R. P., and Nycum, S. H. *Your Computer and the Law.* Englewood Cliffs, N.J.: Prentice-Hall, 1976.

Boehm, B. W. "Software Engineering: R&D Trends and Defense Needs." *Research Directions in Software Technology*, Cambridge, Mass.: M.I.T. Press, 1979, 44–86.

Brandon, R. H., and Gray, M. *Project Control Standards.* Princeton, N.J.: Brandon/Systems Press, 1970.

Brooks, F. P., Jr. *The Mythical Man-Month.* Reading, Mass.: Addison-Wesley, 1978.

Browne, J. C. "Performance Analysis and Evaluation: The Connection to Reality." *Research Directions in Software Technology*, Cambridge, Mass.: M.I.T. Press, 1979, 557–583.

"Capacity Planning: Predicting Your Future Computer Needs." Interview with L. R. Bonner. *Computer Decisions*, Feb. 1980, 64–70.

Castaldi, R. E. "Capacity Planning at Lone Star." *Datamation*, April 1979, 146–152.

Coffman, E. G., Jr. (Ed.). *Computer and Job/Shop Scheduling Theory.* New York: Wiley, 1976.

Cooke, L. H., Jr. "Planning for Growth." *Datamation*, Dec. 1979, 181–186.

Dalal, J. R. "DDP Entails Change of Management Style." *Computerworld*, July 30, 1979, SR/4.

291

"Data Entry Productivity." *Computer Economics Report,* Oct. 1980, 4.

Dopuch, N., Birnberg, J. G., and Demski, J. *Cost Accounting.* New York: Harcourt Brace Jovanovich, 1974.

Dunn, N. "Getting the Most Out of Your Data Center." *Computer Decisions,* May 1979, 68–73.

Ferrari, D. *Computer Systems Performance Evaluation.* Englewood Cliffs, N.J.: Prentice-Hall, 1978.

Ferreira, J. "IRM: An Evolutionary Mosaic." *Infosystems,* Oct. 1979, 82–90.

Freed, R. N. "Computer Contracting Is Changing for the Better." *Computer Decisions,* June 1979, 82–93.

Freedman, D., Pisani, R., and Purves, R. *Statistics.* New York: Norton, 1978.

Gaade, R. P. R. "Picking Up the Pieces." *Datamation,* Jan. 1980, 113–118.

Gibson, C. F., and Nolan, R. L. "Managing the Four Stages of EDP Growth." *Harvard Business Review,* Jan.–Feb. 1974, 76–88.

Hampton, D. R., Summer, C. E., and Webber, R. A. *Organizational Behavior and the Practice of Management.* Glenview, Ill.: Scott, Foresman, 1968.

Harvey, S. B. "Bridging the Planning Gap." *Infosystems,* Oct. 1979, 108–114.

Holmes, F. W. "Confluent Technologies Pervade IRM." *Infosystems,* Oct. 1979, 92–98.

Horngren, C. T. *Cost Accounting: A Managerial Emphasis.* Englewood Cliffs, N.J.: Prentice-Hall, 1972.

International Data Corporation. "Computing for Business into the 80s." *Fortune,* Oct. 1980.

Johnson, R. W. *Financial Management.* Boston: Allyn & Bacon, 1971.

Krauss, L. I., and Macgahan, A. *Computer Fraud and Countermeasures.* Englewood Cliffs, N.J.: Prentice-Hall, 1979.

McFadden, F. R., and Suver, J. D. "Costs and Benefits of a Data Base System." *Harvard Business Review,* Jan.–Feb. 1978, 131–139.

McFarlan, F. W. "Management Audit of the EDP Department." *Harvard Business Review,* May–June 1973, 131–142.

McFarlan, F. W., and Nolan, R. L. (Eds.). *The Information Systems Handbook.* Homewood, Ill.: Dow Jones-Irwin, 1975.

McGuire, J. S. "Corporate, DDP Needs Must Be Balanced." *Computerworld,* July 30, 1979, SR/7.

Morley, E., and Silver,.A. "A Film Director's Approach to Managing Creativity." *Harvard Business Review*, March–April 1977, 59–70.

Nolan, R. L. "Plight of the EDP Manager." *Harvard Business Review*, May–June 1973, 143–152.

Nolan, R. L. "Controlling the Costs of Data Services." *Harvard Business Review*, July–Aug. 1977, 114–124.

Nolan, R. L. "Managing the Crises in Data Processing." *Harvard Business Review*, March-April 1979, 115–126.

Orlicky, J. *The Successful Computer System.* New York: McGraw-Hill, 1969.

Parker, D. B. *Crime by Computer.* New York: Scribner's, 1976.

Patrick, R. L. "Probing Productivity." *Datamation*, Sept. 1980, 207–210.

Rhodes, W. L., Jr. "The Disproportionate Cost of Data Entry." *Infosystems*, Oct. 1980, 70–76.

Strassmann, P. A. "Managing the Costs of Information." *Harvard Business Review*, Sept.–Oct. 1976, 133–142.

Van Rensselaer, C. "Centralize? Decentralize? Distribute?" *Datamation*, April 1979, 88–97.

Wagner, E. R. "Price-Slashing 4300 Forces Competition to Ledge." *Data Management*, Nov. 1979, 8.

Weinberg, G. M. *The Psychology of Computer Programming.* New York: Van Nostrand Reinhold, 1971.

Whitmarsh, J. "Disaster Recovery Centers Springing Up." *Computerworld*, Dec. 10, 1979, 55–57.

Index

Acceptance tests, 274
Allocation method, 219–221
Annual maintenance, 240
Annual report, 78–95
Application cost, 227
Application rates, 226
Application resource estimate, 162,
    175–177
Attended equipment, 195
Auditability, 174
Availability
   interactive, 90
   on-line, 91, 193
   resource, 5, 162
Average cost per job, 86–87, 92
Average hours per job, 87–88

Back-up
   empty shell, 257
   full-floor, 257
   off-site, 258
Batch rerun percentage, 84, 90, 91, 94
Benchmarks, 203
Benefits, 210, 213–214, 240
"Big pot," 219
Bottlenecks, 185–186
Brainstorming, 132
Budget
   benefits, 210, 213–214
   capital expenditures, 208
   DP, 35–36
   expense elements, 208–209
   fixed expense, 209, 210

fixed income, 209
income elements, 209
operating, 208
presentations, 211–214
salary plan, 210
time frame, 208
variable expense, 209, 211
variable income, 209, 210
zero-base, 213
Business exposure, 63
Business skills, 28
Buzzwords, 57

Capital asset, 208
Capital expenditure budget, 208
Career path, 125, 141
Chargeback, 92, 219, 221–223, 226,
   231–232
Communications control, 114
Computer resource, 18, 19
   total, 25, 196, 249
Confidentiality, 270–271
Console messages, 191
Contracts, 270–275
   checklist, 270
   confidentiality clause, 270–271
   delivery date, 272
   payment terms, 274
   renewal provisions, 273–274
   term, 270
Control
   communications, 114
   complexity of, 148